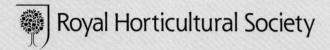

Royal Horticultural Society

GROW YOUR OWN
VEG & FRUIT
YEAR PLANNER

EDITOR-IN-CHIEF
JANE COURTIER

MITCHELL BEAZLEY

GROW YOUR OWN VEG & FRUIT YEAR PLANNER
Royal Horticultural Society

First published in Great Britain in 2009 as *Grow Your Own Kitchen Garden Year*
by Mitchell Beazley, an imprint of Octopus Publishing Group Ltd,
Carmelite House, 50 Victoria Embankment, London EC4Y 0DZ
www.octopusbooks.co.uk

An Hachette UK Company
www.hachette.co.uk

Revised edition 2012

Reprinted 2014, 2015

Published in association with the Royal Horticultural Society

ISBN 978-1-84533-733-9

A CIP record of this book is available from the British Library
Set in Caecilia, Frutiger, Garamond, Glypha, and Interstate
Printed and bound in China

Publisher: Alison Starling
Commissioning Editor: Helen Griffin
Editorial Director: Tracey Smith
Art Director: Pene Parker
Jacket Designer: Juliette Norsworthy
Designer: Nichola Smith
Senior Editor: Ruth Patrick
Editor-In-Chief: Jane Courtier
Copy Editors: Louise Pateman, Joanna Chisholm and Stephanie Milner
Senior Production Controller: Lucy Carter
Production Controller: Sarah Kramer
Proofreader: Lynn Bresler
Indexer: Helen Snaith
RHS Publisher: Rae Spencer Jones
RHS Consultant Editor: Simon Maughan

The Royal Horticultural Society is the UK's leading gardening charity
dedicated to advancing horticulture and promoting good gardening.
Its charitable work includes providing expert advice and information,
training the next generation of gardeners, creating hands-on
opportunities for children to grow plants and conducting research
into plants, pests and environmental issues affecting gardeners.
For more information visit **www.rhs.org.uk** or call 0845 130 4646.

Royal Horticultural Society

GROW YOUR OWN
VEG & FRUIT
YEAR PLANNER

| contents

| Foreword

Not since the days of the 'Dig for Victory' campaign during the Second World War has the RHS seen such a surge of interest in growing your own food. In 1941, as part of the 'Dig for Victory' campaign, the RHS issued what was to become its most iconic publication ever, *The Vegetable Garden Displayed*. So successful was it, that it was translated into German at the end of the war to assist with the reconstruction of the German domestic economy.

Nearly seventy years later, The Royal Horticultural Society is at the heart of a brand new movement to encourage gardeners to grow their own. In 2007, the Grow Your Own campaign began when the Society and the BBC collaborated on a new television series, *Grow Your Own Veg*. Through the programme, nursery woman and BBC *Gardener's World* presenter Carol Klein – a keen vegetable grower herself – visited gardeners up and down the country to learn more about the subject. These included allotment experts, willing to share their secrets and enthusiasm, as well as amateurs who were trying their hand at growing their own edible crops for the first time.

Like the television series, the accompanying book of the same name was a runaway success, quickly reaching the top of the bestseller list. Together the RHS, the BBC and Carol Klein had tapped into the mood of the moment; a growing demand to discover how to grow your own food, fresher and tastier than shop-bought produce, with none of the air miles, packaging or chemical inputs. All across the country, more and more gardeners were taking up allotments, and in the mid-winter of 2007 when the series was first aired, a legion of soon-to-be veg gardeners was inspired. Such was the demand for *Grow Your Own Veg*, a sister title, *Grow Your Own Fruit*, was published in 2008.

But what we then discovered is that gardeners wanted to plan their veg and fruit ahead, month by month, and needed help with the planning. As a result we have created *Grow Your Own Veg & Fruit Year Planner*. This is in an easy-to-use format that guides and inspires the reader through vegetable and fruit growing year round, arranged month by month. In this book you will find advice on setting up your plot, and techniques and methods for successful growing and harvesting of fruit and vegetable crops, plus suggestions on the best varieties of fruit and veg available today.

Growing Your Own has just as much relevance today as it did in 1941, as gardeners are not only saving money by growing their own produce but finding that growing fruit and vegetables is a pleasurable and healthy activity that the entire family can take part in at home. Today, people of all ages and from all walks of life are reliving domestic values of yesteryear. Now, as it did seven decades ago, the RHS continues to play a vital role in helping the public to find the information it needs to get growing, through the advice the Society shares with its members. As we find ourselves in the middle of yet another gardening revolution, we hope that this important book, which is core to the values of the RHS, inspires and enthuses you to become part of that revolution and encourages you to start Growing Your Own.

FIGS *(above left) are a low maintenance – not to mention delicious – fruit to try in your garden. The trees grow large over the years, so if you have a small garden, keep them in check with seasonal pruning.*
CRUNCHY YOUNG LETTUCES *(left) are a staple of the summer vegetable garden, and can be arranged in the plot to create a beautiful patchwork of colours and textures.*

Inga Grimsey
Former **Director General, The Royal Horticultural Society**

| Introduction

We have become much more discriminating about our food in recent years. We want to know exactly how it has been produced; many people are increasingly unhappy about the fact that fruit and vegetables in supermarkets and greengrocers may have been sprayed with numerous pesticides, fed with chemical fertilisers and washed with chlorine before they land on our tables. We like to know where our food is from – is it local, or has it been flown thousands of miles to give us an expensive, out-of-season treat? Flavour is also a matter of prime importance; no-one wants to eat bland, tasteless fruit and vegetables just because the varieties chosen have a long shelf life and are easier for the commercial grower to pack and transport. But so often, that is what we've had to put up with.

While the range of produce available has increased in response to these demands, prices have increased, too. There may be lots of premium products out there now,

but all of them carry a premium price tag. Organic produce, tomatoes on the vine, unusual salad leaves, potato varieties specially selected for their flavour... it would be very easy to run up a large bill in no time. Even then, the produce we select has most likely spent a lot of time being transported over many miles and sitting around in warehouses or on the supermarket shelf, meaning it is hardly at its freshest.

Why grow your own?

Growing your own fruit and vegetables brings satisfaction on many levels. There is always something especially thrilling about harvesting a crop that you have raised from seed, no matter how many times you have done it before – it brings back a connection with the earth that too often tends to be lost in the busy modern world. Healthy living is now one of our major concerns, and growing your own wins on two counts: both in the gentle exercise of gardening itself and in the quality produce we grow. It is easy to eat your 'five a day' (or more) when you have a range of delicious fruit and vegetables just waiting to be picked in your own back garden.

Growing crops means you know exactly what has happened to your food in its lifetime; what type of soil it has grown in, and what fertilisers, pesticides or weedkillers have been used. If you want to eat organic produce, you can be absolutely certain of its provenance. You can select varieties for their flavour, not just their appearance and shelf life, and you can have the fun of growing age-old 'heirloom' varieties that have been rejected by large-scale producers because they don't have sufficient commercial qualities, even though they might be exceptionally good to eat.

'Food miles' are another consideration. Is it really worth buying a pack of French beans that have travelled from Africa or strawberries flown in from the United States? Part of the pleasure of crops is their seasonality; the first new potatoes of summer, the eagerly anticipated short weeks of asparagus cutting; parsnips sweetened by a touch of frost – they are all made more enjoyable when we have to wait for their proper time. When fresh strawberries and runner beans are available all year round there is no doubt they lose something of their savour and, in any case, out-of-season crops are usually only a pale imitation of the real thing.

With so many crops, freshness is vitally important. A squeaky-crisp lettuce cut straight from the garden bears no relation to the limp offering on a supermarket shelf, and there is far less waste when faded outer leaves don't have to be thrown away. Sweetcorn is at its very sweetest when cooked within minutes of picking; in fact, it's said you should make sure the pan of water is on the boil before you cut the cobs. And few things can beat the flavour of a juicy peach eaten straight from the tree.

The perfect hobby

If you are on a tight budget, growing your own crops can offer a real saving, especially if you're careful in choosing what to grow. High-value crops like asparagus and raspberries are particularly cost effective, and runner beans produce an enormous crop from a relatively small piece of ground. With careful planning, you can be eating home-grown food virtually all year round, either fresh or

RADISH is a hardy vegetable that adds crunch and spiciness to salads. It is fast-growing, maturing in as little as four weeks, and will store for several days in the fridge once harvested, placed in a polythene bag.

from store, and can even produce very welcome gifts of home-made preserves and pickles from your plot.

For many people, kitchen gardening becomes a fulfilling hobby that lasts a lifetime. You don't need a huge garden; it is an enjoyable challenge to see just how many crops you can grow in windowboxes, pots and hanging baskets, on a tiny patio or balcony. Children, too, love to grow something they can eat, and gardening can set them on the right road to healthy eating.

Whether you are a novice gardener or an old hand, it is often difficult to remember exactly what you should be doing when, and it's easy to miss a sowing date or forget to order plants in time. This book will help you keep on top of everything, from preparing your plot, to planning what to grow, to problem solving. The month-by-month guide will keep you up to date on all the tasks that need doing and there is plenty of detail on useful subjects such as selecting the best varieties, growing food in pots and ensuring good fruit pollination. Above all, you will find the real satisfaction that comes from growing your own, and thoroughly enjoy the process along the way.

CHINESE CHIVES (above right) have white flowers that illuminate the kitchen garden in late summer, contrasted here by curly purple-red kale and the glossy green leaves of Swiss chard.

THE VIBRANT COLOURS AND TEXTURES of vegetables (right), both in their prime and when they are starting to run to seed, are demonstrated in this early summer potager.

| Growing in a small space

If, like most people these days, you don't have a house with an extensive vegetable plot or an orchard, don't worry – there's plenty you can grow in even the smallest garden. A courtyard, patio or balcony can house a range of containers.

Balconies

Many residents in flats have balconies as their only outdoor space. Far from being a place devoid of suitable growing areas this offers many opportunities. Not only do balconies often provide a sheltered environment but they also, by their very nature, have plenty of vertical wall space, which can be adapted to fruit cultivation using restricted tree forms such as fans, espaliers and cordons, or climbing plants such as runner beans.

Many balcony gardens are in cities or by the coast, where the climate tends to be milder than in other locations, giving gardeners with balconies the opportunity to cultivate some of the more tender crops, which would otherwise struggle outdoors in temperate areas. Tomatoes, peppers and aubergines thrive on a sunny balcony, and growing climbers such as grapevines up balcony supports offers shade in summer and creates an ornamental feature, as well as providing a yield of fruit. It is even worth trying real exotics such as citrus and pomegranates in favoured areas.

Before you get carried away, however, do make sure your balcony is structurally sound and will hold the extra weight of your crops and the soil they grow in. Wet soil is surprisingly heavy, as you will know if you have ever tried to move a large tub around. Be extra careful with pots on walls or hanging baskets – they must be securely supported so there is no danger of them being knocked off and falling on some unfortunate person below.

Courtyards and patios

These usually provide gardeners with more space than balconies, allowing a wider range of crops to be grown. They are often sheltered and sunny (though there will always be some in the shade) and usually surrounded by plenty of vertical wall space. Many patios have beds for plants, but even if the area is completely paved there is enormous scope to grow fruit and vegetables in containers there.

Raised beds

If you have sufficient room, a raised bed will increase the range of plants that can be grown. Think of a raised bed as a large, specially constructed container with no base, so that the growing area is higher than the ground. Its sides are usually made of wood or brick; you can build it from scratch, or buy a ready-to-assemble DIY raised bed, which is an easier, if more expensive, option.

Ideally beds should be no wider than 1.2m (4ft) so that they can be comfortably worked from both sides. If the bed is being positioned against a wall or fence, make it 60cm (24in) wide. The maximum convenient length for a bed is probably 3m (10ft); any longer can be irritatingly long to walk around. Square or rectangular beds make the best use of a small space and are easier to construct. Fill the bed with compost, or good-quality soil fortified with organic matter, and ensure there is good drainage at the base.

Containers

Growing in containers offers many benefits, particularly for fruit. You can control the size of a plant by restricting its roots in a pot, which also forces the plant to crop more quickly than a tree or shrub in the open ground whose roots have unlimited access to the soil. This is particularly useful if space is limited in your garden because it allows you to maximise your plants' cropping potential. Containerisation also makes both fruit and vegetables much more accessible for harvesting, and easier to protect from pests and diseases, too.

Containers are now readily available in a huge range of materials, the most popular being plastic, terracotta, metal and wood. Terracotta looks very attractive, but tends to dry out more quickly than plastic, and needs more regular watering. To combat this, line the inside walls of the container with thin plastic to reduce moisture loss. Look for frostproof rather than frost-resistant pots unless protection can be given over winter.

PICK CONTAINER-GROWN STRAWBERRIES *as soon as they are ripe. Do this during the warmest time of day. Not only will they taste better but their beautiful fragrance will also be at its most intoxicating.*

TEN BENEFITS OF RAISED BEDS

❋ Raised beds allow easy access and require less bending.

❋ Soil in raised beds warms up quickly, which is good on clay where spring arrives later.

❋ You can plant closer and get higher yields.

❋ Raised beds provide ample growing depth which is good for root crops.

❋ You can import new soil that is most appropriate to your crop.

❋ One raised bed is less daunting than a large veg plot.

❋ Beds can be made to any shape, and from any material to match the style of your garden.

❋ Cloches, netting and plant supports are easy to manage in a raised bed.

❋ Gluts are less likely as crops are grown in short rows or blocks, giving smaller amounts at one time.

❋ Paths around raised beds allow the soil within the bed to remain uncompressed by treading, thereby protecting its structure.

Standing terracotta pots on 'feet' avoids waterlogging and therefore reduces the chance of frost damage and the pot splitting.

Plastic pots are lighter than terracotta (an important consideration when you are moving pots about), dry out less easily and aren't affected by frost. Imitation terracotta pots that look just like the real thing are now available in garden centres.

Metal containers have a smart, modern look. They are frostproof, can be heavy or lightweight and won't dry out like terracotta. Their main potential problem is that they heat up (and conduct the cold) quickly.

Wooden planters, such as Versailles tubs, have a limited lifespan because the wood will rot, though this can be slowed down by lining the inside with plastic sheeting with drainage holes in the bottom.

Almost any shape and size of container can be used for growing plants – from old kettles, large tins and wooden boxes to buckets and wooden crates (lined with pierced plastic), depending on the look you want. Good drainage is important for all containers; check that there are enough drainage holes in the base of the container and make more if necessary. Cover its base with old crocks or stones, and raise it on feet to let the water drain freely. Use either a water-retentive, peat- or bark-based potting compost, or a soil- or loam-based medium such as John Innes to fill the containers; good-quality compost can make a lot of difference to the health of a plant.

Ensure that the pot size is appropriate for what you want to grow. Root vegetables such as carrots need deep pots, while beetroot, which sits near to the top of the soil, and salads need less depth. Big plants such as tomatoes and courgettes, and fruit trees and bushes, require large pots to accommodate their roots. For tall plants that need a stable base, use a heavy pot and fill it with soil-based potting compost.

One of the advantages of containers is that they can be moved in or out of the sun as required, especially if they're on a base with wheels. In general, though, they are often too heavy to keep shifting about, so choose their position with care.

Regular watering will be necessary; do not rely on rainfall to keep your container plants moist, because it may not penetrate the leaf cover of the plants, or be heavy enough to soak down to the roots. Water-retaining granules mixed with the compost when planting make the job easier, and mulching the surface with gravel or other decorative materials not only helps minimise evaporation but also looks attractive. If you have many pots, it might be worth installing an automatic irrigation system.

The relatively small amount of compost in a container will have limited nutrients for plants, so feeding will be necessary. Incorporate a controlled-release fertiliser on planting, or use a general-purpose, balanced liquid feed throughout the season.

Small gardens

For those lucky enough to have a garden, the scope for growing fruit and vegetables becomes even more extensive. Where crops can be grown directly in the ground rather than in containers, maintenance is reduced because watering and feeding demands are much less rigorous, and obviously the more space you have, the greater the range of plants you can grow. Where gardens are small, fruit trees will need to be chosen with care, making use of the dwarfing rootstocks that are available to keep plants compact, and restricted growth forms such as fans and cordons come into their own in small spaces.

Make use of vertical garden space, too; walls and fences make good supports for fan-trained fruit trees and climbing crops such as runner beans. Allow scrambling plants like cucumbers and squashes to ramble over garden sheds and outbuildings.

Where space is limited, why not grow decorative varieties of vegetables and fruits in ornamental beds among the flowers. Many lettuce and salad leaves are available in red, green and purple, with scalloped or frilly leaves, while basil can be dark red and carrots have attractive, feathery foliage. Bushy tomatoes and wigwams of runner beans make interesting additions to a border, while strawberry plants, particularly alpine varieties, make a great edging. Fruit and vegetables certainly don't have to be dull.

EVEN IN A SMALL COURTYARD GARDEN *(top right) it is surprising how careful use of a limited space can enable a good range of fresh produce to be grown and enjoyed.*

STEP-OVER APPLE TREES *(right) are ideal for small gardens, where they can add decoration and function alongside other interestingly coloured or textured vegetables and salads.*

| Know your plot

A good understanding of the geographical aspects of your site is essential if you want to grow food crops successfully. Planting moisture-loving crops in dry soils, acid-loving crops in alkaline soils or sun-loving crops in shady locations will always result in disappointment. It is particularly important to get the conditions right for fruit crops, as most are perennials and therefore grow in the same piece of ground for years or even decades. Making sure they are in a suitable location initially is crucial, because moving them later could be both extremely time-consuming and very difficult.

Assessing your soil

Healthy soil is essential for good crops, but fortunately if your soil isn't ideal you can improve it. Soils consist of minerals, clay, sand and silt, which are coated in and bound by organic materials to produce small lumps called peds; these give structure to the soil and prevent it from becoming a solid mass impenetrable to roots. Peds have air spaces between them, which allow oxygen, water and roots to enter the soil. Working or trampling on your soil, especially when it is wet, ruins the structure – and, remember, the better the soil structure, the better the crop you will be able to grow.

Take a really good look at your soil by digging a narrow, sharp-sided pit about 60cm (24in) deep, and check the colour of the sides. There should be a layer of dark topsoil at least 20cm (8in) deep above a base of paler subsoil. The topsoil should be open and friable, ideally with plant roots visible to their full depth. Hard, compacted soils block growing roots and drainage, so careful attention and cultivation is required to open up the soil.

Once you have examined your pit, fill it with water, cover and leave overnight. If the water is still there the next day, drainage is poor and raised beds or a drainage

TESTING YOUR SOIL

A quick way to identify your soil type is to take a handful of soil, moisten it slightly and then try to mould it in your hands. You can then note its particular characteristics.

Sandy soils are made up of relatively large particles surrounded by air spaces. Water drains easily and there is plenty of air for plant roots.

Predominantly sandy soils warm up quickly in spring; drain very quickly and don't hold onto nutrients well; they are easy to dig and make into a seedbed; and are well-aerated and don't compact easily. To help improve their workability and texture, incorporate organic matter.

Silty soils are composed of medium-sized particles that can be sticky and heavy but are also quite nutrient rich.

Predominantly silty soils warm up relatively quickly in spring; hold onto nutrients well; drain quite slowly; can easily become compacted; are relatively easy to dig; and are generally sufficiently aerated.

Clay soils comprise very small particles that stick together so air is slow to penetrate and drainage is obstructed. They are therefore difficult to cultivate.

Predominantly clay soils warm up slowly in spring; hold on to nutrients very well; can easily become waterlogged; are very prone to becoming compacted; can be very heavy to dig; and can be poorly aerated.

SANDY SOILS (top) feel gritty between your fingers and won't easily stick together to form a ball.
SILTY SOILS (centre) feel silky to the touch and can be rolled into a ball or cylinder relatively easily.
CLAY SOILS (bottom) feel sticky and heavy, and can be rolled into a pencil-thick sausage and then bent into a ring.

system might be needed. Excess water excludes air from the soil and roots can't survive long without air. In effect, the plants drown.

Your soil's texture influences many physical and chemical characteristics of your plot such as nutrient availability, moisture-retention, drainage, fertility and aeration. You therefore need to know whether your soil is made up of clay, sand or silt particles. Roll some of the topsoil between your hands. If it flakes and crumbles, it is low in clay. If it feels gritty between your finger and thumb, it is sandy. A soapy or silky feel suggests silty soil. And if it is easy to roll into a sausage shape, your topsoil is of clay.

Whatever your soil type, digging in well-rotted organic matter, such as garden compost or farmyard manure, and applying mulches of organic matter preserves and enhances its structure, as does working your soil only when it is reasonably dry.

TESTING YOUR SOIL'S pH LEVEL

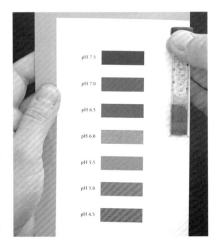

TAKE A SLICE OF SOIL *2.5cm (1in) thick from the top to the bottom of a hole in your garden. Mix the soil sample, then put a little of it into the pH kit's test tube.*

FOLLOW THE INSTRUCTIONS *carefully by adding testing chemicals to your soil sample. Give the tube a good shake, then allow the soil to settle.*

COMPARE THE COLOUR *of the resulting mixture with those on the supplied colour chart. The best match indicates your soil's pH from the area of your sample.*

IS YOUR SOIL ACID OR ALKALINE?

Measuring the pH of your soil enables you to determine whether the soil is acid or alkaline. A pH of 7 is neutral, less than 7 is acid and more than 7 is alkaline. Fruit and most vegetables grow best in a slightly acid soil with a pH of 6.5, although pH 7–7.5 helps reduce club root disease in the cabbage family.

A laboratory test is best (and not hugely expensive), but quick and simple soil testing kits are available from all good gardening stores. To take a soil sample, use a clean trowel to scrape the surface from a small area in, eg, the vegetable garden and dig a hole 15cm (6in) across and 15cm (6in) deep. With the trowel take a slice of soil 2.5cm (1in) thick from the top to the bottom of the hole and place in a clean, dry container. Avoid roots, stones and surface debris.

For the best results, repeat the soil test several times with samples from different areas of the vegetable garden.

If the soil is too acid, spread garden lime (finely ground chalk or limestone) and mix it into the soil in the amounts the test results suggest are needed to raise the pH. Lowering the pH is more difficult, though acidic materials such as sulphur chips can be used. It's usually much easier and more successful to grow acid-loving crops such as blueberries in a container of ericaceous (acidic) compost than to try to adjust an alkaline soil to a more suitable pH.

Weather and climate

One factor that will influence the positioning of specific crops is the site and aspect of your plot, with elements such as light, temperature, rainfall and wind all having an important impact on what crops you can grow.

Light: Most vegetable crops will need as much sun as possible, and few are worth growing where buildings or trees limit the summer sun to less than six hours a day. Some fruits, such as alpine strawberries, acid cherries, red and white currants and gooseberries, tolerate some shade, but others, such as grapes, figs, peaches, nectarines and apricots, love and need sun and warmth. Mapping out your garden to note key areas of shade and full sun is essential before you start planting.

Temperatures: In general, inland and upland areas are colder than coastal regions, and urban areas are usually warmer than the countryside since the warm masonry and paving emit heat at night. The growing season gets shorter the further away you go from the equator, and eventually crops such as squashes and tomatoes cannot be grown outdoors. The longer the growing season for most vegetables the better, especially for frost-sensitive plants such as pumpkins and sweetcorn.

Damage from frosty weather is perhaps most problematic for fruit gardeners. A badly timed late frost can destroy open blossoms as well as any fruitlets, reducing potential yield significantly. Frost can also damage the soft shoots and foliage of various crops, even reasonably hardy crops such as kiwifruits and grapevines.

Local horticultural societies, weather station data (on official forecasting websites) or neighbours are all ideal starting points if you need to obtain details of annual temperature extremes in your area.

Rainfall: Maintaining soil moisture is important for the healthy growth of all crops, and in areas with low rainfall frequent watering will be necessary. Plants near walls and fences are vulnerable to 'rain shadows', and so soil at the base of such vertical structures can become very dry, even in rainy weather.

High levels of rainfall will be a problem if soil drainage is poor – even moisture-loving species will fail to thrive in waterlogged soil. Improve drainage by digging in plenty of bulky organic matter, such as composted bark, plus a 7.5cm (3in) layer of horticultural grit to a depth of half a spade blade. More permanent drainage problems such as those caused by a sloping site or high water table require more substantial treatment, such as the digging of a soakaway or installation of drainage pipes, and in such cases it's frequently easier and more economical to use raised beds or to grow crops in containers.

Wet winters make harvesting and preparing the soil difficult, and can spoil the produce even if there is good drainage. While gardeners in wet districts can stand on planks so that they don't damage the soil, a good alternative is to build raised beds. Winter rains fill the soil with water until it can take no more (usually around mid winter). The surplus then drains away, but the stored rain is available for plants during early summer.

Dry summers can greatly reduce the quantity and quality of crops, and raised beds are useful in areas prone to droughts because the greater depth of fertile soil gives plant roots more to explore for water. Adding organic matter, by mulching or digging in, and not compacting soils allow the equivalent of 5cm (2in) of rain to be stored in the soil – enough to keep plants going for two weeks.

Wind: The majority of tree fruits flower early in the year and so require a sheltered site that attracts pollinating insects (predominantly bees) that are already on the wing. If these beneficial creatures are discouraged from

PEACHES, NECTARINES AND APRICOTS *are best grown as a fan against a sunny, south- or southwest-facing wall if the fruits are going to ripen successfully in temperate climates.*

AREAS WHERE COLD AIR COLLECTS

These are known as frost pockets. Cold air will naturally sink to and collect in the lowest point it can reach, so sloping sites are most at risk. If your garden is in a natural valley do not plant frost-sensitive vegetables or early-flowering fruit trees at the bottom of it, where there will be a natural frost pocket.

visiting flowers by strong winds the fruits' flowers won't be pollinated and resulting fruit set will be very poor. Windy conditions also slow vegetable growth and make cloches and horticultural fleece hard to keep in place.

Hedges make good windbreaks, being cost effective and good for wildlife; fences are an alternative in small gardens and where quick results are wanted. Porous fences (with 50 percent gaps) and hedges are better than solid barriers, which force the wind up, over and down, creating turbulence that can damage plants and fences.

| Preparing the plot

It is well worth taking time and trouble over soil preparation when starting a new fruit or vegetable garden from scratch. After all, it is likely to remain in place for many years, and it is really important to give the growing medium a good start. Proper preparation means avoiding future problems for yourself, as well.

Tackling weeds

Getting rid of persistent weeds at the start could save hours of labour later on. In the vegetable garden there are opportunities to deal with weed growth as the crops are lifted each year. However, the more permanent nature of most fruit crops makes this much more difficult, so for a fruit garden and long-term ornamental planting schemes it is even more important to tackle weeds right from the beginning of the preparation process.

Preliminary cultivation of the soil is worthwhile, even if you intend to follow a no-digging regime later. Young growth of annual weeds such as groundsel, chickweed and fat hen are best hoed off or skimmed off with a sharp spade. While you are digging over the plot, remove as many weeds as possible, including those with deeper roots such as bindweed, dock, thistles and dandelion. Take care that you do not leave any bits of root behind to regenerate. Don't add perennial weeds to the compost heap. Instead lay them out where they are exposed to sun; they will soon dry out and die.

Some weeds are particularly deep rooted and troublesome and are more difficult to get rid of – bindweed, Japanese knotweed and horsetail are among some of the worst. These can be treated with a weedkiller such as glyphosate. This is a reasonably environmentally friendly herbicide, since the active chemical does not remain active in the soil after it has done its work.

If you prefer to avoid chemical weedkillers you can use black plastic sheet mulches to cover troublesome weeds. Plastic sheet mulches are useful for clearing large areas if you prefer an organic approach, but they do need to be in place for three or four years to clear the more persistent perennials. Do not use a mechanical cultivator to clear areas covered with perennial weeds, because the blades chop up the roots into small pieces, each of which may grow into a new plant.

TOOLS

Having the right tools for the job makes vegetable growing much easier and leaves more time for you to enjoy the end result. Good inexpensive tools are sold by DIY or garden stores and are widely available second hand, but buy the best you can afford – they should last you a lifetime. Handle the tools before buying to make sure they are well-balanced and a suitable size, so that they are comfortable to handle. Clean your tools and store them carefully after every job. That way they will last longer and be a pleasure to use every time. Regularly sharpen the blades of tools like spades and hoes, and sand down wooden handles to avoid splinters. A typical starter-kit for growing your own vegetables includes:

- spade
- fork
- push or draw hoe
- trowel and hand fork
- rake
- pair of secateurs
- hosepipe and watering can
- boots and gloves

Cultivation

A new vegetable plot will often benefit from 'double digging', particularly if drainage is poor. This means digging the soil down to a spade's depth (known as a spit) and then thoroughly breaking up the soil at the base of the hole. Freely drained and reasonably fertile soils usually need only single digging – turning over the soil one spit deep. Single digging is generally sufficient for fruit crops, because the majority of fruit tree and bush roots are found in the top 20cm (8in) of soil.

To single dig a new bed, start by excavating a trench to a spade's depth and moving the soil to the far end of the bed. Then dig a second trench behind the first, placing its soil back in the first trench and breaking it up with a fork in the process. Repeat these steps until the whole bed has been dug. Incorporate soil improvers such as well-rotted garden compost or farmyard manure into the soil as you progress, and remove weeds, debris and large stones. Finally, fill in the last trench with the soil excavated from the first one.

Fertilisers and manures

Fertile conditions boost the size, flavour, yield and quality of your crops. Every second or third year vegetables, particularly, benefit from the addition of bulky, well-rotted organic matter, such as garden or municipal compost or farmyard manure to one half or one third of your plot. Fruit trees can be given an occasional mulch with these materials, taking care to keep them away from the trunk.

Greedy crops, such as brassicas, beetroot, spinach and celery, need the boost of a general fertiliser containing roughly equal amounts of nitrogen, phosphorus and potassium. Fruiting vegetable crops such as peas, beans and marrows, as well as fruit trees and bushes, can be given a fertiliser high in potassium, such as sulphate of potash or tomato fertiliser. Potassium is the nutrient that promotes flowering and fruit formation.

WHEN DIGGING UP WEEDS (top) *use a fork to loosen the roots. Dig around perennial weeds such as dandelions carefully to ensure that no pieces of taproot remain in the ground, where they can regenerate.*

BURNING WEEDS (centre) *with a flame gun is a useful way to kill off weed seedlings without disturbing the soil underneath them.*

PLANT THROUGH BLACK PLASTIC SHEET MULCHES (right) *for low-maintenance weed control. It also warms the soil. The sheeting must be secured well at the sides of the bed so it does not blow away.*

Green manures

In nature, the nutrients that plants take from the soil are returned to it once more when the plant eventually dies and rots down. When growing vegetables, the plant's top growth is generally removed so that the nutrients do not get a chance to be returned, which is why you need to add fertilisers to the soil.

Green manuring is a more natural way of doing this than by adding chemical fertilisers, which is why it is popular with organic gardeners. Vacant areas of soil are sown with a quick-growing crop that is dug in before it has matured. This adds bulky organic material to the soil, helping to improve its structure, as well as returning the nutrients from the plant. Green manures sown in autumn will take up nutrients left over by the crops, which would otherwise be washed away by rain, and growing a green manure crop will also help to suppress weed growth.

Plants with deep or spreading roots, such as rye-grass, are particularly useful as they search out nutrients in areas of soil not available to shallower-rooting plants. Leguminous (pea-family) crops are also helpful as they have the ability to enrich the soil by 'fixing' atmospheric nitrogen (converting it to a form that can be used by plants), and this will benefit following crops. Field beans, lupins and clover are among leguminous green manures.

Seeds of various crops suitable for growing as green manures are available from seed companies, either separately or as mixtures.

UNDERSTANDING SOIL FERTILITY

Soil fertility refers not only to the amount of nutrients a soil contains but also to the ground's general health. Just one teaspoon of healthy soil will contain thousands of fungi, bacteria and other microorganisms, all of which are essential in maintaining a balanced plot able to support plant growth.

Most soils tend to be naturally fertile, but sandy and shallow chalky soils will benefit more from the addition of organic matter to enable them to hold on to nutrients. Also, a heavily cultivated piece of land could be devoid of certain nutrients so it's useful to research its history. An allotment bed previously supporting black currants would be low in nitrogen, for example, because these plants have a heavy demand for this nutrient.

IMPROVE YOUR SOIL (top) by adding plenty of well-rotted organic matter such as farmyard manure or your own garden compost.

APPLY FERTILISERS (above) only once you know what crops you are growing – if at all. Surplus nutrients can cause root scorching and ground water pollution.

A THRIVING PLOT (right) is more likely if your plants are grown in soil that suits their particular requirements.

| All about growing

Obtaining strong, healthy plants is the first step in growing good crops, but they need regular care afterwards to fulfil their potential. This is a quick guide to some of the main techniques involved in growing good fruit and vegetables.

Fruit

Planting: The ideal time to plant fruit trees and bushes is in autumn when the soil is still warm from summer, even though containerised plants are available to buy and plant year-round. Bare-root trees, which tend to have healthier root systems, are available in the dormant season. Keep their roots moist until they are planted, which you should do as soon as you reach home.

Dig out a planting hole that is about twice the width of the rootball and the same depth. If there is any compacted soil beneath the ground, break this up using a fork or mattock. Mix the soil from the hole with well-rotted organic matter and controlled-release fertiliser at the rate that is recommended by the manufacturer.

Plant at the same depth as the bush or tree was grown previously in the nursery, using a planting stick placed across the hole to check the level against the soil mark on the stem. When correct, backfill the hole, firming down the soil around the roots as you go.

After planting, you should mulch a fruit tree with a generous amount of well-rotted manure around the base of the plant, but do make sure that the mulch is kept away from the trunk to prevent it rotting. Mulching helps to retain moisture and should suppress some weeds. Its gradual breakdown into the soil makes it a useful soil conditioner, too. Most fruit trees benefit from regular mulching each year in early spring. If applied earlier it can be washed away before it becomes effective.

When buying a tree fruit such as an apple, make sure you choose an appropriate rootstock; this controls the eventual size of the tree. Most gardeners prefer to grow trees on dwarfing or semi-dwarfing rootstocks, which keep trees compact and encourage early cropping. If you are short of space, choose trees suitable for growing as cordons, espaliers, or other restricted forms (see page 59).

Strawberries are one of the most popular fruits, and they can be cultivated in tiny spaces by using specialised planters or other containers. The trailing habit of a strawberry plant makes it a wonderful subject for a hanging basket outside a kitchen window.

PLANTING A BARE-ROOT FRUIT TREE

1 DIG OUT A HOLE *wide and deep enough to accommodate the root system. Hammer in a strong stake to support the tree when young.*

2 PLACE A STICK ACROSS THE HOLE *to ensure that the tree is at the depth at which it was previously planted.*

3 BACKFILL THE HOLE, *firming the soil around the roots using the tips of your fingers. Water the tree in well and secure to the stake.*

PLANT STRAWBERRIES IN A GROWING BAG

1 MAKE SIX PLANTING HOLES *in the surface of the growing bag. Use a knife to cut a cross and then fold back the flaps.*

2 REDUCE A LARGE ROOT SYSTEM *by about half, using a pair of sharp secateurs. This won't damage the plants.*

3 DIG OUT A HOLE *large enough to fit each plant, ensuring the crown is just above the soil surface. Firm each plant in well, then water.*

Staking: Any fruit tree planted in the open ground, as opposed to against a wall or fence, will require staking to ensure that it stays upright and is able to carry a crop of heavy fruit. Position the stake on the side from which the prevailing wind comes to prevent the tree from being blown against the stake and so damaged.

Use tree ties with padding to protect the tree from rubbing against the stake. A pair of tights can be a useful, cheaper alternative because they are flexible and will also cushion the tree from the stake. Tree ties should never be overtight. Check them regularly – at least each winter – and loosen if necessary.

Trees in pots: Any fruit tree can be grown in a pot, so no matter how small your garden is you can be dazzled by a spectacular display of blossom in spring and later tasty home-produce direct from your garden. Select a sunny, sheltered site for your container.

Because it will be very heavy once filled, move the container to its final position before potting up the tree. Place crocks in the bottom of the pot, and stand the pot on feet or bricks to allow it to drain freely. Use a loam-based potting compost such as John Innes No. 3 mixed with some controlled-release fertiliser to fill the pot.

A fruit tree in a pot will need daily watering during dry periods in the growing season, and once it starts to flower it will also require a high-potash liquid feed (such as tomato food) each week until the fruit begins to ripen. Some trees may require staking or another form of support to help them carry the fruit crop. Don't let the tree overcrop because this will stress it owing to its restricted root system.

For the first 3–4 years as it increases in height, replant the tree in a larger pot each year. The eventual size of the container can be as large as you want.

Soft fruit in containers: Soft fruit bushes and plants can also be grown in containers very successfully. Gooseberries, especially standard gooseberries; red, white and black currants, and cane fruit such as raspberries will all grow well in a large pot of loam-based (or a mixture of loam-based and soilless) potting compost. Like trees, they need careful attention to watering in spring and summer.

Strawberries are particularly suited to container growing. Special strawberry planters, towers, and barrels with holes in the sides can be used to pack lots of strawberries into a very small space – ideal for small, patio gardens. The trailing habit of strawberries makes them especially good for growing in a hanging basket, and they do very well in growing bags, too (see above). If the growing bag can be positioned on a raised surface it will take the backache out of weeding and picking, making it ideal for older or less mobile gardeners.

Pruning: Most fruit trees will benefit from an annual removal of branches to encourage vigour and healthy fruit. The main reasons for pruning are: to remove dead, dying and diseased parts of the tree or shrub; to allow air and sunlight into the plant for the optimum development of fruit and to avoid disease; and to improve the appearance of the tree or shrub and allow it to grow to the shape and size you want. Pruning is carried out in both winter and summer, depending on the effect you want to achieve. Remember that pruning trees hard in winter tends to stimulate growth the following season, while pruning in summer will control growth. This is why summer pruning forms such an important part of training restricted forms of tree such as cordons and espaliers.

Pollination: For almost all fruit varieties to produce fruit successfully, their flowers need pollinating. This process is usually carried out by flying insects such as honey bees and bumblebees; however, nuts such as cobnuts and filberts are pollinated by the wind. Many types of fruit are self-sterile and have to be pollinated by another variety of tree growing nearby. Some fruit trees such as 'Victoria' plums and 'Stella' cherries are self-fertile, meaning that they pollinate their own flowers; this is ideal in a small garden because only this one tree is required to produce fruit. However, even self-fertile varieties tend to crop better when another tree is nearby for pollination. Ask a specialist nursery for advice on the best pollinators for the particular varieties you want to grow.

Vegetables

Seed or plants: You can either raise your crops from seed, or you can buy plug plants from a specialist supplier, a local nursery or by mail order. The range of plants available is growing all the time. Seed sowing and plug plants both have their advantages and disadvantages: you will have to weigh up what is better for you and your garden's conditions. Buying in plants is particularly useful if you have a small garden and do not have the facilities for raising plants from seed. It is also a good idea if you want only a small number of plants.

If you want to grow from seed, there are two ways: either in containers or trays for later transplanting, or by sowing direct into drills made in the soil outdoors. Which method you choose depends on the crop as well as the growing conditions at the time of sowing.

Sowing direct outdoors: Soil temperatures of at least 6°C (43°F) are needed for most seed to germinate, and this is

MAKE A DRILL *with a corner edge of a hoe. In dry weather, water the bottom of the drill. Then sprinkle seed thinly and evenly along the row.*

STATION SOW PELLETED SEED *or large ones such as broad beans alongside a guideline of string. Press each gently into the soil and cover.*

likely to be reached by mid spring in most of England, two weeks later in colder districts and two weeks earlier in mild regions of the United Kingdom. In cold areas, covering the soil with a sheet of polythene from mid winter can help to advance spring sowing by keeping the soil dry and thus allowing it to warm up more quickly than it would otherwise have done.

Rake the prepared ground for sowing until you have a smooth layer of finely divided particles over firm, but not too hard, underlying soil. If there are any clods of earth, break them down into fine crumbs by striking them firmly with the back of the rake to shatter them. Rake in a dressing of all-purpose fertiliser, if appropriate.

Make a drill (or groove) in the soil using the corner of a hoe or rake, or by pressing a length of a broom handle into the soil, and sow the seed in the drill in a sparse, continuous flow. Alternatively, sow five or six seeds wherever you want a plant (eg lettuces or turnips), later thinning to one plant. Then draw back the soil with the hoe or rake to fill the drill and firm the soil gently.

Sowing in containers: Some crops such as tomatoes and peppers have to be sown in containers. They need to be sown carly under cover, long before it is warm enough to grow them outside. Other types can be sown in trays and pots to get an extra early crop, or just because it is a more convenient way of raising the plants. Use seedtrays, pots or cell trays filled with a proprietary multipurpose or seed compost. Cover each tray with a glass or plastic propagator top and keep at an even temperature in a greenhouse, cold frame or even on a windowsill indoors. Pot the seedlings up when they are large enough to handle. Gradually harden off before planting outside.

Transplanting: Seedlings in pots, or growing in a seedbed outside, can be transplanted to their final growing positions at the appropriate time and when they have reached a suitable size to handle. When doing this, hold them by a leaf, not by their stem. The stems of seedlings are very fragile, and it is easy to crush them and kill the plant. Leaves, on the other hand, can be replaced. Take care to damage the roots as little as possible.

Transplant seedlings on a dull, cool day, and water them thoroughly before and after transplanting to ensure a quick recovery. Protect newly transplanted specimens from both sun and wind for several days.

MANY SEEDLINGS CAN BE SOWN CLOSELY TOGETHER *as they are small in size, but they will soon need thinning or potting on if they are to develop properly.*

CROP ROTATION

Growing each group of crops on a different piece of land each year can help reduce the build-up of soil pests and diseases. Where possible, aim for a three-year rotation. Crops are grouped according to their likely pest and disease problems and their soil requirements. A common three-year rotation comprises one group containing root vegetables (beetroot, carrot, parsnip, potato etc); another of legumes and fruiting crops (peas, beans, sweetcorn, courgettes etc); and a third group of brassicas (cabbages, broccoli, kale, cauliflower etc). Divide the vegetable plot into three and grow each group in a separate area, rotating the crops to a fresh area each year for three years. Such a rotation also allows you to tailor the soil preparation to the requirements of the different groups of crops; for example adding manure to the section for brassicas but not for root crops (fresh manure causes roots to become misshapen), and liming for brassicas but not potatoes (limey soils encourage potato scab).

| Extending the season

Gardeners can lengthen the season for fruit and vegetables at both ends. In late winter and spring, raising plants under cover or giving them protection with cloches, horticultural fleece and so on gives them a head start in the growing season. At the other end of the year, the same protection techniques can be used to extend the harvest period.

Spring

For vegetables, sowing can start under cover in late winter and very early spring for crops such as tomatoes and onions. This gets the plants growing early so that they are already a good size when it is warm enough to plant them outside, and gives them a long growing season. Ideally a greenhouse should be used for sowing, heated at least sufficiently to remain frost-free. However, a sunny windowsill is also suitable for raising young plants, particularly if you use a white board behind the plants so that they get light from both sides, and not just the front. Alternatively, once the seeds have germinated, give each container a quarter-turn each day so seedlings receive the light evenly.

You can also gain some extra time by covering the soil outside with clear or black polythene where you intend to sow early crops. Cover the soil at least six weeks before the anticipated sowing date; the polythene keeps off the rain and allows the soil to warm up and be ready for sowing up to four weeks earlier than if it was uncovered. After sowing, the polythene can be replaced by horticultural fleece. Such fleece is a very useful, non-woven, plastic fabric that lets in light, rain and pesticide sprays, yet retains some warmth.

If the fleece is suspended over the soil on hoops, you can make sowings under fleece about two weeks before doing so in open ground. Beneath the fleece the plants

A COLD FRAME LID CAN BE PROPPED OPEN *on hot spring days and closed at night when frosts are still possible. In this way the plants inside it will gradually become acclimatised and harden off, ready for planting out if appropriate.*

AN UNHEATED PROPAGATOR *acts like a mini-greenhouse and is perfect for germinating seeds of tender vegetables.*

are protected from the worst frost and flying pests, including birds. Unfortunately slugs and weeds appreciate fleece as much as crops, so you will need to keep an eye out for both. In cold weather, use a double layer of fleece, reducing it to a single layer as soon as possible.

Covering crops with fleece for the early part of their life also encourages an early harvest. When transplants are covered by fleece they can be expected to mature about two weeks before uncovered crops.

Cloches can be used in the same way as fleece. These are really miniature greenhouses, about 50cm (20in) tall, although they can be prone to blowing over in windy weather. Use them to cover tender plants such as aubergines, bush tomatoes, courgettes, melons and peppers, in early summer.

Strawberries may also have their flowers spoiled by a late frost, so drape fleece over the plants when frost is forecast. Strawberries grown under cover in pots in a heated greenhouse or conservatory can be coaxed into fruiting by late spring or early summer, giving you the luxury of an extra-early harvest.

Tree fruits such as apricots, peaches and almonds flower very early in spring, and the flowers are often killed by frosts. Use fleece to protect these, too, covering the trees up on cold nights, but removing the fleece as soon as possible to allow insects to pollinate the flowers. The easiest method of frost protection for container-grown fruit is moving vulnerable plants to a frost-free spot. This could be as luxurious as a heated greenhouse, or as minimal as a sheltered cold frame or porch.

Autumn

As the weather starts to cool in late summer, tender plants such as outdoor tomatoes, peppers and aubergines can be given protection with cloches or fleece to allow the fruits that little extra time to develop and ripen. Enclose the lower parts of tall plants such as tomatoes with two glass or plastic cloches standing on end, or carefully take down plants from their supports, lay them on straw or similar material and place cloches over the top of them.

Move tender container-grown fruit back under cover well before the first frosts arrive. A few vegetables – such as rhubarb, chicory and seakale – can also be taken under cover in autumn and 'forced' in warmth in a greenhouse into early growth. To produce especially tender stems, such vegetables are usually grown in darkness. Trim chicory leaves to 1cm (½in) from the roots, set the plant in moist peat substitute or peat in a box deep enough for the roots to be covered but keeping 1cm (½in) of the crowns above the surface. Leave the pot is a warm, dark place while the chicons form.

Heap straw, dry leaves or dry bracken loosely over rows of vegetables such as carrots to help insulate them from intensely cold weather. Because such protection keeps the soil warmer, this makes it easier to lift the roots through the winter, as otherwise in extreme weather the vegetables can be frozen hard into the soil where they are impossible to dig up until the frost lifts.

FLEECE TUNNELS *are a versatile growing aid, easily moved from crop to crop and providing protection from the elements.*

| Coping with problems

Anyone who has ever grown vegetables or fruit will know that they can be affected by a whole range of problems. These may be cultural – caused by providing plants with less than ideal conditions – or by attacks from various pests and diseases.

Cultural problems

These may result from weather damage, incorrect soil conditions and nutrient deficiencies, among other reasons. Exposed, windy sites are often difficult for plants: tall growers such as Brussels sprouts and cabbages can be damaged by wind rock, and strong winds scorch foliage and stunt growth. Pollinating insects are unable to work the flowers in windy conditions so that fruit crops may be poor.

A heavy clay soil is not suitable for plants that like well-drained conditions, such as many culinary herbs, while very light, free-draining soils will not satisfy hungry and thirsty plants such as brassicas. Fruits such as blueberries need an acidic soil, and will never thrive in alkaline conditions. A shortage of soil nutrients, particularly on chalky soils, can cause a range of distress symptoms such as yellowing between the leaf veins and stunted growth.

A knowledge of the conditions that individual plants require is the first essential for successful cultivation. If the ideal conditions do not exist in your garden it is often possible to overcome the problem by, for example, providing windbreaks, enriching the soil with organic matter, or growing acid-lovers such as blueberries in containers of the correct acidic compost rather than trying to alter the soil's alkalinity in the open ground.

Pests and diseases

The first line of defence is that well-grown plants in optimum growing conditions and with sufficient water and nutrients fend off pest and disease attacks much more readily than plants that are stressed. A certain level of attack can be tolerated, especially if the edible part of the crop is not directly affected, but if action needs to be taken there are various options (see pages 288–295).

Many gardeners do not like the idea of using chemical controls, particularly on edible crops, and in any case an increasingly limited number of chemicals are available for use on fruit and vegetables. When applied correctly, and at the right time, they can work very effectively, but for many people they are seen as a last resort.

Pests: It is possible to boost natural countermeasures to do some of the control work for you. Encourage natural

UNHEALTHY LEAVES *should be removed immediately. These tomato leaves have been affected by magnesium deficiency.*

PEST DETERRENTS *such as these woven wooden plant protectors and orange marigolds may deter pests from kohlrabi and cabbages.*

pest controllers such as lacewings, ladybirds and hedgehogs into your garden by providing them with food and shelter. Also, make life inhospitable for other pests, removing hiding places and limiting access by getting rid of debris and weeds, and raking the soil level to deter slugs. Prevent destructive pests reaching the crop by erecting barriers and mesh. For example, cover a carrot crop with fleece to exclude carrot fly or surround the crop with a 50cm (20in) barrier of plastic sheeting, which will be sufficiently high to exclude this low-flying insect for the next 2m (6½ft) of the plot. Use brassica collars, 7–15cm (2½–5in) across, to prevent cabbage root flies from laying their eggs around the base of a plant.

The next step is, where possible, to choose crop varieties that resist attack, such as fly-resistant carrots. Although mixing plants, for example onions and carrots, to confuse pests is often advocated, there is little evidence that it is effective. Similarly, plants with strong odours such as marigolds are believed by some to protect vegetables from pests; it may or may not work for you – but there is no harm in trying.

When pests do attack, it may be possible to remove them by hand if they are large enough: for example, you can pick the caterpillars of cabbage white butterflies off leaves under attack; and you can hunt down and dispose of snails and slugs at night with the aid of a torch. Such methods, however, can be time-consuming.

The final remedy is to use a chemical control. So-called directed sprays with a physical action (such as oils, insecticidal soaps and fatty acids) will do least harm to helpful insects. Of those that poison insects, the natural ones, such as pyrethrum and derris, are short-lived and mild. Synthetic insecticide will normally persist for longer than natural materials and may be potentially harmful to helpful insects, so they should be used with discretion and strictly according to the pack directions. Bifenthrin (a synthetic version of pyrethrum) is a popular choice.

Diseases: These are caused by infections of bacteria, viruses and especially fungi. Again, plants grown in good conditions are better able to fight off infection than those under stress. There are varieties that have some resistance to disease; for example, potatoes resistant to potato blight, peas that deter powdery mildew and certain cabbage family plants that resist club root.

Many diseases are fungal in origin, and fungicides can often be used as a preventative control, before disease strikes, as well as on plants already affected. Some diseases, particularly those caused by viruses, cannot be treated, and it may be best to remove and destroy affected plants as soon as they are seen in an attempt to limit the spread of the disease.

BEER TRAPS *can be introduced to attract and kill slugs. Check them regularly to ensure they are well topped up.*

BOTRYTIS *can be a problem on soft fruit crops, such as raspberries, particularly in wet or humid weather.*

| Planning what to grow

It's easy to get carried away when you first start planning your fruit and vegetable garden. The temptation is to grow as many different plants and varieties as possible, but you soon realise that you have to be practical if you are to make optimum use of your space.

First of all, consider the resources you have available. Do you have a large garden, so that you can devote a good-sized area to fruit and vegetables? Or is space limited, so that your vegetable plot has to be kept small? Perhaps you have such a small growing area that you will have to make do with a bit of patio space, or dot some vegetables and fruit bushes among the flower beds. Obviously the space available will make a big difference to the type and number of fruit and vegetable plants you decide to grow. Another resource that is often in short supply is time. Someone who has a full-time job or young children to look after is not likely to be able to devote as much time to gardening as, perhaps, a retired person who enjoys a daily session of gardening as their main hobby.

Think about how much time and effort your plants will need. Upright tomatoes, for example, require staking, training and protecting from blight and they crop outdoors for only a few weeks in late summer, while runner beans crop abundantly over a longer period. On the other hand, asparagus almost looks after itself, and once you have established a bed it needs only routine annual maintenance in exchange for up to ten years of abundant produce. If you prefer to avoid periods of intense work, choose crops that need sowing, planting, thinning and weeding over a long period so the work is spread out.

Your gardening skills should also be taken into account – do you have the knowledge and confidence to grow some of the trickier crops, or would you prefer to stick to easy-to-grow, tried-and-tested favourites?

Then, consider your needs. There are some crops that are readily available in the shops, where they are cheap to buy – is it really worth spending a lot of time and effort growing crops like these? It may be better to concentrate on more exotic varieties that are either very expensive to buy, such as asparagus, or that are rarely offered for sale, such as salsify or mulberries. Probably a better use of your space and time might be to grow delicious varieties of early salad potatoes such as 'Pink Fir Apple' than maincrop potatoes, which are cheap and of perfectly adequate quality in the supermarket. On the other hand, a few strawberry plants brought into a porch or cold frame in mid winter would provide you with a punnet of fresh berries when prices in the shops are high and flavour probably poor – indulgent but easy to achieve.

Picking your own produce and getting it from garden to plate in a matter of minutes are some of the joys of growing your own. For some crops, absolute freshness is really important to quality and flavour. There's no comparison between freshly picked salads and the tired, limp leaves of a bought lettuce that's been on the road and on the shelf for several days before you buy it. The sugars in sweetcorn start to turn to starch as soon as the cobs are picked, and sweetcorn that is in the pot within minutes of picking is often sweeter and juicier than any you can buy from a shop. Many soft fruits bruise very easily, and strawberries and raspberries that have been transported hundreds of kilometres are much more likely to be in poor condition than those that have travelled only a few metres between your garden and a plate.

When settling on which crops to grow, you should also take into account your family's likes and dislikes. There's

SHINY, FRESH TOMATOES *(top) picked straight from the vine have an unbeatable taste and tangy aroma.*

FOR AN EARLY CROP OF SWEETCORN *(above) you should sow seed indoors in cold areas and plant out when all danger of frost has passed.*

little point in producing a huge crop of prizewinning parsnips if no one particularly enjoys eating them.

Once you have made a list of what you like, decide how much you require. Unless you have lots of grateful neighbours or a large freezer it can be frustrating to experience the gluts and dearths of a garden's harvest. Careful planning at the outset and use of various storage methods can, however, keep these peaks and troughs to a minimum. Remember that growing too little is better than growing too much and then having to discard produce that you have spent time and money nurturing. Ideally, therefore, plan crops so that something will be ready for picking (or eating from store) right through the entire year.

TOP TEN FRUIT AND VEGETABLES

VEGETABLES

- **Salad leaves:** Bags of mixed leaves are very expensive and not a patch on fresh-cut ones. They are so quick and easy to grow, in containers as well as in the open ground.

- **Tomatoes:** Compact varieties fit in the smallest of gardens. The flavour and aroma of home-grown tomatoes are far superior to anything you can buy.

- **Peas:** Freshly picked peas are a real treat. Grow sugar snap varieties for minimum waste and a heavy crop.

- **Carrots:** Fresh-pulled, young carrots are deliciously crunchy and sweet, and they are quick and simple to grow, especially in light soils.

- **Runner beans:** These must give one of the best returns on space, allowing you to make use of vertical surfaces such as walls and fences. Keep them watered while flowering and they will give a huge crop that freezes well.

- **Courgettes/marrows:** These are easy to grow, crop heavily right up to the first frosts, and are available in a wide range of shapes and colours.

- **Leeks:** Invaluable as a supply of fresh vegetables in winter; they will withstand even very severe winter weather.

- **Potatoes:** Grow the early varieties, harvested before blight becomes a problem later in the season, and less-common varieties not found in shops. Potatoes can even be grown in a tub if you don't have much room.

- **Cabbages:** Although they need protection from pests such as caterpillars, cabbages can be grown all year round, and a whole range of different varieties is available.

- **Radishes:** Super-speedy and easy to grow, peppery, crisp radishes have a long season.

FRUIT

- **Strawberries:** Everyone's favourite fruit! They can be cultivated in the ground or in pots on the patio, and can even be forced for an early crop when prices in the shops are sky-high.

- **Raspberries:** Although these usually need to be provided with some form of support, they are easy to grow, particularly the autumn-fruiting varieties.

- **Plums:** Tolerant of a range of soils and conditions, plums give a heavy crop. Go for the best-flavoured varieties, such as gages.

- **Black currants:** Easy to look after and very productive, this health-giving fruit is always popular.

- **Blackberries:** Plump, juicy cultivated blackberries are far superior to even hedgerow fruits, and provide a welcome late-season crop.

- **Apples:** Trained forms can fit into small spaces, and if appropriate varieties are grown the fruits will store well right through winter.

- **Blueberries:** A 'superfruit', packed with healthy nutrients. Always plant blueberries in acidic soil; they are easily grown in containers.

- **Cherries:** As well as their delicious fruit, cherries provide beautiful blossom in spring, fiery autumn leaf colour and interesting bark year-round. Watch out for birds.

- **Gooseberries:** Increasingly rarely available in the shops, gooseberries provide fruit both for cooking and, from dessert varieties, for enjoying straight from the bush.

- **Melons:** The heady scent of a perfectly ripe melon is unmistakable. A greenhouse is required to get the best crop.

early spring

The cold, dark days of winter are behind us; the days are lengthening and the weather is, at last, warming up. The growing season now starts in earnest, and there are plenty of sowings to be made indoors and out. Fruit trees and bushes are bursting into growth, and some of the earliest flowering types are already in full blossom.

In early spring, night frosts and cold spells are common, so care must be taken not to push ahead too quickly. A few bright, breezy days help to dry out the soil ready for sowing; covering areas for early sowings with cloches or polythene will keep off the rain and hasten the process along. Make sure you have plenty of supplies of compost, trays and pots for the busy sowing and potting season ahead.

vegetables | GENERAL ADVICE

Make a clean start | Double check that old crops and weeds have been removed from the vegetable plot and clean up where necessary.

Tackle weeds | Hoe young weeds the moment they appear. It is worth preparing the seedbed just to encourage weed seeds to germinate so that you can kill them before you sow. Once the surface weed seeds have germinated and been removed, few others will sprout and you will have a clean bed.

Rake seedbeds | As soon as the soil is dry enough, rake it level and create a fine tilth. This means breaking down any clods of soil until it is all an even consistency of fine crumbs.

Fertilise the soil | Most vegetable gardens need feeding. On a dry day, spread general-purpose fertiliser in the recommended proportions on the pack.

Time sowing carefully | In some areas, the soil is often still rather too cold to get good results from sowing seed directly onto the soil. If in doubt, wait until weeds begin to emerge; when they germinate, the chances are your seed will too. It is better to wait a week or two than to sow in poor conditions.

Use plastic mulch | Cover prepared soil with black polythene to keep it weed-free and moist, ready for sowing.

Prepare containers for sowing | Fill containers with compost and keep it moist, ready for sowing vegetables. If they are kept in the greenhouse, the compost will be able to warm up before the seeds are sown.

Sow vegetables outside | Sow broad beans, calabrese, early carrots, lettuces, onions, parsley, parsnips, peas, radishes, rocket, salsify, scorzonera, spinach, spring onions, turnips and herbs such as dill and chervil where they are to grow. If frost and winds are a problem, cover the sown area with horticultural fleece or cloches.

Protect carrots and cabbages | Cover all carrot and cabbage-family crops with horticultural fleece to exclude cabbage root fly and carrot fly, which are on the wing in mid spring. The adults lay their eggs near the plants' roots and the larvae eat the roots when they hatch out. Covering the plants with fleece means the flies cannot get near to them to lay their eggs.

Make successional sowings | Once seedlings from the first sowings of many crops are a few centimetres tall, make further sowings to get a continuous supply. Peas crop for about two weeks in summer; to extend the season you can sow up to four times in spring for a regular supply. Since salad crops become unappetising very quickly, sow seed little and often.

Water dry seedbeds | With the soil still moist from winter, you seldom need to water in spring, but cold dry winds can parch seedbeds, so check on their condition and give a light watering where necessary.

Thin seedlings | As soon as seedlings can be handled, start thinning them out where they are too crowded. Most seedlings are best thinned out to their final spacing in several stages rather than all at once. Where appropriate, transplant some of the thinnings to fill in any gaps in the row.

Sow seed indoors | Sow aubergines, beetroot, celeriac, celery, peppers (including chillies), tomatoes and tender herbs (such as basil) ideally in a greenhouse, or indoors on a bright windowsill if no greenhouse is available.

Sow crops for transplanting | Sow Brussels sprouts, leeks, summer cabbages and cauliflowers in pots and cell trays indoors, or in an outdoor seedbed. These can be transplanted to their final position later in spring.

Plant crowns, tubers and sets | Plant asparagus crowns, tubers of early potatoes and Jerusalem artichokes, and onion sets and shallots.

Order plug plants | If you have decided not to raise your own plants from seed, order plug plants from mail-order suppliers as early as possible.

Resow failures | If crops fail to germinate, sow again with fresh seed. This is why you should always hold some seed in reserve. Some failures will occur, particularly if weather conditions have been poor, with an unexpected cold snap after sowing, for example, or if pests such as mice have taken pea and bean seeds.

Apply slug controls | Seedlings are very vulnerable to slug damage, so use some form of slug control to keep them at bay. Slug pellets containing a molluscicide should be used sparingly and as directed on the pack. If you prefer not to use pellets, various organic alternatives such as aluminium sulphate powder and ferric phosphate are available.

Net seedbeds against pests | Birds dust bathing in seedbeds can be very destructive. Nets will help to keep them out, and will also prevent cats from digging the soil.

CONTINUE TO HARVEST THE LAST WINTER CROPS *in early spring, such as kale, winter cabbage and parsnips.*

vegetables | WHAT TO DO NOW

ONION FAMILY

Leeks

Start leeks from seed

Sow leeks in a seedbed outside from now to mid spring for plants to mature in autumn. Rake the soil to a fine tilth and sow thinly in drills 15cm (6in) apart and 1cm (½in) deep.

Onions and shallots

Sow onions and shallots

Sow as soon as the soil is workable to give a late summer crop. Sow thinly in rows 30cm (12in) apart in well-prepared soil.

Start onions from sets

Plant sets from now to mid spring to crop from mid to late summer. Sets are baby onions and, being partly developed already, they grow rapidly and are particularly useful when the growing season is short. Just before planting, thoroughly rake the top few centimetres of soil and incorporate a general fertiliser. Mark out rows 25–30cm (10–12in) apart, and push the sets into the soil with 7.5–10cm (3–4in) between each one, the pointed end uppermost and the tip just visible. Protect from birds.

CABBAGE FAMILY

Brussels sprouts

Sow Brussels sprouts

Sow Brussels sprouts outdoors from now to mid spring. Prepare a firm seedbed and sow thinly in rows; the seedlings should appear within 7–12 days. Seeds can also be sown now in modules under cover for planting out later.

Cabbages

Sow cabbages

Red cabbages need an early spring sowing as they are slow growers. Autumn cabbages can be sown from now until late spring.

SOWING CABBAGE SEED

EVENLY SPRINKLE *a good number of seeds across a whole tray of compost. Allow a finger width between each seed.*

COVER THE SEEDS *with a thin layer of seed compost and then gently firm this down by hand or using the bottom of another seed tray.*

WATER THE COMPOST *carefully so that it is evenly soaked. Leave the seeds to germinate in a sunny place. Keep the compost moist.*

BEANS AND PEAS

Broad beans

Sow broad beans

Sow outside from now on, depending on the weather. If the soil temperature is low, cover it with polythene for a couple of weeks before sowing, or sow the seed under cover, one per root trainer or small pot, to plant out later.

When sowing outside, sow a few extra seeds at the end of the row for gapping up any failures later. Sow 10–15cm (4–6in) apart, in rows 60cm (24in) apart. They need a sunny, sheltered site because mature plants, when bushy and weighted with pods, are liable to wind damage.

If you have autumn-sown beans, delay your first spring sowing until the weather is warm enough for the autumn beans to have put on some strong new growth. Then you'll have a second crop to follow on from the first.

Runner beans

Prepare for runner beans

If you have not done so already, dig plenty of well-rotted organic matter into the soil where you intend to grow runner beans. They need lots of moisture, particularly while flowering and setting pods, and organic matter will help hold on to soil moisture to keep it available to the roots. Dig a trench and add well-rotted compost or manure to the base; you can also add a layer of old newspaper to act as a sponge. Leave the trench open for spring rains to saturate the newspaper.

Peas

Sow peas

Make a first sowing outside if the weather is warm enough. Do not be tempted to sow into cold, wet ground because germination will be poor. If spring is slow to arrive, warm the soil by covering it with polythene before sowing then protect the seedlings with fleece.

A traditional method of sowing peas, which works well with shorter varieties, is to make a flat trench with a hoe, 5cm (2in) deep and about 25cm (10in) wide. Water the trench first, then sow the seeds 5–7cm (2–2¾in) apart in three rows along the bottom of the trench. Press the seed in a little to ensure it does not become displaced when the trench is backfilled with soil, then firm the ground lightly with the back of the hoe.

PEA VARIETIES

Like potatoes, peas are grouped by the time they take to mature. Earlies take around 12 weeks, second earlies 13–14 weeks, and maincrops 15–16 weeks. The earlies can be sown throughout the summer.

Some pea varieties have wrinkled seeds, whereas some are round and smooth. Generally, the latter are hardier and are used for the very early sowings, but they lack the sweetness of wrinkled varieties, which are best for summer sowings. CLOCKWISE FROM TOP: 'Sugar Ann' AGM, 'Delikata' AGM, 'Oregon Sugarpod' and 'Sugar Lord'

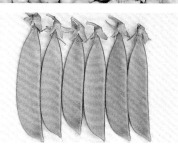

Both dwarf and semi-leafless varieties can also be sown in small blocks. Lay the seed in a staggered pattern on the soil so that each one is 15cm (6in) apart. In loose soil, simply push in the seed to a depth of 5cm (2in); otherwise use a trowel.

Sowing seed in a single row, or pair of rows, works best for taller varieties because it makes it easier to support them. It also gives increased air ventilation around the plants, helping to prevent powdery mildew and making weeding easier. Make a single V-shaped drill, 5cm (2in) deep, water the base and sow the peas 5–10cm (2–4in) apart. You can add a second row, providing it is 30cm (12in) away, and insert supports between the two.

PERENNIAL VEGETABLES

Asparagus

Plant asparagus crowns

One-year-old asparagus crowns can be planted now. It is important that the ground is ready on delivery because the fleshy crowns mustn't dry out. If planting is delayed, wrap up the roots in wet newspaper.

The bed system produces high yields in a relatively small space, with one bed consisting of three rows of crowns, spaced 30cm (12in) apart each way. On heavy soil, make sure the bed is slightly raised and mounded up to improve drainage.

Dig a trench for each row, 15cm (6in) deep, and carefully spread out the fragile roots. Cover with 7.5cm (3in) of soil and water in well.

TO PLANT ONE-YEAR-OLD ASPARAGUS CROWNS, *dig a trench for each row, 15cm (6in) deep, and carefully spread out the fragile roots. Cover with 7.5cm (3in) of soil and water in well.*

Mulch established asparagus beds

Apply a balanced organic fertiliser and a 5cm (2in) thick mulch of organic matter before the spears emerge to help suppress weeds, retain moisture and protect the early spears from frost. This also helps prevent the soil forming a crust (called 'capping'), which causes bent spears.

Globe artichokes

Plant globe artichokes

Buy globe artichokes as small, pot-grown plants and grow them 90cm (3ft) apart in the vegetable garden, or space them out in a big flower border. You should remove any flowerheads produced in the first year.

Globe artichokes aren't fully hardy and need a sunny, sheltered site with well-drained, moisture-retentive soil to which plenty of organic matter has been added. Avoid growing them in shade or in a frost pocket, or in heavy soil that gets waterlogged in winter. The best yields are obtained in cool, moist summers that allow plants to build up plenty of foliage.

Always try to buy named varieties, which give more reliable crops than unnamed seed-raised plants. Established plants should be mulched now with well-rotted manure, keeping it away from the stems, and fed with tomato fertilizer.

Jerusalem artichokes

Plant Jerusalem artichokes

Tubers of Jerusalem artichokes can be bought from greengrocers, while named varieties of known quality are available to buy from specialist suppliers. Larger tubers can be cut into egg-sized portions provided they have two or three buds. Enrich the planting site with organic matter and plant clean, healthy tubers now, each one 15cm (6in) deep and 60cm (24in) apart. If you are planting in rows, they will need to be spaced 90cm (3ft) apart.

Ideally, provide a sunny position with well-drained, moisture-retentive soil. However, because the plant tolerates heavy, shady and dry sites, it can be raised in areas where other crops won't grow (such as under trees and next to hedges), although the yield will be lower.

The artichoke is a useful crop on new sites because its roots help break up the soil. It can also be grown as a windbreak since it grows to 3m (10ft) high when planted in two or three rows, but it will need support on open sites. Jerusalem artichokes need careful positioning because of the shade they cast, and they can spread aggressively.

Rhubarb

Sow or plant rhubarb

Pot-grown rhubarb plants can be bought and planted now. One or two plants should be enough for most people, but if more are required space them 1m (3½ft) apart. Provide a sunny position and well-drained, moisture-retentive fertile soil. Before establishing a new bed, add plenty of organic matter and remove all perennial weeds. Avoid heavy soil, which can rot the fleshy crowns.

The cheapest method of obtaining plants is to grow them from seed. Seedlings are generally virus-free, but they can be variable in quality. Sow between now and mid spring in a prepared seedbed, or in 9cm (3½in) pots.

Rhubarb responds well to feeding. A spring topdressing of pelleted poultry manure or well-rotted farmyard manure helps, but avoid direct contact with the crowns.

CARROT SEEDLINGS (top) should come up in around 14 days when sown in spring. Crops will benefit from a fleece covering to protect them from carrot fly, which is on the wing in mid spring.

WHEN SOWING BEETROOT SEED (above), the best way to make it germinate quickly is to soak it overnight. Sow short rows every 14 days to provide a continuous crop.

ROOTS AND STEMS

Beetroot

Sow beetroot

Sow beetroot outdoors from now through to summer, sowing a short row every couple of weeks in order to have a regular supply of tender roots. Soak the seed overnight before sowing. Mark out straight rows using a string line or bamboo cane, water the drill if the soil is dry, and sow the seed thinly, 2.5cm (1in) deep, in rows 30cm (12in) apart.

Seedlings should appear in 10–14 days. Thin to 10cm (4in) between seedlings as soon as possible. Grow beetroot in an open sunny site in well-drained, fertile soil. Light, free-draining soil produces the best early crops because it warms up more quickly than heavier ground.

Carrots

Sow early carrots

Sow a variety suitable for early crops such as 'Amsterdam Forcing' or 'Early Nantes'. Seeds will germinate more quickly if the soil is warm, having been covered with polythene or cloches for several weeks.

All carrots require an open, sunny site and well-drained fertile soil, but you need to find out exactly what type of soil you've got and choose varieties to suit. To grow long-rooted carrots, such as 'St Valery' or 'Autumn King', you need a good loam or sandy soil that can be deeply cultivated to at least one spade's depth. If your soil is shallow, stony or heavy clay then opt for stump-rooted or round carrots such as 'Chantenay Red Cored' or 'Parmex', rather than long-rooted types that are likely to develop stunted or forked roots. If the soil is completely unsuitable or space is limited, try growing short-rooted types in containers or growing bags.

Use a string line or bamboo cane to mark out lines, then use a draw hoe or trowel to create drills 1cm (½in) deep with 15cm (6in) between the rows. If the soil is dry, water the drill and allow it to drain before sowing. Sprinkle the fine seed along the drill, cover with a thin layer of soil and firm down.

Sow carrots sparingly to avoid the need for thinning later on because the scent of the crushed foliage attracts carrot root fly. Growing carrots with other plants such as spring onions or annual flowers (such as cornflowers and larkspurs) is a traditional but, unfortunately, not very effective way of limiting carrot fly damage.

Celeriac

Sow celeriac under cover

Sow the tiny seed thinly in pots or modules filled with seed compost mixed in equal parts with fine vermiculite. Then cover the seed with vermiculite and germinate in a propagator at a temperature of about 15°C (59°F). Transfer the pot-grown seedlings into individual biodegradable pots of multipurpose compost once the first true leaves have formed, with one plant per section.

Make sure the plants have good light and that the temperature stays above 10°C (50°F). Sow early, as it needs plenty of growing time for the roots to reach a good size.

Florence fennel

Sow Florence fennel under cover

Sow in a warm greenhouse or propagator on a sunny windowsill. Fill pots or modular trays with seed compost, firm gently, water well and allow to drain. In each pot, sow several seeds 1cm (½in) deep, spaced a little apart from each other, then cover with compost. Place in a greenhouse or on a sunny windowsill and, once the seed has germinated, thin to leave one seedling per pot.

Fennel tends to bolt to seed if the roots are disturbed, so it's important to keep root disturbance to a minimum when planting out. This is why seed should be sown in individual or modular pots. Keep plants evenly moist and plant out in around four to five weeks – don't leave them in their pots for too long or they are more likely to bolt.

Parsnips

Sow parsnips if conditions are right

Parsnips need a long growing season so are traditionally sown very early. They like a sunny position and grow well in most well-drained soils, ideally one that is light and sandy. In colder areas, or on heavy clay soils, results will be more satisfactory if you wait for a few weeks. Do not add organic matter to the soil the same season as sowing, as this may cause forked roots. If the soil is shallow or heavy and stony, choose a short-rooted variety such as 'Little Gem' rather than a very long-rooted type.

Choose a site improved with well-rotted compost or manure the previous year. A week before sowing, rake over the soil, adding a general fertiliser, then rake the surface to a fine crumbly texture to prepare a seedbed.

Make a drill 1cm (½in) deep with a hoe. If the bottom of the drill is dry, dampen it before sowing. Sow three seeds every 15cm (6in) and lightly cover them with fine soil. Space the rows approximately 30cm (12in) apart. Parsnip seed is notoriously slow to germinate, taking several weeks before the first signs appear.

PARSNIP SEEDS *are notoriously slow to germinate, so try sowing fast-maturing vegetables such as radishes around them to make good use of the space. Parsnip seeds also store badly, so use a fresh batch each year.*

PREPARE THE GROUND FOR PARSNIPS *by thoroughly raking over the soil, mixing in a general fertiliser, then raking the surface again to create a fine, crumbly texture, ready for the seeds.*

Sow radishes along the row between the sowing stations of the parsnips. These will mark the row while you are waiting for the parsnips to show, and by that time the radishes will be ready for pulling, so you will have made good use of the available space.

Potatoes

Prepare for potato planting
Just ahead of planting, dress the ground with a general fertiliser and rake well to break up any large clods. Avoid growing potatoes in waterlogged ground, low-lying spots where frosty air could collect and very light, free-draining soil. Start your seed potatoes into growth by sprouting or chitting them (see page 276).

For early crops, increase the soil temperature by covering the site with black plastic several weeks before planting; this helps to accelerate growth. You can plant the tubers through holes made in the plastic.

Plant early potatoes in containers
Use large 10 litre (2 gallon) tubs at least 30cm (12in) deep and half fill them with compost. Place in a well-lit and ventilated frost-free greenhouse or porch. Place a chitted potato in each container and cover with 10cm (4in) of compost. Top up with further compost as the plant grows.

WHEN CHITTING POTATOES, it can take four to six weeks for them to sprout, after which they will be ready for planting. When planting chitted potatoes, take care not to damage any of the delicate new shoots.

Crops will be small, but you will be able to enjoy potatoes well before any are available outdoors. Choose a first early variety such as 'Maris Bard', 'Swift' or 'Rocket', which could be ready in seven or eight weeks.

SALADS

Cucumbers

Plant cucumbers under glass
If you have a greenhouse heated to a constant minimum temperature of 21°C (70°F), cucumbers can be planted now. They thrive in large pots (minimum 10 litres), in growing bags or in the ground. Containers need to be filled with rich, fresh potting compost, and beds need plenty of well-rotted organic matter.

Radishes

Sow radishes
Use an early variety such as 'French Breakfast' for an early spring sowing. Sow seed thinly, in drills 1cm (½in) deep that have been watered beforehand, and cover with a cloche or a layer of fleece. Thin the seedlings to at least 3cm (1½in) apart; overcrowding makes them spindly and may delay or prevent the roots from developing fully.

Being fast growers, radishes are ideally suited to a number of small successional sowings throughout the season and can be sown from now until early autumn. They can be grown among slower-maturing crops and to fill gaps where a couple of lettuces or a few beetroots have been harvested. They are best pulled when the roots

SOWING SMALL RADISH SEED means you will inevitably end up with rows of tightly packed seedlings, but they can be easily thinned to avoid overcrowding and prevent spindly growth.

are small and tender. In dry conditions they might run to seed or produce tough and pithy or hot, peppery tasting roots. Radishes can also be grown as a cut-and-come-again crop (see page 120) for their spicy leaves.

Tomatoes

Sow tomatoes

Sow tomatoes under cover in a pot or tray of moist seed compost and cover lightly with another layer of seed compost. If you don't have a heated greenhouse or propagator, place the container in a polythene bag (with a label if you're growing more than one variety), and put it in a warm place, such as an airing cupboard. Wait several days and then check daily for signs of germination.

Once shoots emerge, move the container to a warm, well-lit spot and let the seedlings grow. Pot them up individually into 8cm (3in) pots as soon as they are large enough to handle, and keep the potting compost evenly moist. Tomatoes usually germinate easily and you are likely to have plenty of seedlings, so keep a few as spares in case of emergencies and throw out or give away the rest to friends or family.

Since tomatoes are sensitive to frost, they can be planted outside only once all risk of frost has passed. If you are intending to grow them outdoors, do not sow until about eight weeks before planting time. If tomatoes are sown too early, the seedlings will become leggy before it is safe to plant them out.

START TOMATO SEEDS OFF INDOORS *and move them to a warm, well-lit spot as soon as the shoots emerge. You are likely to have plenty of seedlings and, if you get it right, will be picking plenty of tomatoes.*

SPINACH AND CHARD

Spinach

Sow perpetual spinach

For an early crop, sow seed indoors in modules now and plant the seedlings outside once the soil has started to warm up. A spring sowing outdoors will keep you in leaves all summer (see right).

Sow in rows 45cm (18in) apart and space seeds 30–38cm (12–15in) in the row. Sow two or three seeds at each station in case some don't germinate, and thin to the strongest seedling later. Seedlings can take a long time to show, often up to a few weeks.

TENDER VEGETABLES

Aubergines

Sow aubergines

Sow indoors now at 21–30°C (70–86°F). Sow 8–10 seeds per 9cm (3½in) pot, and then move to individual pots when they are large enough to handle.

Okra

Sow okra indoors

Okra is a half-hardy annual grown for its fleshy seed pods, known as gumbo or ladies' fingers, which are used in African and Indian cookery. It demands a hot, humid environment; if you don't have a greenhouse or polytunnel to grow it in, it will need to be grown under cloches or frames in the sunniest site you can find.

Okra seed doesn't remain viable for long, so buy it fresh or save your own each year. Since okra seedlings will damp off and collapse in cold wet soil below 18°C (65°F), sow in individual 9cm (3½in) pots of well-watered seed compost and place in a heated propagator in a well-lit position at 25°C (77°F). Don't let the seed dry out before germination occurs.

The seed will germinate quickly at the high temperatures needed but can quickly become leggy, so remove the pots from the propagator as soon as the seedlings emerge. Continue growing at 22–30°C (71–86°F), and use tepid water when watering.

| Making a raised bed

Growing vegetables in a raised bed has several advantages over growing them in the ground. Think of a raised bed as a large, specially constructed container with no base. The sides are usually made of wood, brick or stone blocks, the choice depending on cost, appearance and available materials. Ready-to-assemble DIY raised beds are an easy option but tend to be more expensive.

Ideally beds should be no wider than 1.2m (4ft) so that they can be comfortably worked from both sides. If the bed is being positioned against a wall or fence, make it 60cm (24in) wide. The maximum convenient length for a bed is probably 3m (10ft); any longer can be irritatingly

RAISED BEDS *can be built at a low level (above), ideal for small spaces, or up to 1m (3ft) or table-top height depending on your needs.*

WATER RAISED BEDS *in dry weather (right) and mulch to prevent evaporation because they dry out more quickly than open-ground beds.*

long to walk around. It can be any shape, but square or rectangular beds make the best use of a small space and are easier to build.

Planning a raised bed

In a plot of 3 x 3m (10 x 10ft), you can fit two square beds of 1.2 x 1.2m (4 x 4ft) for vegetables, salads and herbs. Separate them with a path 60cm (24in) wide to give easy access in all weathers without the cultivated soil being compacted under foot. To prevent weeds from growing on the path, pin a permeable ground-cover fabric to the soil using metal staples then cover with a layer of ornamental bark or gravel at least 5cm (2in) deep.

To make the beds, use 15 x 2.5cm (6 x 1in) planks for the sides, held together by 5cm (2in) square stakes that are 30cm (12in) long. Long beds will need extra staking along the sides to prevent the weight of soil bending the planks. When a bed is

EDIBLE HERBS AND FLOWERS *can slot into the smallest spaces to provide fresh ingredients for your table or simply add a bit of colour to raised beds.*

sited on a firm surface such as a patio, use corner brackets that are the same depth as the planks and just stand the bed in place.

Cut the wood to the correct length, making two sides of each bed 5cm (2in) shorter than the other two sides to allow for the width of the timber they will butt up to. Screw the sides

on to the stakes to make the frame, pre-drilling holes to prevent the wood splitting. Prepare the soil by forking over the area to ensure good drainage, then place the frame on the soil and hammer the stakes into the ground. Fill the bed with suitable compost, or soil fortified with organic matter.

MAKING A RAISED BED

ASSEMBLE THE FRAME *of the raised bed by attaching the wooden plank edges to the stakes using galvanized screws.*

HAMMER THE CORNER STAKES *of the frame into the ground with a mallet. Use an old piece of wood to protect the frame.*

FORK OVER THE GROUND *in the bottom of the raised bed before filling it. This will help drainage.*

fruit | GENERAL ADVICE

Last chance to winter wash | Winter washes are applied during the dormant season to destroy overwintering pests and their eggs. They cannot be sprayed when the plants are in growth, so this is a last chance to use them. Tar oil winter washes are no longer available, but have been replaced by a winter tree wash containing natural plant oils.

Before using winter wash, check that the growth buds on trees and bushes have not begun to break, or the new growth will be scorched. Protect plants that are growing nearby, and spray on a still day so that wind won't carry the spray where it's not wanted.

Mulch trees and bushes | Apply a mulch around fruit trees, nuts and bushes as long as the ground isn't frozen. This helps to keep in soil moisture, as well as helping to prevent weed growth and supplying some nutrients as it gradually rots down. Use well-rotted farmyard manure or garden compost, but make sure the mulch is kept away from the trunks and stems otherwise it might cause rotting.

Control aphids | Aphids (greenfly and blackfly) can affect most fruits. Damage is particularly noticeable a little later in the spring and in early summer, but they often colonise new growth early in the growing season. By sucking sap they weaken the plant, distort growth and, most importantly, spread harmful viruses for which there is no control.

Do not spray plants with insecticides when they are in blossom because of the risk of killing beneficial pollinating insects. When spotted, colonies can be squashed between finger and thumb, or dislodged with a powerful jet of water from a hose. When plants are not in flower an insecticide can be used, following the manufacturers' instructions to the letter.

Keep on top of weeds | The key to good weed control is to act while the weeds are still young and never let their growth get out of hand. Keep weeding regularly right through the spring to summer.

Repot or topdress container-grown fruit | This is the time to move container-grown fruit trees and bushes on to the next size pot or, if you don't want to pot them on, to topdress them with fresh compost.

When repotting, remove the plant carefully from its pot by grasping the stem. Crumble away some of the old compost from around and on top of the rootball, being careful not to damage the roots. Make sure there is sufficient drainage material in the base of the larger pot, and a layer of fresh compost. Put the rootball on top of the compost and fill in round the sides of it with more compost, using a piece of wood or a similar tool to push it firmly down the sides so there are no air gaps. Finish off with a thin layer of compost over the top of the rootball and water thoroughly.

If the plant is already in as large a pot as you want, scrape some of the surface compost away with a trowel, again making sure you don't damage the roots. Mix fresh compost with some slow-release fertiliser granules and use this to replace the compost you have removed.

Protect early blossom from frost | Almond, plum, peach, apricot, cherry and nectarine trees flower very early, and their blossoms (and later, fruitlets) must be protected from frost if they are to survive. Drape a double layer of horticultural fleece or even old net curtains over the trees. Erect a tent of canes around the plant to hold the fleece away from the blossom – if touching, it will allow the cold to penetrate through to the flowers.

It is much easier to protect blossoms from frost when the trees are grown as trained forms against a wall or fence than if they are freestanding. If the plants are growing in containers, they can be moved to a frost-free position (such as a conservatory) when frost is forecast. Strawberry plants are also subject to frost damage when flowering, causing the yellow centres of the flowers to turn black in the middle. They can be protected with a covering of fleece or glass or plastic cloches.

It is important to remove the frost protection from fruit as soon as possible, as insects must have access to the flowers during the day in order to pollinate them.

Hand-pollinate blossoms | Where trees are grown permanently under cover (for example nectarines or apricots in a conservatory), flowers should be hand pollinated to ensure good fruit set. Hand pollination is also useful for early flowering outdoor trees, as pollinating insects are scarce early in the season.

Traditionally, hand pollination is carried out with a rabbit's tail, gently pushing it into the flower and transferring its pollen to the surrounding blossom. These days it is more common to use a soft brush or even cotton wool. This should ideally be carried out each day throughout the flowering season.

Feed tree fruits | Plums, cherries, cooking apples and pears are hungry feeders. Apply a high-nitrogen fertiliser to these plants now, sprinkling it around the root zone, following the manufacturer's instructions.

Mulch acid-loving soft fruit | Give blueberries, cranberries and lingonberries a mulch of well-rotted organic matter, but not spent mushroom compost as this is too alkaline. Sulphur chips can help to acidify the soil.

EARLY FRUIT BLOSSOM, *like this plum, is vulnerable to frost so it's essential to site the trees in a sheltered spot where insects can access the blooms and exposure to frosts can be minimised.*

fruit | WHAT TO DO NOW

Apples

Train pyramid apples

Continue to train pyramid apples by shortening the leader by two thirds, each time cutting back to a bud on the opposite side to the previous year. Remove any branches lower than 45cm (18in). Continue in this way until the pyramid reaches its intended height.

Apricots

Train apricots

Apricots have a similar fruiting habit to plums and peaches and so are managed in much the same way. The fan-trained form is popular for apricots.

Cherries

Water cherries when necessary

As well as providing frost protection for early blossoms, ensure trees are kept well watered during the early stages of fruit development to avoid excessive 'run-off', when some fruits turn yellow and fall off. Run-off occurs in three main stages: when unpollinated flowers and blooms with immature embryos are shed; when pollination is incomplete; and when fruits swell but are then aborted because they have suffered a growth check through lack of moisture, inadequate food reserves or excessively cool temperatures or frost.

Citrus fruits

Feed and water citrus plants

Citrus plants growing in conservatories or other protected locations require more water now that they are starting into growth after the winter. Citrus are hungry plants and respond well to regular feeding. This is the time to switch from the winter feeding regime to a summer feed. The bulk of flowering and fruit ripening occurs in winter,

A PERMANENT FRAME *around a wall-trained apricot (top) makes the job of protecting vulnerable early flowers and embryo fruit from frost much easier. In summer, netting can be draped over it to deter birds.*

CITRUS FRUITS SHOULD BE THINNED OUT *(above) to ensure that the remaining fruits are able to swell and ripen sufficiently, even though it is tempting to leave all the fruit on.*

when they need a balanced fertiliser; conversely summer is a period of leaf growth so a high-nitrogen fertiliser is preferred. Switch back from summer to winter feed in mid autumn. Specialist summer and winter citrus fertilisers are available from many garden centres or citrus nurseries.

Thin out citrus fruits

Most citrus plants should be limited in the number of fruits they carry for the best results; a plant 1m (3ft) tall should bear no more than 20 fruits. Kumquats, however, are the exception – they don't need thinning. Topdress the containers of your citrus plants with fresh compost.

Mulberries

Feed mulberries

Apply a topdressing of general fertiliser over the root area now. Mulberries are attractive trees with very well-flavoured, juicy fruits, but are not commonly grown, perhaps because they are slow growing and do not start to crop for around five years after planting.

Peaches and nectarines

Fan-training a peach

The cheapest way of obtaining a fan-trained peach is to train it yourself but, as it will establish quickly, it is important to train the fan when young in order to set a good branch framework. Select a feathered maiden and, once growth has started in spring, remove the central leader, cutting back to the lowest of two side branches, one on either side of the plant. They should ideally be about 40cm (16in) above the ground. If upright shoots are not removed, they will tend to hinder the development of the fan.

Train the side branches onto canes attached to wires, angling them to about 45 degrees. These two branches are sometimes referred to as 'ribs'. Remove any other sideshoots. Prune the ribs back by about one third to an upward-facing bud. This will stimulate buds to break along the pruned branch.

The following year, in early spring, cut back this new growth by about two thirds to stimulate further growth. The basic structure of the fan will now be

---

TRAIN AND PRUNE PEACHES AND NECTARINES

Pruning of peaches and nectarines should always be carried out once the trees have started into growth, not in the dormant season. This applies to all stone fruits, including plums and cherries; pruning in the dormant season increases their susceptibility to canker and silver leaf disease. Peaches and nectarines can be treated in the same way because their flowering and fruiting habits are the same; both form fruits on the wood produced in the previous year. The pruning technique is sometimes called 'replacement' pruning because it consists of replacing older branches with new growth from the current year. Pruning involves looking towards the future – one year in advance of the current year. If pruning more than one peach or nectarine tree, disinfect secateurs between trees to prevent passing on potential infections.

---

complete, with about eight ribs, or branches. Once the fan has been established, start pruning in early spring when the plant is in growth.

Remove any undesirable shoots, such as ones coming off the trunk and where they are going to cause congestion. It is important to leave all the swollen fat buds, which will become the current year's flowers and subsequently the fruit. Identify the vegetative buds or shoots as these will bear next year's crop.

Leave one new vegetative bud or shoot towards the base of the branch and another one half way up the branch. The shoot at the base will be used for next year's replacement, while the second one can be a backup in case the basal shoot fails. The terminal bud (in the tip of the branch) can also be left.

SOFT FRUIT

Blackberries and hybrid berries

Train cane fruits

Untie canes of blackberries and hybrid berries that have been bundled together for the winter and train them onto arches or supports before the buds burst into growth.

Blueberries

Feed blueberries

Apply a topdressing of ericaceous (lime-free) fertiliser to the soil at half the recommended rate and cover it with a 7.5cm (3in) layer of ericaceous mulch material such as composted conifer clippings. Keep plants well watered, especially during spring and summer, using rainwater wherever possible.

Ensure the soil has a constant pH of 5.5 or lower, to avoid plants developing lime-induced chlorosis and associated iron deficiency. Sulphur chips can be used to lower soil pH, but where soils are not naturally acid it is easiest and most successful to grow blueberries in containers of ericaceous compost.

BLUEBERRIES FLOWER EARLY IN SPRING, *their bell-shaped blossoms being pollinated mainly by bees. Consequently a sheltered position, which bees prefer, helps achieve the best yields.*

Gooseberries

Train gooseberries

The pruning for a gooseberry trained as a bush or standard is the same and is based on the principle that gooseberries fruit on old wood and at the base of the previous year's wood.

As soon as the plant starts to grow, shorten the central leader (if there is one) back to the highest branch on a two-year-old gooseberry bush with a short leg (trunk) and four or five equally spaced branches. Then cut back the leader on each branch by one third to inward-facing buds to retain the upright habit – most gooseberries have a tendency to flop outwards and therefore quickly lose their shape. Cut back any sideshoot that has formed along the main branches to one or two buds.

Strawberries

Keep strawberries weed free

Weed frequently between the rows of strawberry beds to

GOOSEBERRIES AND CORDONS

WHEN GROWING GOOSEBERRIES *as cordons, keep plants compact by cutting back new growth to one or two buds and replacing some of the older branches altogether.*

SELECT A STRONG LEADER *and cut it back by about one third shortly after planting. On established cordons, cut the leader back to a bud above the top of the supporting cane.*

GOOSEBERRIES GROWN AS CORDONS *take up little space in the garden, allowing a range of different varieties to be grown and making harvesting easy.*

PLANTING COLD-STORED STRAWBERRY RUNNERS

COLD-STORED STRAWBERRIES *can be planted now and will fruit within 60 days. Trim large root systems by about half using sharp secateurs before planting.*

MARK OUT A PLANTING LINE *across the bed using a taut string. Alongside it, set a plank with the correct spacings marked 35cm (14in) along its length and make the holes.*

DIG A HOLE *large enough to fit the plant roots along each line, then backfill and firm in, ensuring that the crown of each plant is level with the soil surface.*

keep the plants weed free and prevent any competition for water and nutrients. However, take care not to damage the plants, especially if you are using a hoe – it is very easy to sever a strawberry plant from its roots with one ill-judged push of the hoe.

Help strawberry pollination

If strawberry plants are covered by polythene cloches to protect the flowers from frosts and encourage strong growth, roll up the sides when the plants are flowering to allow pollinating insects access to them.

Pollinate greenhouse strawberries

Growing strawberries under glass is an easy way to get an early crop, but the flowers are not very accessible to pollinating insects. Brush over the open flowers gently with your hands to help the job along.

Sow alpine strawberries

Sow seed of alpine strawberries in pots or trays of moist compost in a propagator or heated greenhouse, and pot on the seedlings into individual pots when they can be handled easily. They can be planted out in late spring. The small, sweet, aromatic fruits will be produced in summer; they are not as juicy as large-fruited strawberries but have a very special flavour of their own.

Prepare for strawing down plants

Within the next few weeks strawberries will need to be surrounded by straw or fibre mats to keep the developing fruits clean and help prevent them from being attacked by fungus diseases. It is a good idea to get supplies in now so you have everything you need. Straw is easy to find in urban areas – it is sold as bedding in pet shops – and fibre mats – available from garden centres – sell quickly as summer approaches.

POSITION A FIBRE MAT *around each strawberry plant. These fibre mats will help prevent weeds and also protect the fruit from touching the ground.*

VINE FRUIT

Grapes

Care of grape vines

The pruning of grape vines must be completed while the plants are completely dormant, as they will bleed sap excessively if they are pruned once growth has started (see left). Do not carry out any major pruning of vines now – it is too late to be safe.

Melons

Sow melons for growing under cover

Sow up to four seeds in a small pot, water well and place in a heated propagator at 20–25°C (68–77°F) in a well-lit site. Sow an extra pot in case of failure – you can always give these away if they all germinate.

Germination should occur in less than one week, after which the compost should be kept moist but not saturated. Once three or four leaves have formed, remove the plants from the propagator and grow at 18–20°C (68–70°F). If you can't provide these conditions, buy young plants from a garden centre later in the season. In cool-temperate climates, melons are best grown in a greenhouse or in a warm, protected microclimate, such as against a very sunny or sheltered wall, or under cloches or frames and black plastic mulches. Only in warm-temperate climates will melons grow successfully without protection or shelter. If you are intending to grow melons outside, delay sowing until mid spring.

NUTS

Cobnuts and filberts

Time to prune

Prune cobnuts and filberts now if this was not done in late winter. Remove older, thicker stems to encourage the production of new growth, which will carry more flowers than the older wood.

The trees make useful informal hedging, and the lower half of the main stems can be cleared of sideshoots so the ground beneath the canopy can be planted with shade-tolerant crops such as alpine strawberries.

Feed nuts

Apply a topdressing of general-purpose fertiliser to cobnuts and filberts. This will help to increase the crop.

SOWING MELON SEED IN CONTAINERS

FILL A SMALL POT *with seed or general potting compost and firm it down gently into the container.*

SOW UP TO FOUR SEEDS *per pot. Lay the seeds on their side and then label and date the pot.*

COVER THE SEEDS *with a thin layer of vermiculite. Place in a warm, well-lit place while the seeds germinate.*

| Understanding fruit tree forms

Fruit trees can be grown in a variety of different forms to suit the size of your garden. For small gardens, restricted forms such as cordons, fans, espaliers and step-overs are particularly ideal as they will make maximum use of the space they are in as well as adding ornamental value. Fruit trees can also be incorporated into fences or other boundaries by training them as an espalier, step-over or fan to create an attractive feature. Only spur-bearing (not tip-bearing) varieties can be trained in this way. If in doubt about whether a particular variety is suitable, ask your supplier for advice.

MATURE ESPALIERS (above) make excellent ornamental screens and can be used to partition a garden in an eye-catching way.

BUSH TREES, like this 'Cox's Orange Pippin' apple (right), are a good way to train trees and bear a lot of fruit. But they do take up space.

Restricted tree forms

Cordon

This simple form is popular in a small garden as several varieties can be crammed into a small space. The tree is usually planted as an oblique cordon (shown) at an angle of 30–45 degrees, and has fruiting spurs along the stem. Can also be grown as a double-stemmed (or U-shaped) cordon. Use 'M9', 'M26' or 'MM106' rootstock for apples and 'Quince A' or 'Quince C' for pears.

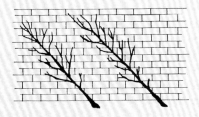

Espalier

Probably the most intricate way to grow a fruit tree against a wall or fence. A central stem is trained upwards with pairs of opposite branches trained horizontally along a system of wires. There are usually three or four tiers. Fruit spurs are encouraged along these horizontal branches. Use 'M26' or 'MM106' rootstock for apples and 'Quince A' or 'Quince C' for pears.

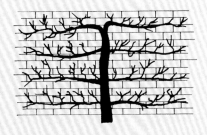

Fan

Perhaps one of the most attractive and popular tree form shapes, a fan has a short trunk in the centre of the plant and then branches radiating out on either side into a fan shape, usually to cover a wall or fence. Use 'M26' or 'MM106' rootstock for apples and 'Quince A' or 'Quince C' for pears.

Spindle and pyramid

The tapering shape of a spindle lets sunlight reach most parts of the tree. A pyramid is kept to a tighter cone and needs a little more pruning, but the neater growing habit appeals to some. Both are 2–2.5m (6½–8ft) high. Use 'M26' or 'MM106' rootstock for apples and 'Quince A' or 'C' for pears.

Step-over

Ideal for edging paths and borders. They are supported by one wire pulled tightly between two posts. Best grown on 'M27' or 'M9' rootstock. Pears are too vigorous for this form.

Unrestricted tree forms

Bush

The traditional choice for a small garden, an open-centred tree is trained on a trunk 60–75cm (24–30in) long. It is sometimes called an open-centre goblet. Use 'M27', 'M9', 'M26' or 'MM106' apple rootstock and 'Quince A' or 'Quince C' for pears.

Half-standard

Just a larger version of the bush tree, a half-standard has a taller, clear trunk of about 1.5m (5ft). It is a smaller alternative to a standard tree. For a half-standard, use 'MM106' or 'MM111' rootstock.

Standard

The largest fruit tree form, which usually has a clear stem of 2m (6½ft) and an open-centred crown, so requires a big garden. The tree could reach 7m (23ft), so also consider how the fruit will be picked. For a standard, use 'MM111' or 'M25' apple rootstock and Quince for pears.

mid spring

This is one of the busiest months in the garden. The weather is good for growing and the crops are surging ahead – but so are the weeds. From now on, right through the growing season, you have to be ever vigilant, or weeds will quickly take over. As plants put on more growth, pests, too, are on the increase. Watch out for aphids in particular colonising the tender young growing tips of plants.

There are plenty of seeds to sow and crops to plant out, but even though the weather is improving, it is still too risky to start sowing some of the more tender vegetables outdoors without protection.

This is the month to enjoy the magnificent blossoming of fruit trees, with the flowery promise of heavy crops to come.

vegetables | GENERAL ADVICE

Water seedbeds | Cold, dry winds can soon parch seedbeds, and a light watering in these cases is helpful. In general the soil is still moist from winter, so deep watering is seldom necessary.

Thin seedlings | Start thinning seedlings as soon as they are large enough to be handled. In some cases, thinnings can be used to fill any gaps further along the rows, but this technique is not suitable for root crops such as parsnips and carrots, as it will result in stunted or misshapen roots.

Resow failed seed | Early-sown crops are always more subject to failure, particularly if there has been an unexpected cold spell after sowing. Where necessary, resow crops, but ensure you have allowed enough time for slow-germinating seeds (such as parsnip) to emerge.

Guard against slugs and snails | Tender young seedlings are very attractive to slugs. Protect them with slug controls or deterrents.

Protect carrots and cabbages | If you have not already done so, use fleece to cover crops of young cabbages and carrots to exclude cabbage root fly and carrot fly, which are on the wing now.

Make successional sowings | Make further sowings of crops such as lettuce, peas, beetroot, radish, carrots and turnip to ensure a continuous supply.

Sow sprouting broccoli and calabrese | Sow early varieties of sprouting broccoli in seedbeds or modules now, ready for transplanting to the garden in a few months' time. Calabrese are best sown directly where they are to grow.

Prepare the seedbeds thoroughly by forking over the soil and raking the surface to produce a fine, crumbly texture. Stretch a length of string as a guide and draw out a straight 1cm (½in) deep drill by dragging a measuring rod, hoe or broom handle along the line. If the bottom of the drill is dry, lightly water before sowing. Sprinkle the seed thinly along its length, cover with soil and firm gently by lightly patting down.

The seedlings should appear within 7–12 days. Thin out seedbed-raised plants so that they are 7.5cm (3in) apart. Weed the seedbed regularly, either by hand or by carefully hoeing between the lines. Slugs and snails will quickly devour seedlings, so pay particular attention to their control. Young plants are usually readily available from garden centres in late spring if you have no room or do not get around to sowing your own.

YOUNG LETTUCE, CARROT AND CORIANDER PLANTS *make an attractive feature in the spring vegetable garden. Close spacing helps to keep down weeds.*

vegetables | WHAT TO DO NOW

ONION FAMILY

Garlic

Water during dry weather
During spring and early summer, an occasional thorough watering during dry spells will improve the yield. Don't water once the bulbs are large and well formed, because this could encourage rotting.

Leeks

Sow outside
Leeks can be sown now to mature in autumn. The growing instructions are the same as for leeks sown in early spring (see page 40).

CABBAGE FAMILY

Broccoli and calabrese

Sow seeds for transplants
Sow early varieties of sprouting broccoli in seedbeds or modules now, ready for transplanting to the garden after a few months. Calabrese are best sown directly where they are to grow. Prepare the seedbeds thoroughly by forking over the soil and raking the surface to produce a fine, crumbly texture.

Stretch a length of string as a guide and draw out a straight 1cm (½in) deep drill by dragging a measuring rod, hoe or broom handle along the line. If the bottom of the drill is dry, lightly water before sowing. Sprinkle the seed thinly along its length, cover with soil and firm gently by lightly patting down.

The seedlings should appear within 7–12 days. Thin out seedbed-raised plants so that they are 7.5cm (3in) apart. Weed the seedbed regularly, either by hand or by carefully hoeing between the lines. Slugs and snails will

SOW CAULIFLOWER OUTSIDE *in mid spring. Seedbed-raised seedlings can be transplanted as soon as they are large enough to handle.*

quickly devour seedlings, so pay particular attention to their control.

Young plants are usually readily available from garden centres in late spring if you have no room or do not get round to sowing your own.

Cabbages

Cut heads as they are ready
Cut off the plants close to the ground with a sharp knife, or remove young leaves as and when they are needed. After harvesting the first spring and early summer cabbages, cut a cross in the top of the stump, about 1cm (½in) deep, and the plant will produce a cluster of smaller heads within about five weeks.

Cauliflower

Sow indoors or outside
Either sow the seed directly where it is to grow (thinning to final required spacing), raise the crop in a seedbed for transplanting later or germinate seed in modules. For

direct sowing, mark out a row with string and form the drill with a tool handle or measuring stick. The standard-size summer varieties are ready to harvest in as little as three months from a spring sowing. Seed can be sown from now until late spring.

Kale

Sow in seedbeds

Thoroughly prepare the soil before sowing by raking the surface to a fine, crumbly texture. Use a length of string as a guide and make a 1cm (½in) drill to sow the crop. The seedlings should appear within 7–10 days. Kale sown between now and late spring can be transplanted to its final position in six to eight weeks' time and will be ready to harvest as winter and spring greens.

Kale has many advantages over other brassicas. It tolerates a little shade, is completely frost-hardy, and is not so vulnerable to the pests and diseases that afflict the others. It can also be grown in virtually any soil, including impoverished, wet, loose and poor ones. However, adding well-rotted organic matter, such as manure or garden compost, or hoeing a granular fertiliser such as pelleted chicken manure into the surface, will improve the crop.

BEANS AND PEAS

Runner beans

Sow under cover

Sow seeds in pots of sowing compost in a greenhouse, propagator or on a windowsill indoors, sowing two seeds per pot, 5cm (2in) deep. It is too early to sow runner beans outdoors yet.

Peas

Support seedlings

Put supports in place before the young plants become top heavy and flop over. For dwarf and shorter varieties, twiggy pea sticks, chicken wire attached to stakes or string and stakes are fine. For taller varieties, trellis, bamboo canes and netting are more appropriate. Blocks of semi-leafless peas are self-supporting.

It is easy to underestimate just how sturdy such supports need to be, especially in windy weather. The foliage of fully grown plants acts like a sail and everything could go flying, so make sure that the supports are strongly tethered.

PLANT PEA SEEDLINGS *into the ground, when they are about 10cm (4in) tall. Insert supports around the plants. Remember to acclimatise the seedlings first so they don't suffer a shock.*

USE TALLER VARIETIES OF CLIMBING PEAS *to edge the kitchen garden, or their simple outlines to create attractive divisions between sections of a bed.*

ROOTS AND STEMS

Parsnips

Sow outside

If the weather was too cold or wet for sowing parsnips in early spring, seed can be sown now.

Thin seedlings

When the seedlings appear, thin them out to leave the strongest one of the three and hoe regularly to keep weeds down. Large, easy-to-peel roots are obtained by wide spacing of plants and the absence of weeds. Parsnips are highly drought-resistant plants that need watering only once every 10–14 days if the foliage starts to wilt.

Potatoes

Continue planting tubers

The two methods are to dig a trench or to plant in individual holes. Handle each sprouted potato carefully so you don't knock off any of the shoots, and plant 15cm (6in) deep. Space 30cm (12in) apart, with 60cm (24in) between rows for earlies and 40–75cm (16–30in) for maincrops. Closer planting often results in smaller potatoes at harvest time.

You can also plant potatoes through black plastic sheeting by simply cutting holes in it. Doing this means they won't need earthing up. Some rare varieties are not available as seed potatoes but as virus-free microplants.

These should be planted out as any other type of seedling, after the last frosts, to the same spacing.

Earth up early varieties

As soon as the first shoots emerge from potatoes planted earlier, start the process of earthing up by drawing up soil around and over them to produce a rounded ridge. This will prevent the shoots being damaged by a late frost. Alternatively, cover with fleece if frost is threatened.

You will need to continue the earthing up process at one- to two-week intervals until the ridge is around 20–30cm (8–12in) high; this kills weeds, helps prevent blight and stops the tubers from being exposed to the light and turning green and poisonous. You do not need to earth up potatoes growing under black plastic sheeting as they are already protected from light and the plastic prevents weed growth. During dry spells, give potatoes an occasional but thorough watering. Plenty of water early on in the plants' development will lead to initiation of tubers and a heavy crop later (see right).

DIG A TRENCH *15cm (6in) deep, then space your potatoes 30cm (12in) apart. Leave a gap of about three years before growing potatoes in the same spot to avoid the accumulation of soil-borne pests and diseases.*

SPROUTING SEED POTATOES *before planting helps to give an earlier crop, but the tubers need to be handled carefully to avoid knocking off the fragile sprouts.*

SALADS

Chicory

Sow indoors or outside

Sow chicory seeds from now through to summer, either directly into the ground, or in modules under warmer conditions for later planting. Sowing in modules is usually preferred since germination from outdoor sowings can be patchy, and bolting (where the plant makes flowers instead of leaves) can be a problem in cool spring weather. Take care when transplanting the chicory seedlings because they do not respond well to root disturbance.

Chicory grows best on a light soil with a reasonable amount of organic matter mixed in to keep the soil moist. Although chicory grows happily in full sun it doesn't mind a bit of shade, which makes it ideal for growing between taller crops.

Lettuce

Continue sowing outside

Sow lettuce in a position in full sun on moisture-retentive, reasonably fertile soil. Sow seed thinly in drills 1cm (½in) deep. Final spacing in the row will be from 15cm–30cm (6–12in), depending on the variety; see the seed packet for individual instructions. Water in well and ensure the seedlings get plenty of sunlight. Alternatively, rows of lettuce seeds can be sown more densely as a leafy cut-and-come-again crop (see page 120).

Thin earlier-sown seedlings

Thin out lettuce seedlings as soon as they can be handled comfortably. First thin them to half their final spacing, with a further thinning later on to leave them at the correct distance. With care, the thinned seedlings can be transplanted, provided this is done in cool weather and plants are well watered afterwards. Replanting them among slow-maturing crops like brassicas is an effective use of space. Thinnings can also be eaten.

Radishes

Keep roots growing steadily

Water regularly in dry weather to prevent plants from bolting or becoming woody. Irregular watering can result

THERE ARE SCORES OF LETTUCE VARIETIES *to choose from, each with its own flavour, texture and colour. Growing instructions will vary slightly depending on the variety, so always read the seed packet.*

SPLIT RADISH ROOTS *are caused by irregular watering and can lead to infections that make the roots virtually inedible, so make sure you water plants regularly, particularly in dry weather.*

in splitting of the roots, while lush, leafy growth instead of root development may be caused by overwatering.

Tomatoes

Space out seedlings

Tomatoes are very sensitive to frost, so plants that are raised indoors can be planted outside only once all risk of frost has passed. To keep the young plants sturdy they need plenty of light. Space them so the leaves do not touch, in the brightest place you can find.

Tomatoes grown to maturity in a greenhouse, conservatory or even a porch will fruit earlier and for longer, particularly if their positions are heated – but even a cheap polythene tunnel will help keep your tomatoes snug and speed up ripening. When growing plants in the open, a sunny, sheltered site is essential, such as against a sunny wall. Enrich their planting positions now with plenty of well-rotted organic matter and tomato fertiliser.

In an unheated greenhouse or conservatory, tomato plants can be set out now, once they are 15–23cm (6–9in) tall, spacing them 45cm (18in) apart. If the plants have become rather leggy, plant them more deeply.

If tomatoes are likely to occupy the same site for several years, growing in containers or bags, where the compost is removed each year, is best otherwise pests and diseases are likely to build up in the soil.

TOMATOES IN A SMALL SPACE

Where space is really short, tomatoes can be grown very successfully in hanging baskets or windowboxes. Most seed catalogues have a range of trailing varieties specially bred for growing in small containers.

Fill the container with good quality potting compost and mix in some moisture-retaining granules to make watering easier. Plant three trailing tomatoes to each medium- to large-sized basket or windowbox.

Suitable tomato varieties to use include 'Garden Pearl', 'Tumbling Tom Red', 'Tumbling Tom Yellow' and 'Maskotka'.

PLANTING TOMATOES IN A GROW BAG

PLACE THE BAG IN A SUNNY POSITION *and cut a cross in the plastic, peeling it back to expose the compost.*

SPACE THE SLITS *about 45cm (18in) apart. Don't try to pack the plants too close together or they will shade each other.*

MAKE HOLES *in the compost and gently ease in each seedling (they should be sturdier than shown and starting to form their first flowers).*

Spinach

Sow outside

Sow the seed directly where it is to grow in drills about 1cm (½in) deep in rows 30cm (12in) apart. Spinach is more of a prima donna than perpetual spinach, refusing to perform if conditions are not right and running to seed very quickly in dry conditions. It needs plenty of moisture at the roots and lots of nutrients, so apply a general fertiliser and do not attempt to grow it in dry soil with low fertility. Add plenty of well-rotted manure or compost to the soil before sowing. Sow it in a spot that can be lightly shaded in summer to help keep the soil cool and moist, and consider intercropping with taller vegetables that will cast a dappled shade over the spinach during the midday heat.

If you like spinach, be generous with your sowing so that you can gather great handfuls for the steamer or wok – it cooks down to almost nothing. Since spinach will not easily germinate in hot weather and tends to bolt if sown too early, make sowings from now until early summer for summer leaves, and then in autumn for a supply of leaves into winter.

Don't forget that baby spinach leaves also make great salads. To grow small salad leaves, make a wide drill and scatter the seed thinly across it. You should not need to thin the seedlings.

SPINACH SEEDLINGS *won't germinate easily in hot weather, so sow from now until early summer. Make successive sowings of small amounts every few weeks for a continuous supply of fresh leaves.*

Winter squashes and pumpkins

Sow seed indoors

Sow seed indoors or in a frost-free greenhouse in the same way as for marrows and courgettes, about one month before the last expected frost. Winter squashes and pumpkins need a long hot growing season to ripen fully, so choose early ripening cultivars, such as 'Waltham Butternut' or pumpkin 'Neon'. You must also time your seed sowing to give plants the maximum growing time outdoors.

Courgettes, marrows and summer squashes

Sow seed indoors

Sow seed in pots indoors about one month before the last predicted frost in your area. The seeds of courgettes, marrows and summer squashes are large and flat and can be prone to rotting, so sow them on edge, two to a 9cm (3½in) pot. Remove the weakest seedling straight away if both germinate.

Sweetcorn

Sow seed indoors

Sweetcorn needs a long season for the cobs to mature. This means that for an early crop in cold areas you should sow the seed indoors now and plant out when all danger of frost has gone. Choose an early variety such as 'Dickson' or 'Honey Banatam'. Supersweet cultivars such as 'Dynasty' are more difficult to germinate and the seed is more likely to rot in cool, damp conditions, so use a heated propagator if you have one.

Sow in modules or individual pots at 20–27°C (70–80°F) and plant out after all risk of frost is over.

MARROW, COURGETTE OR SQUASH?

These are all closely related members of the same family – cucurbita – and there is often confusion over exactly what is meant by each term.

Courgettes, also called zucchini, are just immature marrows; the fruit of any marrow variety can be picked when young and used as a courgette. However, conventionally marrows are striped dark and light green while courgettes are dark green and not striped, so most seed catalogues list different varieties for each use. Popular marrow varieties are 'Long Green Bush' and 'Badger Cross'. Traditional courgette varieties include 'Defender' and 'Patriot', but there are now lots of different colours and shapes available – the spherical 'Eight Ball', bright yellow 'Golden Dawn' or creamy green 'Clarion', for example.

Summer squashes taste similar to courgettes but include the more unusual shapes of the family. Scallop-edged patty pan types such as 'Sunburst' or 'Green Buttons' are popular, and 'Early Golden Crookneck' has curved, club-shaped fruits. Finally there are the winter squashes, which are harvested when ripe and will keep for much of the winter. Their flesh is drier, sweeter and nuttier than summer varieties and they come in a wide range of shapes. Good varieties include 'Cobnut' and 'Crown Prince'. Pumpkins are a type of winter squash usually grown for very large fruits, such as 'Hundredweight'.

Chillies

Pinch out young plants

Pinch out the growing tips of chilli peppers when plants are 20cm (8in) tall to encourage bushiness and prevent plants becoming top heavy. The sideshoots can be pinched out again later if lots of small fruit are needed.

CHILLI PEPPER SEEDLINGS (top) *enjoy a well-drained and moisture-retentive soil. When plants reach 20cm (8in) tall, pinch out the growing tips to encourage bushiness and stop them becoming top heavy.*

AN ABUNDANCE OF CHILLI PEPPERS (above) *illustrates how pinching out the sideshoots a second time later can benefit fruiting, ideal if you need lots of small peppers.*

fruit | GENERAL ADVICE

Plant fruit trees | This is the last chance to plant bare-root trees. Ideally container-grown trees should be planted now, too; although they can be planted all year round, they will establish more quickly and be easier to care for if they are not in full leaf at planting time.

Feed fruit in pots | Apply a balanced liquid feed to fruit trees growing in containers.

Check on fruit pests | Fruit trees and bushes can be attacked by a number of pests including aphids, apple sucker, pear sucker, pear midge and caterpillars. Watch out for any problems and take action early – insecticide spraying must be done before the blossoms open because of the risk of otherwise harming beneficial pollinating insects. Insecticides containing bifenthrin are useful for the control of a wide number of insect pests, but read the instructions carefully before using.

Protect flowers from frost | Continue to protect early-flowering trees from frost by covering them with a double layer of horticultural fleece, but remove this to allow pollinating insects access to the flowers by day.

Apply protective fungicide sprays | If any of your fruit suffered from fungus diseases last year, this is a good time to give a protective spraying with a fungicide such as myclobutanil or mancozeb. Apples and pears, black currants and gooseberries often benefit from a spraying now, but it is not necessary unless disease was evident last year. As with all garden chemicals, follow the pack instructions carefully.

Remove grease bands | Remove grease bands from trees and burn them to destroy any pests.

CHERRY TREES flower early in the year, so it is important to continue covering them at night throughout mid spring, where practicable, to protect against frosts if a good crop is to be expected.

fruit | WHAT TO DO NOW

TREE FRUIT

Apples and pears

Protect against scab
If scab has occurred in previous years, start preventive fungicide sprays with myclobutanil or mancozeb at bud-burst. Continue to spray at intervals as recommended on the pack. Scab causes dark patches on the leaves followed by brown or black corky scabs on the surface of the fruit.

Watch out for mildew
Developing shoots on apples are often affected by powdery mildew, which forms a white coating on the leaves and distorts and stunts growth. Control with the fungicide myclobutanil, following the pack directions.

Continue formative training of espaliers
The maiden whip to form an espalier should have been planted in late autumn (see page 230) and cut back to 45cm (18in) above ground to encourage buds to break just beneath the cut. Two of the shoots that should have developed just below the initial cut will now become the first horizontal tier. Train the top shoot up the vertical cane attached to the wire, so the stem grows upwards.

AN ESPALIER'S TIERS OF HORIZONTAL BRANCHES *should be trained along supporting wires. Patience is required to create an espalier, but it is very effective once established.*

GRAFT FRUIT TREES

Tree fruits can be propagated by whip and tongue grafting now. This involves taking a shoot from the tree you want to propagate (called the scion) and grafting it onto a rootstock. It's not a common procedure for gardeners but is useful if, for example, you have an existing tree of an unknown or commercially unavailable variety that you want to increase.

Scion wood should have been collected in mid winter when it was fully dormant and stored in a refrigerator (see page 267). The scion is prepared by making a long sloping cut below a healthy bud. The rootstock is cut down to about 30cm (12in) from ground level and a similar but opposite sloping cut made at the top of the stem. A tongue is then made by cutting into the exposed surface of the cuts on both the scion and the rootstock so that the two lock snugly together. It is important to get the sloping surfaces at exactly the same angle so they fit without any gaps. Use a very sharp grafting knife and practise making cuts on spare pieces of stem until you have perfected the technique.

Bind the scion and stock firmly using grafting tape and cover any exposed surfaces with grafting wax. The graft should callous over after a couple of months and the tape should then be removed.

THE SLOPING SURFACES *on both the scion and the rootstock need to be at exactly the same angle (left) so they lock together without any gaps. Bind them together using grafting tape (right).*

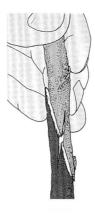
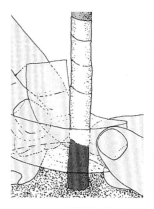

To form the next tier, select a vigorous shoot from either side of the main trunk and tie each to a cane placed at 45 degrees to the main stem. Remove other shoots growing from the main stem. The following year, the shoots of the new tier can be repositioned at 90 degrees. Repeat this process each year until the desired amount of tiers has been created.

A low-growing step-over apple tree can be created by training it as a single-tiered espalier, with the two topmost shoots trained horizontally in opposite directions along a supporting wire, 45–60cm (18–24in) high, that is pulled taut between two posts. Step-overs make an intriguing and productive edging to a fruit or vegetable garden.

Cherries

Feed and train trees
Cherries are vigorous growers and will benefit from a topdressing of general-purpose fertiliser now.

To form a fan, train a feathered maiden to strong horizontal wires spaced 38cm (15in) apart. At bud-burst, cut the central leader back to two healthy sideshoots. On each side of the leader, secure a sturdy bamboo cane tightly to the wire supports at an angle; tie the sideshoots to form the framework of the fan.

Citrus

Increase humidity
Mist citrus plants regularly when flowering begins and maintain a minimum temperature of 14°C (57°F).

Figs

Plant outside or in containers
Figs need a warm, sunny site. They can be grown against a south- or south west-facing wall, where they can be trained as a fan, or in containers. This is a good time for planting trees using either method.

To encourage figs to bear good crops of fruit it is advisable to limit their root system; by restricting its vegetative growth, the plant will channel its energy into reproduction and should bear more fruit. Growing a fig in a container will restrict its roots effectively. Another advantage is that it can be moved before winter arrives

into an unheated greenhouse or even a shed or porch. The container can also be plunged into the ground if you want the fig as a permanent feature in one place.

Start the plant off in a 25cm (10in) container, and as the plant grows repot it each year, until it is eventually in a 45cm (18in) container. Use a pot with plenty of drainage holes and lots of broken crocks at the bottom. Standing the container on bricks helps excess water to drain away.

TIE WALL-TRAINED FIGS *to a sturdy support (top) to form a strong framework. New shoots may attempt to grow away from the support; tie these in or remove them.*

FAN-TRAIN OUTDOOR FIGS *against a sunny wall (above). Train two side branches, one for each side of the fan, and as they grow, tie in the sideshoots so they are evenly spaced.*

If you intend to plunge a containerised fig into open ground, fill a 30–40cm (12–16in) pot with John Innes No 3 compost and plant the fig, then position the pot well into the ground.

Another method of root restriction is by creating a planting pit. Dig a hole 60 x 60 x 60cm (2 x 2 x 2ft). Line the sides of the hole with patio slabs, setting them 2.5cm (1in) proud of the ground to prevent the roots from spreading over the top of the soil. Leave the bottom unlined; instead fill the hole with rubble or broken bricks and crocks to 10–15cm (4–6in) deep, which will prevent roots penetrating the soil underneath. After planting, backfill the hole using ordinary garden soil or a loam-based potting compost.

Plums, damsons and gages

Mulch and feed trees

On established trees apply a mulch of well-rotted farmyard manure to help retain soil moisture, keep down weeds and provide nitrogen. This can be supplemented with a topdressing of dried poultry pellets or non-organic nitrogen fertiliser such as sulphate of ammonia.

Quinces

Mulch roots

Apply an organic mulch, 7.5cm (3in) thick, to help keep the roots of quince trees cool and moist.

QUINCES ARE ORNAMENTAL *as well as productive. Their single, large, bowl-shaped flowers are borne in abundance in spring and are followed by colourful fruits. The trees are easy to look after and are not prone to many of the more common fruit problems.*

Cranberries and lingonberries

Feed with ericaceous fertiliser

Apply a liquid ericaceous fertiliser at half the recommended rate, especially if yields have been low. Water plants with rainwater wherever possible, keeping the soil moist at all times. To encourage plants to spread, maintain a layer, 2.5cm (1in) deep, of horticultural grit or sharp sand on the surface of the bed or pot.

Raspberries

Feed and mulch plants

Topdress summer and autumn raspberries, blackberries and hybrid berries, such as tayberry, with a general-purpose fertiliser and mulch with low-nutrient organic matter such as garden compost or composted bark chips. Alternatively, topdress with well-rotted farmyard manure. Make sure the mulch is placed away from the new canes and the crown.

Strawberries

De-blossom spring runners

Spring-planted strawberry runners should have their blossoms removed in their first year so they put all their energy into getting established.

EARLY STRAWBERRY CROPS *can be grown under tunnel cloches, as shown, or in a greenhouse. Remember to keep these plants watered while they are covered.*

Pick fruit under glass

If you have potted strawberry plants being forced in a heated greenhouse the first fruits will be ready for picking any time now. Check the plants for aphids and red spider mite and treat as appropriate.

APHIDS ON STRAWBERRY LEAVES *pose a risk because they can transmit harmful viruses for which there is no cure. See the fruit pests and diseases chart on pages 294–295 to find out how to control them.*

VINE FRUIT

Grapes

Train newly planted vines

To train vines planted in late autumn (see page 237) using the guyot system (see page 259), select three or four new shoots and tie two shoots – one in each direction – to two low, fixed wires to form the fruiting arms of the vine. The remaining one or two shoots are spares; tie them up vertically. Remove any shoots that appear further down the trunk. Prune both of the vertically trained shoots so they form spurs of two or three buds; the new growth that comes from these will be used to replace the fruiting arms next year. Do not prune established vines now.

Adjust greenhouse ventilation

Temperatures inside the greenhouse shoot up rapidly on sunny days, even though the weather outside may be chilly. Automatic ventilators will ensure the greenhouse does not become overheated when you are not there, but keep a check on the temperature with a maximum/minimum thermometer to ensure the vents are working properly. If necessary, automatic ventilators can be adjusted, usually by simply screwing the arm to allow them to open at a higher or lower temperature.

Kiwifruit

Mulch with bulky organic matter

Once the ground has warmed slightly and the soil is moist, surround kiwifruit with a mulch of bulky, well-rotted organic matter to a depth of at least 7.5cm (3in). This will help suppress weeds, retain soil moisture and keep the extensive root system cool.

Melons

Sow in pots for growing outdoors

Sow one seed per 9cm (3½in) pot, water well and place in a heated propagator at 20–25°C (68–77°F) in a well-lit spot. Germination should occur in less than a week, after which the compost must be kept moist but not saturated.

Once the first true leaves appear, remove the plants from the propagator and grow on at 18–20°C (64–68°F). If you can't provide these conditions, you can buy plants in garden centres later in the season.

Select an early variety for growing outdoors; try 'Sweetheart', 'Edonis' or 'Outdoor Wonder', for example. Growing in a cold frame or under cloches will give better results, especially in cooler regions.

NUTS

Mulch with bulky organic matter

Maintain a 7.5cm (3in) thick layer of bulky organic matter such as well-rotted garden compost or farmyard manure around the root zone of almonds, cobnuts and filberts. Avoid the mulch touching the tree trunks directly to deter rotting of the collar. This will help retain soil moisture through the summer, essential for healthy development.

APPLY A BULKY ORGANIC MULCH *around the base of nut trees in mid spring. This will help young trees to establish and retain soil moisture through summer to ensure healthy nut development.*

Plant cobnuts and filberts

This is the last opportunity to plant bare-root trees. Make sure they are watered thoroughly if the weather turns dry in the weeks after planting. For the best crops, plant more than one variety to ensure good pollination. 'Kentish Cob', 'Butler' and 'Ennis' are good varieties, as is 'Merveille de Bollwiller', which will pollinate any of the others.

LATE-FLOWERING ALMOND

Almonds are difficult to grow in cold and exposed gardens because the early spring flowers are subject to damage by frosts. A new variety of almond, 'Mandaline', has been specially bred to flower at this time of year, when the worst of the frosts have usually passed.

| How to ensure good pollination

For almost all fruit trees to successfully produce fruit, their flowers need pollinating – for pollen grains from the male anthers of a flower to be transferred to the female stigma. This is usually carried out by flying insects but nuts such as cobnuts and filberts use the wind.

Some fruit trees such as 'Victoria' plums and 'Stella' cherries are self-fertile and pollinate their own flowers. This is ideal in a small garden because only one tree is required to produce fruit. But even self-fertile trees tend to crop better when another tree is nearby for pollination.

Most fruit trees, however, have self-incompatible flowers, so require another growing nearby to pollinate them. Successful cross-pollination generally requires trees of the same fruit type; for example, an apple will pollinate another apple tree while a pear tree can't pollinate an apple and vice versa. Also, the trees may need

to be different varieties of the same fruit; two 'Golden Delicious' apples will not cross-pollinate each other. Some apples and pears are 'triploids' that won't pollinate other trees and need two pollinators themselves.

Pollination partners

Fruit trees are classified into flowering groups so that it is easy to choose two varieties that will flower at the same time. Trees should be chosen from the same group or from ones either side, as flowering periods usually extend into each other. Opposite are the pollination groups of some popular varieties.

MOST TREE FRUIT – *even self-fertile varieties – rely on bees (above) and other insects to transfer pollen from one flower to the next.*

Apples

GROUP 1 'Gravenstein' (triploid), 'Vista-bella'
GROUP 2 'Beauty of Bath', 'Egremont Russet', 'Idared', 'Reverend W. Wilks',
GROUP 3 'Bountiful', 'Bramley's Seedling' (triploid), 'Cox's Orange Pippin'*, 'Discovery', 'Kidd's Orange Red'*, 'Spartan', 'Worcester Pearmain'
GROUP 4 'Ashmead's Kernel', 'Ellison's Orange' (below), 'Gala', 'Tydeman's Late Orange'
GROUP 5 'Gascoyne's Scarlet' (triploid), 'King of the Pippins', 'Newton Wonder', 'Suntan' (triploid)
GROUP 6 'Court Pendu Plat', 'Edward VII'
GROUP 7 'Crawley Beauty'

* 'Cox's Orange Pippin' is incompatible with 'Kidd's Orange Red' despite being in the same group.

Pears

GROUP 2 'Louise Bonne of Jersey', 'Packham's Triumph'
GROUP 3 'Concorde', 'Conference', 'Merton Pride' (triploid), 'Williams' Bon Chrétien'
GROUP 4 'Beth' (below), 'Catillac', 'Doyenné du Comice'

Cherries

GROUP 1 'Early Rivers' (si)
GROUP 2 'Merton Glory' (si), 'Noir de Guben' (si)
GROUP 3 'Van' (si), 'May Duke' (psf), 'Roundel' (sf), 'Starkrimson' (sf)
GROUP 4 'Bigarreau Napoléon' (si), 'Lapins' (sf), 'Stella' (sf) (below), 'Sunburst' (sf)
GROUP 5 'Bigarreau Gaucher'** (si), 'Florence' (si), 'Merton Late' (si), 'Nabella' (sf), 'Morello' (sf)
GROUP 6 'Bradbourne Black'** (si)

** 'Bigarreau Gaucher' and 'Bradbourne Black' are incompatible with each other.

Plums and gages

GROUP 1 'Jefferson' (si), 'Monarch' (sf)
GROUP 2 'Denniston's Superb' (sf), 'Coe's Golden Drop' (sf), 'Ariel' (psf)
GROUP 3 'Czar' (sf), 'Opal' (sf), 'Pershore' (sf), 'Victoria' (sf) (below)
GROUP 4 'Cambridge Gage' (psf) (bottom), 'Oullins Gage' (sf)
GROUP 5 'Marjorie's Seedling' (sf), 'Pond's Seedling' (si)

sf *self-fertile*
psf *partially self-fertile; gives a better crop if cross pollinated.*
si *self-infertile; must be cross-pollinated.*

late spring

Even in the coldest regions we should have seen the last of the spring frosts by late spring. Young plants raised under cover can be planted out safely after gradual hardening off; vegetables such as runner beans and sweetcorn can be sown outside, and tender fruits that have spent the winter under cover can be brought back out into the garden. Keep the hoe close at hand to deal with weeds and be prepared to water plants in dry spells.

Bees and other insects should have been busy among the fruit blossoms and swelling fruitlets will be visible as the petals fall. Even at this early stage we need to watch out for fruit pests such as sawflies and codling moth; they are on the wing and ready to attack.

Best of all in late spring, there should be some new season's crops to harvest – fresh lettuces and radishes, baby carrots, overwintered broad beans and succulent asparagus spears.

vegetables | GENERAL ADVICE

Protect against pests | By now, crops should be pushing up well. Since carrots, parsnips and cabbage-related crops are still vulnerable to pests, keep them covered with fleece or insect-proof nets for as long as possible.

Continue weeding | Weed growth is at its peak. Hoeing between crops on dry days reduces handweeding to a minimum. Use a well-sharpened hoe, slide it flat along the ground and sever weeds from their roots – do not use the hoe to try to dig weeds out of the soil. On a dry, bright, breezy day, the top growth of chopped off weeds will soon wilt and die; weeds that have been dug up and left lying on the soil surface with a little soil around their roots may well regrow.

Thin out seedlings | Crops will now be growing very fast, so thinning is a priority to avoid spoiling all the hard work you've already invested. Overcrowding will lead to an increased risk of disease as well as increasing the competition for nutrients and water.

Seedlings can be thinned in stages rather than being thinned to their final spacing straight away. For example, if the final spacing is 30cm (12in) between plants, thin them first to 15cm (6in) apart, and then a little while later to 30cm (12in). This gives you more leeway in case some seedlings die or are damaged by pests or disease, and the larger seedlings from the second thinning can often be transplanted to make another row.

Keep tidy | Remove weeds and debris and tidy edges and paths to keep the vegetable plot looking good, as well as being productive. Tidiness also helps prevent accidents in the garden (leaving less around for you to lose or trip over) and deprives slugs and other pests of shelter.

Avoid seedling diseases | Seedlings are vulnerable to fungal diseases such as damping off. Fungicidal seed dressings are no longer available to gardeners, but disease can be avoided by sowing at the optimum time when the soil is warm and not too wet. Watering seedlings raised indoors with copper-based fungicides also protects them. However, disease can often be avoided altogether by using clean containers and clean water.

Seedlings sown direct outside should be thinned to a suitable spacing (see left) as this will increase air circulation around them and avoid the humid conditions that fungal diseases thrive on.

Buy in plants | If you have not raised your own plants, garden centres are usually well stocked with small pots of tender and other crops. The best ones sell quickly, and those that don't soon deteriorate under garden-centre conditions, so buy as soon as possible even if you have to keep them under fleece or on a sunny windowsill until you are ready to plant.

Many seed catalogues also sell a good range of young vegetable plants, but you may be too late to order some of them if you have not done so already.

Continue sowing | There are still important crops to be sown. Beetroot, calabrese, carrots, lettuces, onions, parsley, parsnips, late peas, radishes, rocket, swedes, spinach, spring onions, turnips and herbs (such as parsley, dill and chervil) can all be sown in the ground where they are to grow.

Make successional sowings | Continue to make regular small sowings of various vegetables for a steady supply to harvest, but remember that by the time plants sown now mature later in the summer, tender crops such as French beans, courgettes and tomatoes will also be ready. In the heat of mid summer the likes of lettuce, spinach and radish won't stay in good condition for more than a few days but will quickly deteriorate, so adjust the amount of seed you sow accordingly.

Sow tender crops indoors | Sow frost-sensitive crops such as courgettes, cucumbers, French beans, marrows,

melons, pumpkins, squashes and sweetcorn under glass.
All produce fast-growing plants, so it is important not
to sow them too early, otherwise you will have plants
becoming large and leggy as they wait to be planted out
while frosts still threaten.

Small seed makes small seedlings and these take a
long time to put on good growth (carrots and onions are
good examples), whereas large seed (such as peas, broad
beans and marrows) produce large seedlings that get off
to a flying start. If you garden in the warmer southern
areas of the country you can sow these outdoors from
now to early summer and they will still have enough
time to crop well. In colder areas, however, it is safer to
start them indoors.

Harden off earlier-sown crops for transplanting |
Many of the transplants sown earlier in spring will be
ready to go outdoors after hardening off. Harden plants
off by gradually acclimatising them to the cooler
outdoor conditions. Start by putting them outside in a
sheltered spot on a mild day and returning them under
cover in the evening. Then leave them out day and night,
and finally move them to a more open position near to
where they are to grow.

Brussels sprouts, salads, summer calabrese,
cauliflowers and cabbages in particular appreciate
early planting out, even if a temporary fleece covering
is required in cold snaps.

Catch up on sowing and planting | There is still time
to sow and plant crops that should ideally have been
raised earlier in spring – they invariably catch up. In fact,
with badly drained gardens in cold exposed sites it is
better to wait until now; early spring sowing is too risky.

Increase greenhouse ventilation | As the sunshine
gets stronger, it is important that greenhouses are
sufficiently ventilated. Even on a chilly day, sunshine
will push up the temperature inside the greenhouse
very quickly and delicate seedlings could be badly
affected. Automatic ventilators provide the best control,
particularly if you are not around during the day to
open and close the vents as the weather changes.

GIVE YOUNG PLANTS *the best possible chance by weeding regularly,
thinning seedlings, watering well in dry spells and keeping pests and
diseases at bay. A tidy vegetable plot is a productive one!*

vegetables | WHAT TO DO NOW

Leeks

Transplant young plants

The time to transplant is when the young leeks are
about pencil thick. Water thoroughly the day before
transplanting and lift using a fork. Make wide, deep holes
– 15cm (6in) deep and 5cm (2in) across – and drop a single
seedling in each. Don't backfill with soil, but simply fill
each hole with water to settle the soil around the roots.

General

Sow crops for transplanting

Raise transplants, including cabbages and cauliflowers
for autumn, spring and winter, and purple sprouting
broccoli, in pots or cell trays under glass, or in
a seedbed outdoors.

Broccoli and calabrese

Plant out seedlings

Set young plants from seedbeds or pots in their final
positions when they are roughly 10–15cm (4–6in) high,
watering them well before transplanting. Ensure that
the prepared planting site is well firmed by shuffling up
and down all over it on your heels. Rake flat and repeat
until no dips or hollows remain. Plants sown direct
where they are to mature should now be thinned to
their final spacing.

For calabrese, leave 45cm (18in) between the rows,
and 30cm (12in) between plants within the row. Space
purple and white sprouting broccoli at 45cm (18in)
between both rows and plants. The wide spacing will
ensure good air circulation around the plants and help

WATER LEEKS THOROUGHLY *after transplanting (top). Repeat as
necessary during long dry spells.*

PROTECTIVE COVERINGS *of fine or medium netting (above) are
very useful when it comes to growing brassicas, as they keep many
of the common pests at bay – such as cabbage white butterfly
caterpillars and pigeons.*

prevent diseases. Dig a hole big enough to accommodate the roots and deep enough for the lowest leaves to be near the soil surface. Plant seedlings 2.5cm (1in) deeper than in the seedbed to give them good anchorage and water in. Net the crop against insects and pigeons.

Make sure plants never go short of water as they develop, which will prevent the formation of good flowering heads and could result in fungal diseases. Reduce competition for moisture and nutrients by carefully hoeing off the tops of any weeds around the plants the moment they appear.

Brussels sprouts

Transplant young plants
Transplant Brussels sprouts when they are roughly 10–15cm (4–6in) high. If the seedlings have been grown in modules, transplant them when the roots begin to show through the bottom of the tray.

Allow 76cm (30in) between the plants and the rows. Resist the temptation to squeeze in more plants, because the distance makes picking easier and the improved air circulation will help to prevent fungal diseases. Plant the seedlings so that the soil is level with the first set of true leaves, and keep well watered. Continue to water the crop regularly while it is establishing, and during dry spells.

TRANSPLANT BRUSSELS SPROUTS SEEDLINGS, *making sure that you allow enough space around them for air to circulate over the leaves as this will help to prevent fungal diseases.*

Broad beans

Provide sturdy supports
Use string roped around a series of stakes or strong bamboo canes to provide support for broad bean plants; in exposed sites they will fall over in the wind or stems will break off under the weight of the swelling pods unless they are well staked. If seedlings are only just showing through, long, strong, twiggy prunings can be used to create an unobtrusive network of support.

On early-sown crops, young beans will now be appearing at the base of the plant. This is the time to 'pinch out' the growing tips in order to concentrate the beans' energy on pod formation. Nip off the top of the stem with two pairs of leaves attached. Removing the shoot tips may also help to prevent attack by aphids, but these need not be wasted as they make a tasty green vegetable when lightly cooked.

French beans

Sow outdoors or under cover
Sow French beans outdoors now under cloches, or in pots under cover in cooler areas, sowing one or two beans per 9cm (3½in) pot of sowing compost. These are tender plants that need warm conditions to thrive. Unprotected outdoor sowings are only worth making in mild areas in warm soil – covering the soil with plastic several weeks before sowing is helpful.

Peas

Support growing plants
Provide peas with twiggy sticks or netting stretched between sturdy posts to climb up. Some varieties of pea, such as the semi-leafless 'Endeavour' or 'Markana', are almost self-supporting if grown in a block, but most will be easier to pick and be more productive with supports.

Sow for succession
To maintain a steady supply of peas through the season, there are two main strategies. Either sow an early variety every four weeks until midsummer, or sow a maincrop

variety from now until midsummer with another sowing of an early variety in early summer. Early peas grow more quickly than maincrops. Good early varieties to grow include 'Feltham First' and 'Early Onward', while reliable maincrops include 'Hurst Green Shaft' and 'Ambassador'.

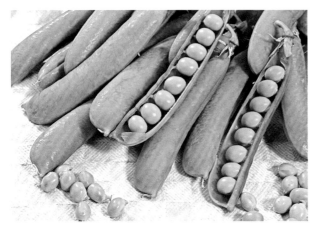

PEA 'EARLY ONWARD' *(top) is a reliable variety with a high yield of blunt-ended pods that are carried in pairs.*

CUT ASPARAGUS SPEARS *(above), including any thin or bent ones, as this will stimulate the dormant buds in the crown into growth. Freshly cut asparagus will keep for up to one week in the fridge, if stored up-right in a small amount of water (replaced daily).*

PERENNIAL VEGETABLES

Asparagus

Start cutting spears

The short asparagus season usually begins around now. In established beds, cut off each spear just below soil level when it's roughly 15–20cm (6–8in) tall. It is essential to cut every spear, even those that are thin (known as 'sprue') or bent ('crooks'), because this stimulates the dormant buds in the crown to grow. Spears grow quickly in warm weather and beds need checking over daily once they start to emerge.

It is essential not to over crop asparagus in its early years; if you do, future yields will be severely reduced. One-year-old crowns of 'F1 hybrids' can be harvested for six weeks one year after planting (or two if they are open-pollinated) and for eight weeks in subsequent years. Seed-raised 'F1 hybrids' can be harvested for six weeks two years after planting (or three if open-pollinated) and for eight weeks thereafter.

Jerusalem artichokes

Stake where necessary

Once stems are 30cm (12in) tall, pile up the earth around the roots to make plants more stable. Weeding shouldn't be necessary because the quick-growing foliage smothers out other plants. There is also no need to feed. You may need to stake plants on windy sites to deter wind rock, which can cause the stems and the tubers to rot, reducing the yield. An alternative is to cut back any stems that are over 2m (6½ft) tall by about one third, but don't be tempted to cut off any more or the yield will suffer.

ROOTS AND STEMS

Beetroot

Weed and water young plants

Water beetroot thoroughly every 10–14 days during dry spells. A lack of water causes woody roots, while a fluctuation in water supply can cause splitting and an excess of water will result in the production of leaves at the expense of roots. Regularly handweed close to the plants and hoe the soil between the rows, but keep the blade well away from the roots because they will 'bleed' if damaged.

Carrots

Thin seedlings and protect from pests

Thin carrot seedlings to around 5cm (2in) between plants; the thinnings are often large enough by this time to use as baby carrots. Water the crop several hours before thinning to make the job easier. Weed the rows every couple of weeks by hoeing between them, but handweed close to the plants to avoid damaging the roots with the hoe. The scent of bruised foliage attracts carrot root fly, so thinning or weeding is best done in the evening to reduce the length of time the plants are vulnerable.

From late spring to summer, cover or surround the crop with a barrier of fleece, fine mesh or polythene to help prevent an attack of carrot fly. The low-flying insects lay their eggs next to the plants and the larvae tunnel into the carrots leaving unsightly holes.

Sow for succession

Switch to sowing maincrop carrot varieties for the rest of spring and summer. For a regular supply of vegetables for your kitchen, make sowings every three to four weeks until late summer. Carrots are generally ready for harvesting about 12–16 weeks after sowing.

HOE THE SOIL *between rows of beetroot, being very careful to keep the blade well away from the roots so they don't get damaged and bleed. Regularly handweed close to the plants.*

Celeriac

Harden off and plant out seedlings

Celeriac seedlings raised under cover should be acclimatised to outdoor conditions before being planted out over the next couple of weeks. Space the seedlings 30cm (12in) apart in rows 45cm (18in) apart, and water in well. Protect the young seedlings from slugs and snails.

Florence fennel

Sow outside

Florence fennel can be sown in the open once all danger of frost has passed, from now until midsummer. Plants should mature around 14–16 weeks after sowing, so a direct-sown crop will be later than one started off earlier under cover (see page 44).

Mark out straight lines and make a shallow drill 1cm (½in) deep. Water if dry and allow to drain before sowing the seed thinly. Space rows 45cm (18in) apart. It is a good idea to make several sowings over a period of several weeks as insurance against poor germination or bolting caused by low or fluctuating temperatures. The

SURROUND CARROTS *with a 50cm (20in) barrier of fleece, fine mesh or polythene to exclude carrot fly, which flies close to the ground and leaves its destructive larvae next to the plants.*

direct-sown seedlings need to be thinned once they have germinated and are growing strongly, leaving around 20cm (8in) between each plant.

Florence fennel is fussy. It thrives in a sunny, sheltered site with rich, moisture-retentive soil, ideally free-draining and with lots of organic matter. Avoid heavy clay, stony or poorly drained ground. It is probably best not to bother growing it if you can't meet its exacting requirements because the plants will bolt if they become stressed.

Plant out earlier sown seedlings

Container-grown plants from an earlier indoor sowing can be planted out from now to very early summer, depending on whether you live in a mild or cold area. Acclimatise plants to outdoor conditions for a couple of weeks, then plant out at 20cm (8in) spacings and water in well.

Potatoes

Continue earthing up

Continue to earth up potatoes as shoots emerge. In many gardens the risk of frosts will be over now, though in some areas late frosts may still occur; if frost is forecast, remember to cover the shoots completely to protect them. Earthing up is also important to prevent the tubers from being exposed to the light and turning green – green patches on potatoes are bitter and poisonous.

EARTH UP POTATOES by drawing soil up around the crops into a mound to stop weeds and to help prevent blight and keep the tubers from being exposed to the light, which can turn them poisonous.

Swedes

Sow direct outside

Sow swedes directly where they are to grow in well-prepared soil. Sow thinly in 1cm (½in) deep rows spaced 38cm (15in) apart; thin the seedlings in stages until the plants end up 23cm (9in) apart.

Swedes like to grow in full sun and well-drained, moisture-retentive soil, following a crop from the previous year that required the addition of plenty of organic matter, such as compost or well-rotted manure. This encourages strong growth and lessens the chances of the roots rotting over winter.

Since swedes are members of the cabbage family and prone to club root if grown on acid soil, check its pH before sowing and add a dressing of lime, if necessary, to increase the alkalinity. A moderate dose of general-purpose fertiliser prior to sowing is a good idea.

Turnips

Harvest young roots

Start pulling turnips when they reach the size of a golf ball. Do not let them develop any larger than a small orange, as beyond this they become woody and much less tasty – check the size of the roots first by pulling back the foliage. Tender young roots can be thinly sliced or grated for eating raw in salads, as well as being cooked.

The roots will be ready in about 6–10 weeks from sowing, depending on the variety grown. With successional sowing, the season for turnips can run well into autumn.

SALADS

Cucumbers

Sow indoors and out

Put the large seed on edge to prevent rotting, 1cm (½in) deep in a small pot of moist seed compost, one seed per pot, and place in a warm spot (a heated propagator is ideal). Grow on in a heated greenhouse or on a sunny windowsill. Be careful not to overwater and, once the first true leaves have expanded, move to a 13cm (5in) pot.

Outdoor varieties are best started indoors now, sowing three seeds in a small pot. Plant out as soon as the

HARVEST RADISHES *by taking hold of the top growth and easing them out with a fork, trowel or even a plastic plant label. Don't leave them in the ground for too long when mature.*

rootball holds together. In warm areas, sow three seeds 2cm (¾in) deep where the cucumbers are to grow and thin to one plant when big enough to handle. Be careful to plant in moist soil and avoid soil touching the base of the stem. Cloches or fleece will increase soil temperatures and also greatly boost growth and yield.

Radishes

Harvest regularly

Pull up radishes as soon as they are large enough to eat. They do not last well in the ground but will store for several days in the fridge if they are first rinsed, patted dry and placed in a polythene bag. Use sliced or grated in salads and sandwiches.

SPINACH AND CHARD

Perpetual spinach

Sow outside

If you are growing large leaves for cooking, space the plants well to let them spread. Sow seed in rows 45cm (18in) apart, with 30–38cm (12–15in) between plants, putting a few together as a precaution in case some don't germinate. Good spacing also helps prevent downy mildew, which can occur with poor air circulation if

plants are too close together. Seedlings can take a long time to show, often up to a few weeks. When they do appear, thin to leave the strongest in each group.

For small leaves in salads, grow as a cut-and-come-again crop (see page 120). Make a wide drill a few centimetres across and then scatter seed thinly along and across it, letting the plants grow closer together.

Perpetual spinach tolerates a little shade, particularly in summer, and grows well in moist soil, though it puts up with drier conditions than true spinach. Leaves are ready for harvesting from eight weeks after sowing; baby leaves for salads are ready after only about two weeks.

Plant out seedlings

Perpetual spinach that was raised earlier in modules indoors can be planted out now.

Spinach

Choose varieties carefully

As the weather gets warmer and drier, spinach is likely to run rapidly to seed. Choose a variety which is slow to bolt, such as 'Emelia', or change to perpetual spinach or Swiss chard.

THE SHINY, CRINKLY LEAVES *of fresh spinach are rich in iron and folic acid. Perpetual spinach is the easiest kind to grow and a spring sowing will keep you in leaves all summer.*

Swiss chard

Sow outside

Sow Swiss chard now for summer and autumn picking at the same spacings as perpetual spinach (p89). Although the leaves of Swiss chard taste similar to spinach, it is a member of the beet family. The leaves have prominent midribs, which can be cooked as a separate vegetable; these can be creamy white, pink, yellow or red according to the variety. Like perpetual spinach, it is far less fussy about growing conditions than true spinach and is a good alternative for dry soils where true spinach quickly bolts.

SQUASHES, MARROWS, PUMPKINS AND SWEETCORN

Courgettes, marrows and summer squashes

Harden off and plant out seedlings

Harden off and set out plants raised in pots when the seedlings have two or three leaves. If the soil is poor, dig a deep planting hole and mix lots of well-rotted manure or compost into the soil before planting; this helps to hold on to the soil moisture that the plants need.

Laying down a polythene mulch and cutting planting holes in it will also help retain moisture and suppress weeds. However, plastic is a breeding ground for slugs so be vigilant if you use this method, particularly when the plants are small and vulnerable to attack. Alternatively, water the plants in well then place a mulch of well-rotted organic matter over the surface.

Plants can also be sown outdoors now, direct where they are to grow. Improve the soil as above, then sow two seeds per station, thinning as soon as possible to one seedling. Outdoor sowings will often overtake plants that have been raised indoors.

Courgette plants tend to be quite compact and bushy, and should be spaced about 90cm (3ft) apart. Summer squashes and marrows are more likely to be trailing plants and can take up much more room, needing spacings of up to 1.8m (6ft).

All plants in this group (see left) thrive in hot summers and need the sunniest position available. In the variable and often cool weather of spring, plants benefit from the protection of a cloche. Once the weather is reliably warm, the cloche can be removed.

Winter squashes and pumpkins

Plant out after frosts

Winter squashes and pumpkins can also be planted once the risk of frost has passed. These plants like fertile, moist soil and the sunniest, most sheltered spot available; they need a long hot summer to do really well. Improve the soil before planting with general-purpose fertiliser. Water the plants in thoroughly and mulch the soil around them. Erect a cloche over them or cover with fleece if the weather turns really chilly.

TENDER VEGETABLES

General

Set out greenhouse plants

Plant tender crops such as aubergines, peppers and tomatoes in greenhouse borders or growing bags. Those that are going to be grown outside will need a few more weeks yet under glass before they can be moved out into the garden.

TOMATO PLANTS, *above, grown under cover in a greenhouse will fruit earlier and for longer. Plant them and other tender vegetables in greenhouse beds or growing bags now.*

| How to grow vegetables in containers

Even if you have room only for assorted pots, tubs and windowboxes in your garden, you can still grow a range of produce, from herbs to salads and tomatoes. To make an attractive feature, arrange the containers in groups near the kitchen. A huge range of pots and planters in different shapes, sizes and materials is now readily available to buy in shops and garden centres, so you should certainly be able to find some that suit your garden and taste, and your individual needs. There are a few key points to container gardening that you need to follow, and you'll soon be enjoying a productive patio.

CONTAINERS MADE OF NATURAL MATERIALS *(above) are a great choice as they blend in and let the vegetables take centre stage.*

COMMON SAGE *(right), like many herbs, thrives in the restricted environment of a pot and adds a decorative touch to a tiny potager.*

The key points

Size
Ensure that the container size is appropriate for what you're growing. Root vegetables such as carrots need deep pots, while beetroot sits near to the top of the soil so requires less depth. Shallower pots are also fine for salads. Big plants like tomatoes and courgettes need large pots to accommodate their roots.

Drainage
Good drainage is vital. Check there are enough holes in the base of the pot and drill more if necessary. Cover the base with old crocks or stones and raise it on pot feet. Use a light, free-draining compost with added grit. For growing bags, make a few holes in the bottom or snip off two of the corners to allow for water drainage.

Watering
Do not rely on rainfall as it may not penetrate the leaf cover or be heavy enough to soak to the roots. Mix non-organic water-retaining gel in with the compost when planting; it swells when wetted and releases water gradually back into the soil. Mulching the surface with gravel looks good and minimises evaporation. Use a water-retentive soilless potting compost (there are plenty of peat alternatives available) or a soil- or loam-based medium such as John Innes potting compost for vegetables.

Feeding
Pots hold a relatively small amount of compost and so plant nutrients are limited. If frequently watered, the nutrients may also be flushed out. Adding a controlled-release fertiliser on planting will help, or use a general-purpose feed. Nitrogen-rich fertilisers encourage leafy growth so are good for crops such as spinach, chard and lettuce; phosphorus-rich fertilisers help root growth so use for root crops; potassium-rich fertilisers aid fruit and flower formation and are good for crops such as tomatoes and courgettes. In practice, any balanced liquid feed is satisfactory.

Position
The advantage of pots is they can be moved around as needed, especially when on a base with wheels. But in general they are too heavy to keep shifting about, so choose a position with care. Avoid windy areas when growing climbers. An open windy site can dry out a pot as quickly as one in hot sun, but vegetables dislike shade.

CONTAINERISED VEG (top left) *make an attractive feature when grouped on a patio.*
FEED FRUITING CROPS *such as peppers (above) with a tomato fertiliser.*

fruit | GENERAL ADVICE

Take care of pollinating insects | Without pollinating insects such as bees, there would be very little fruit. While crops are in blossom, do not spray trees with insecticides because of the risk of killing the pollinators. Give bees and other insects a helping hand by growing plants that provide food for them out of season. Ivy that is allowed to flower is an excellent source of both pollen and nectar in late autumn, and willow provides valuable food in early spring.

Water fruit when necessary | In a dry spell, fruit trees can become stressed through drought. Take particular care with the water requirements of newly planted trees and those in containers or growing against a wall.

Give pollinators access to flowers | Ensure that plants growing in fruit cages, conservatories or under cloches (such as strawberries) remain accessible to pollinating insects. Hand-pollinate blossoms where necessary.

Watch out for frosts | Listen out for forecasts of late frosts and protect blossoms as necessary. Generally, the later the frost, the more harm it does, as trees are further forward in growth and more vulnerable to damage. However, in most areas lean-to frost protection can soon be removed from fan-trained peaches, nectarines, apricots and almonds.

Feed fruit trees in pots | Use a balanced liquid feed to give containerised fruit a boost. Follow the instructions on the pack.

APPLE BLOSSOM *puts on a stunning spring display, enticing in bees and other insects to pollinate it. Do not spray with insecticide while fruit trees are in flower to ensure these beneficial insects come to no harm.*

fruit | WHAT TO DO NOW

TREE FRUIT

General

Deal with over-vigorous trees

Fruit trees that are growing too strongly will not only outgrow their space, but will make leafy growth at the expense of fruit. Winter pruning makes growth even more vigorous, so prune strong-growing trees only in summer.

Bark ringing will also slow down vigorous trees; this involves removing a thin strip of bark from around the trunk with a very sharp knife and is carried out at this time of year. In general, though, this is a job for an expert, as it is easy to damage or even kill the tree if you are not careful.

Keep fan-trained trees in shape

Remove wayward shoots on fan-trained trees and tie in better-placed ones.

Check fruit set

Poor fruit set can be caused by frost damage to flowers, poor flowering or inadequate pollination. The appearance of only a few flowers might be a result of heavy pruning, inadequate nutrition or the build-up of old, unproductive wood. Prune trees correctly and try an early spring application of high-potash fertiliser to promote better flowering. Many fruit crops require cross-pollination by another variety to set a crop; fruit catalogues have details of suitable pollinators. If fruit set is poor now, make a note to take suitable action to remedy it for future years.

Apples and pears

Deal with apple sawfly

Adult sawflies lay eggs at flowering time and the larvae tunnel into the fruit, often leaving a ribbon-like scar behind on the apple surface. They then eat their way back out of the apple and pupate to form a new generation of adults. Fruits are distorted and may fall early. Maggot holes filled with brown waste matter ('frass') can be seen where the larvae have left the fruit. Look for damaged fruitlets and pick them off and destroy them before the larvae have a chance to emerge. If sawfly has been a serious problem in earlier years, trees can be treated with bifenthrin one week after petal fall.

Obtain codling moth traps

Codling moths will soon be on the wing, laying their eggs on apple fruitlets. The larvae tunnel into the fruit in a similar way to apple sawfly (above), but codling moths are even more common and can cause a great deal of damage to your crop.

A good way to control them is to use glue traps baited with pheromone, which can be hung in apple trees to attract and trap the male moths. Originally they were designed simply to indicate when the moths were active so that chemical controls could be applied more effectively, but by trapping the males they reduce mating activity and cuts down the numbers of caterpillars. They make a useful organic control for gardens.

A GOOD SHOW OF FLOWERS *on apple (above) and pear trees should indicate a good fruit set. Apples and pears make beautiful trees, with their blossom in spring to their colourful fruit in autumn.*

Cherries

Keep trees watered

Cherries can suffer from 'run-off' – when developing fruits turn yellow and fall off – if they receive a check to growth at this time of year, either through lack of moisture or excessively cool temperatures. There is little we can do about the temperatures, but we can make sure the trees are kept moist at the roots in dry spells.

Prune young trees

Formative pruning of cherry trees should be carried out now; like other members of the family, cherries are pruned only when they are in growth, as pruning in the dormant season encourages silver leaf disease.

Trees being trained as fans (see page 74) should have a strong sideshoot tied loosely to each angled bamboo cane. To avoid snapping the stems, untie and lower the canes as the season progresses until the desired angle is reached. As the tree's framework develops, tie new main stems onto canes already secured to the wires, the aim being to develop a framework of well-spaced branches radiating from the centre of the tree. Rub off or prune unwanted shoots as they appear.

Figs

Bring plants outside

Container-grown figs that were moved into an unheated greenhouse in autumn can be brought back into the open garden now. Fan-trained trees that were protected with

SPRING FIGS GROW LARGE *in cool climates but rarely ripen in time, then summer embryo figs form at the branch tips and ripen a year later.*

CHERRY TREES *naturally shed some of their immature fruits, pictured above, but this can be overly excessive if there is a check in growth or inadequate pollination.*

straw and fleece over winter can have the insulation removed as the weather warms.

Repot figs in containers

Repot figs every couple of years even when they have reached their established size. Remove them from their container, gently tease out their roots from the rootball, then replant them into fresh John Innes No 3 soil-based potting compost.

Peaches and nectarines

Feed and water trees

Give peaches and nectarines an occasional application of a high-potash liquid fertiliser such as tomato fertiliser, and keep the area around the root zone free of weeds. Regularly water the trees as the fruits start to swell. This is particularly important for trees planted near walls as the soil here tends to be very dry from now right through the summer. Water container-grown trees almost every day during the growing season and give them a high-potash feed every couple of weeks.

Plums, damsons and gages

Control plum sawfly

Adult sawflies lay their eggs at the base of plum blossom, and when the larvae hatch they crawl into the fruit. As

HARVEST GOOSEBERRIES IN TWO STAGES. *Before the crop is fully ripe, thin half the crop to use in cooking.*

LET THE REMAINDER *of the thinned gooseberries sweeten on the bush, then pick them as required.*

the fruits are eaten they often exude a sticky black liquid from the entry holes of the pest, and the fruits tend to fall before they are ripe.

Where this pest is a problem, plum trees can be treated with bifenthrin one week after petal fall. Plum moth larvae also attack ripening fruits and can be controlled using pheremone traps hung in the trees (see apple codling moth traps p95).

Festoon trees for good fruiting

Festooning (see below) is a useful technique to encourage plums and gages to fruit more heavily and to restrict the size of the tree. It is an ideal technique for young standard or pyramid trees.

TYING DOWN ('FESTOONING')

A tree's reward is more when the branches are laid horizontally because it slows up the vegetative growth and allows fruit buds to develop along it. Spindle trees are trained around this principle by developing a series of almost horizontal branches to create the tiers. In spring or late summer, loop string gently over the ends of the branches and tie them downwards to nails banged into the base of the stake. Alternatively, attach small weights to the ends of them. Remove the strings or weights a few weeks later, after the branches have set in their new positions.

SOFT FRUIT

General

Protect soft fruit from birds

Bird protection is vital if you don't want to lose a lot of your crop. A fruit cage is the best answer, but netting vulnerable crops also helps. Some birds such as blackbirds and pigeons don't wait for fruits to ripen and will strip a bush in minutes, so get protection in place early.

Gooseberries

Start to thin for larger fruits

Thin out gooseberry fruits to leave well-spaced berries to swell and provide large fruits. About one quarter to a half of the berries can be removed, depending on the size of the crop. If you wait until the berries are a reasonable size, the ones removed can still be used for cooking and therefore won't be wasted.

Raspberries

Check canes for disease

Cane spot disease causes oval purple or brownish spots with silvery centres on the canes of raspberry, blackberry and hybrid berries. The spots enlarge, weakening the canes, which may then die. Prune out and burn affected canes as soon as you see them and spray the rest of the plants with copper fungicide.

Thin raspberries

If raspberry rows are crowded, thin out the canes to leave about six to eight strong canes per plant. This will give a better crop than allowing them to remain crowded, and enables you to keep the pathways clear to access the plants and control weeds.

Strawberries

Pick forced fruit

Strawberries growing in a heated greenhouse or under cloches should be ready for picking now (see right).

De-blossom young plants

Remove the flowers from strawberry runners planted this spring so they put their energy into getting established.

Plant out alpine strawberries

Seedlings sown in early spring should be planted out now. Space them in rows 75cm (30in) apart with 30cm (12in) between plants in the row. They make a good decorative edging for borders, or they can be grown in stone walls, as ground cover or in cracks in paving.

RASPBERRY BLOSSOM *is pretty and sits on lush green foliage, which the plants will need to sustain during summer when the fruits are swelling. Thin out crowded canes now to produce a better crop.*

Plant cold-stored runners

Continue to plant strawberries bought as cold-stored runners between now and early summer, and they will fruit 60 days after planting.

FRUIT NETTING IS ESSENTIAL *if birds are a problem, but if your fruit and vegetable garden suffers from troublesome squirrels, the netting will have to be made from wire to stop them getting in and ruining your crops.*

TUCK A LAYER OF STRAW *under strawberry plants to help keep the strawberries clean and free from rot. Remove it after cropping because it can encourage slugs and botrytis.*

PREPARE FOR PLANTING MELONS OUTDOORS *by digging plenty of well-rotted organic matter into the planting site. Cover the prepared area with a cloche or plastic mulch to warm the site before planting.*

Straw down beds

Tuck clean straw around and under strawberry plants in beds; this gives the developing fruits a clean surface to rest on and protects them from soil splashes, grey mould (botrytis) and (to some extent) attack from slugs. Where slugs are a problem, you can apply a slug control to the soil surface before putting the straw in place. Bags of straw can be bought from pet shops or strawberry mats from garden centres to surround the plants instead.

VINE FRUIT

Grapes

Ventilate and feed greenhouse varieties

On bright days during spring and summer, ventilate the greenhouse or conservatory. Do not damp down the floor and staging when the vines are flowering (see right) – pollination requires dry conditions. Gently shake flowering branches to help spread the pollen and aid pollination.

Give grapevines an application of high-potash liquid fertiliser, such as tomato feed, and ensure they are watered frequently.

Kiwifruits

Take softwood cuttings and tie in shoots

Select shoots about 10cm (4in) long, trim off the lower leaves and insert in a pot of compost in a heated propagator. Semi-ripe cuttings in summer and hardwood cuttings in winter are sometimes more successful than those taken at this time of year. Tie the fast-growing shoots in to the support framework regularly to keep the plants tidy.

Melons

Harden off for planting outside

Gradually accustom indoor-raised melon seedlings to outside conditions. Dig plenty of well-rotted organic matter into the planting site and place cloches or frames and black plastic mulches over the prepared area to warm the ground in advance.

TIE IN NEW KIWI SHOOTS *using a figure-of-eight knot as they appear if a productive plant is required. Left to its own devices, a newly planted kiwi will quickly become unruly.*

| How to grow fruit in small spaces

The main limiting factor most gardeners face is space and very few have the room for an orchard. Luckily, however, there are a variety of ways to help the fruit gardener get the most from his or her plot.

Maximising your fruit

Naturally compact fruits

Plant breeders have developed many naturally compact varieties and dwarfing rootstocks, mainly because commercial growers can then harvest a greater fruit yield per hectare. However, home gardeners can also enjoy their benefits by growing these varieties and rootstocks. For example, blueberry 'Sunshine Blue' or 'Misty', nectarine 'Nectarella' and peach 'Bonanza' are all compact varieties, as are the Ballerina apple trees 'Charlotte', 'Maypole', 'Telamon', 'Trajan' and 'Tuscan', which have spur systems around a main vertical stem.

Restricted forms

Tree fruits can be trained to develop a framework of compact growth on which fruiting spurs develop, which adds ornamental value as well as saving space. Cordons, fans, espaliers, step-overs (see page 59) and festooned trees (see page 97) all make maximum use of the space available.

Easy pollination

Some varieties need to be pollinated by a different variety of the same plant in order to develop fruit, which means

STEP-OVER APPLE TREES *(above) do not carry a heavy crop of fruit, but they are an excellent way of growing apples even in a tiny space.*

growing two plants instead of one. Where space is limited, it's a good idea to choose self-fertile crops, such as currants and gooseberries, which do not need a pollinating partner. However, you can have more than one variety of apple, pear, plum, peach or nectarine on a small plot by growing what's known as a 'family tree'. This is a rootstock onto which a number of compatible varieties have been grafted, giving the gardener maximum crop variability from minimum space.

Long-season crops

Extend the fresh harvest period by weeks if not months by growing varieties of fruit that crop for longer than others. For example, by growing perpetual strawberries such as 'Mara des Bois' and 'Albion' you will be provided with a steady supply of fresh fruits from early summer until mid autumn, rather than a sudden peak in early or midsummer, as is often the case with conventional summer-fruiting varieties.

Storage potential

Fruits that store well enable you to continue enjoying them for an extended period. By choosing varieties that have a long storage life you can continue to eat them raw, which also allows you to benefit from their maximum vitamin content. Many fruits also freeze well or can be dried or made into preserves.

Dual-purpose varieties

The more uses you can get out of a particular fruit the better, especially if space is an issue. Some fruits – notably apples, pears, plums, gooseberries and cherries – have

STRAWBERRIES IN GROWING BAGS *or other containers are free from soil problems and can be raised off the ground away from slugs. They will also be easier to harvest.*

dual-purpose varieties that are suitable for both cooking and eating raw. By focusing on growing these more versatile types, you can maximise the use of your space.

Plant protection

The fresh harvest period of fruit can be extended at either end of the growing season by the use of cloches, frames, greenhouses or conservatories. This is particularly useful for lower-growing crops such as strawberries and blueberries, which can easily be covered by a cloche or frame, and for fruits in pots that can be moved under cover. Extra protection in spring can allow fruits to be harvested three or four weeks earlier than those left uncovered, and a protective covering at the end of the season will shield later-maturing varieties right up until the first hard frosts, ensuring successful yields from all your fruit.

TREE FRUITS *such as apples can be grown in pots to restrict growth and encourage fruiting.*

early summer

Now there is real warmth in the sun and plants respond by growing apace. Seedlings start to jostle for space and need our urgent attention to thin them out; weeds grow just as quickly and must be dealt with before they get out of hand.

There are still plenty of sowings to be made and transplanting to be done. Dry spells are not uncommon at this time of year, so we may need to get busy with the watering can, especially on newly planted crops. Fast-growing crops such as peas and beans need support systems to keep them in shape before they start to flop.

In the fruit garden, strawberries will be turning pink and summer raspberries will be coming into season – the advance guard of the delicious fruit crops we can look forward to over the next few weeks.

vegetables | GENERAL ADVICE

Keep planting | As space becomes available, cultivate the ground, add fertiliser and sow or plant suitable varieties to keep cropping going throughout the season.

Transplanting tender crops | Courgettes, cucumbers, French beans, marrows, melons, pumpkins, runner beans, squashes and sweetcorn can be sown outdoors in sheltered, mild districts, where they are to grow. Being sown in the ground means they will develop superior root systems, which helps them to grow fast. They won't require as much watering as transplanted crops.

Thin out earlier sowings | Start thinning out seedlings early before they get overcrowded, as overcrowding makes them weaker and more prone to disease.

Plant out hardy plants | All remaining cabbages, cauliflowers, celery, celeriac, broccoli and leeks should be planted out as soon as possible.

Sow crops prone to bolting | Some crops bolt to seed if they encounter cold nights and/or short days: these include chicory, endive, Florence fennel and Oriental greens such as Chinese cabbage. By the end of early summer it should be safe to sow all of these outdoors.

Make extra sowings | In warm districts, it is worth sowing crops such as French beans, runner beans and courgettes in cell trays to plant out as soil becomes free after harvesting later in the summer.

Keep weeds under control | Weed growth should slow down in summer, but survivors of spring weeding sessions will need pulling out before they can set flower and scatter their seed. Always remove weed seedlings as soon as you see them before they have time to establish.

SOW CROPS DIRECTLY *if you can. It saves time potting on, but beware of pests. Crops that need a long season, like squash and sweetcorn, benefit instead from an earlier sowing and should be transplanted now.*

vegetables | WHAT TO DO NOW

ONION FAMILY

Garlic

Harvest early bulbs

The earliest varieties should be maturing now; most mature around mid summer. Plants are ready to harvest when the stems begin to yellow and bend over. Use a fork to loosen the bulbs from the soil, then spread them out in the sun to dry, ideally on wire mesh or netting so that the air can circulate around them. Keep them dry.

To store garlic bulbs once they have dried, knock off the dry soil, place the bulbs in a net bag and hang it up in a cool, dry shed or garage. Alternatively, the stems can be plaited together to form a traditional garlic rope.

Leeks

Earth up plants

Draw soil up around the base of leek plants as they develop to extend the length of the tender, white blanched stems.

Onions

Start to lift autumn-sown varieties

Overwintered onion varieties such as 'Senshyu' that were sown last autumn will soon be large enough for use. Lift bulbs as you require them, but leave the rest in the ground to develop and ripen fully.

ONION BULBS *begin to swell during early summer. It is essential to keep them well watered and free from weeds at this stage in the plants' development.*

ALL ABOUT GARLIC

There are two main types of garlic: hardneck and softneck. The one you come across in supermarkets is the softneck type; it has a white, papery skin and forms many cloves. It is popular with commercial growers because of its long keeping qualities.

Hardneck garlic produces a hard, woody flowering stalk in early summer known as a scape, which is removed in order to encourage the formation of larger bulbs. The scapes are edible and considered a delicacy. There are fewer but larger cloves to each hardneck bulb than softneck varieties, and they have a thinner outer covering. Their flavour is generally held to be superior to softneck varieties.

When using garlic in dishes such as stir-fries, be careful not to let it burn in hot oil because it becomes bitter in taste. The characteristic smell is caused by an organic compound called allicin, which also gives garlic its antibacterial properties that has made it one of the most valued plants for centuries. It is easy to grow and its juicy bulbs will transform your cooking – you'll never want to go back to shop-bought garlic once you've grown your own.

CABBAGE FAMILY

Cabbages

Plant out young plants

Unless the seeds were direct-sown where they are to grow, plant out the young cabbage plants into prepared, firmed soil by early summer for summer and autumn cabbages.

Water in dry spells

As long as cabbages are watered thoroughly immediately after transplanting, they need little water. In prolonged dry spells, a thorough soak every 10 days will be enough. When hearts begin to form, generous watering will greatly improve head size; just one watering can make all the difference.

Harvest spring and summer cabbages

Spring and early summer cabbages can be harvested now. Round-headed varieties such as 'Derby Day' and 'Primo' should be cut when the heads are full and firm. Pointed varieties such as 'Greyhound' can be cut as greens before they have hearted up, but by this time they should be producing tight, firm heads.

THE SMALL JUICY HEADS *of early summer cabbages can be pulled when they feel firm and hearty. After harvesting, cut a 1cm (½in) cross in the top of the stump and it should resprout in about five weeks.*

Apply high-nitrogen feed

Summer, autumn and winter cabbages can be given a feed containing fertiliser with a high nitrogen content before they get too big.

Kale

Sow outside

Kale produces a harvest of tender sideshoots in spring when there is not much else about; 'Hungry Gap' is one of the best-known varieties. Kale dislikes being transplanted, so sow it in the ground now directly where it is to crop. Thoroughly prepare the soil before sowing by raking the surface to create a fine, crumbly texture. Use a length of string as a guide and make a 1cm (½in) drill. The seedlings should appear within 7–12 days.

Sow kale for salads

Mature kale is well known as a winter vegetable, but it can also be grown as a baby leaf for salads. One of the best varieties for this use is 'Nero di Toscana', an Italian variety with very dark green, strap-shaped leaves with a deeply puckered surface. They add an interesting colour and texture to summer salads and have a spicy, peppery flavour. Sow thinly in short rows at intervals between now and mid summer, either in the vegetable garden or in a container. Leaves are ready for picking within about 30 days, and should be cut when they are young and tender.

PUDDLING IN *is traditional when planting brassicas, and cabbages are robust if this method is used – place the plant in the hole in the ground and fill with water several times before adding soil and firming well.*

Broad beans

Harvest young pods

Harvest beans when they are small, before the flesh becomes starchy and the skin bitter. Take pods from the base of the plant first and work your way up. It is best to use scissors or secateurs to snip off the pods; sometimes they hang on tightly to the stem and you can uproot the plant while trying to tug them off.

French beans

Sow outside

Sow in a warm, sheltered site in single rows 45cm (18in) apart, or in double rows 23cm (9in) apart with 45cm (18in)

START TO PICK BROAD BEANS (top) *in early summer when the pods are full but still fresh. Use scissors or a pair of secateurs to snip off the pods as they can sometimes hang on tightly to the stem.*

REMOVE THE MORE MATURE PODS (above) *from the bottom of the plant first and carefully open them. The beans should be a good size and firm to the touch.*

USE BROAD BEAN PODS

A large basket of freshly picked broad beans can yield a disappointingly small amount of beans once they are shelled out – the pods are very thick and fleshy. You don't have to waste the pods, though; top and tail them, slice them thinly and boil until tender. They look and taste like runner beans, and the downy inside of the pod isn't evident once they are cooked. It is only worth treating young pods like this as older pods can be too coarse and fibrous.

between the pairs of rows. Space seeds 10cm (4in) apart within a single row, or 15cm (6in) apart in a double row. Sow some spare seeds at the end of the rows for gapping up failures. Continue to sow seeds every couple of weeks from now until mid summer for a succession of beans.

Set out container-grown plants

Set out young plants sown earlier in pots under cover once they are 8cm (3in) tall, spacing them 15–20cm (6–8in) apart. Dwarf beans are best grown in small blocks where neighbouring plants provide support and protection.

Support climbing varieties

Dwarf French beans are the most commonly grown, but there are climbing varieties available, too. The simplest, most traditional support structure is a bamboo cane wigwam or a double row of canes. The canes should be about 20cm (8in) apart, and a minimum of 1.8m (6ft) tall. Grow one plant per cane to avoid congestion.

Climbing beans can also be trained up a trellis, over arches or along fences to make the most of their beautiful white or lilac flowers and ornamental pods. Whichever way you choose, they will usually need some initial encouragement to propel them in the right direction. Tie in young shoots because they can unwind from canes in windy weather.

Protect newly germinated seedlings

If you are caught out by a spell of unexpectedly cold weather after sowing, cover the plants with fleece or even newspaper until it is warmer. Young seedlings are also prone to attacks from birds (especially pigeons and partridges), which can strip entire sowings. Windy weather is another problem, since it can desiccate leaves, and damage any climbing stems that weren't tied in. The best solution to both birds and wind is a supporting layer of twiggy branches around young plants, which will later prevent dwarf varieties from flopping on the ground under the weight of the beans (see right).

Runner beans

Set up supports

Set supports in place before sowing or planting on well-prepared soil. Runner beans are tall plants and should be positioned so that they will not shade other plants in the vegetable plot. Construct a strong, secure support at least 1.8m (6ft) tall with canes 20cm (8in) apart. Remember that once the beans have grown over the supports, their leafy stems present a large surface to the wind, so the whole structure can be easily blown over just when it is coming to its peak. Use guy ropes to keep the structure secure where necessary.

Sow plants in the open

Sow one seed at the base of each cane in well-prepared soil, sowing several spares at the end of the row to gap up any failures. Alternatively, sow two seeds to each cane if conditions are not ideal. The large seeds should be pushed into the soil about 5cm (2in) deep.

Set out earlier-sown plants

Runner beans sown earlier in pots under cover can be planted out when all danger of frost has passed. Harden the plants off thoroughly and plant with a trowel, one plant at the base of each cane. Firm and water in well.

Peas

Water growing plants

Once flowering has begun, plants must have enough water for the pods to swell properly. During dry spells, check the soil moisture (dig under the surface near the plants to see if the soil is damp at root level) and if necessary give the crops a good soaking once or twice a week. Apply a thick organic mulch to lock in the moisture.

Sow an early variety

There is still just time to make a sowing of an early or second early variety of pea for a late crop.

GETTING RUNNER BEANS TO CLIMB

The young stems of runner beans sometimes have trouble getting an initial hold on their supports, particularly where smooth bamboo canes are used. Winding a little rough textured twine around the base of each cane gives them something to cling on to.

Wind fast-growing shoots carefully around the canes and tie them in loosely where necessary, as they usually need a little help to get climbing. It is important to twine the shoots in the right direction, otherwise they will simply unwind themselves again. Looking at it from the beans' point of view (that is, looking up from below), the stems twine in a clockwise direction; if you are looking down on the top of the stems they twine anti-clockwise.

RUNNER BEAN SUPPORTS *can make an attractive garden feature. This slender obelisk frame made of thin galvanised metal is strong enough to take the weight of heavy climbers.*

Asparagus

Stop cutting spears

It is time to stop cutting asparagus seven or eight weeks after the start of the harvest. This gives the plants time to build themselves up for next year's crop. Give beds a dressing of balanced fertiliser once cutting has finished.

Look for asparagus beetle

Asparagus beetles are small black beetles with yellow spots, and they can do a great deal of damage to asparagus plants. You can often find rows of their small black eggs laid up the stems of spears as you cut them. Rub off any eggs you find and destroy any beetles or their greyish larvae as soon as you see them.

Globe artichokes

Harvest main heads

Harvest heads as they become ready. Large terminal

IMMATURE ARTICHOKE FLOWERHEADS *should be harvested with secateurs just above a leaf junction. Do it before the scales start to open otherwise they will become tough.*

heads are produced first, followed by a smaller secondary flush. Harvest plump heads with secateurs before the scales start to open or they will become tough. If you don't intend to eat the head straight away, leave a length of stalk attached and stand it in a glass of water in the fridge, where it will keep for up to a week.

Plant out seedlings

Harden off artichoke seedlings gradually and plant them out from now until mid summer. Seed-raised plants are of variable quality, so you will need to keep a careful eye on the performance of the plants when they begin to crop. Mark weaker plants to be removed, and then propagate the best ones by offsets.

Rhubarb

Pull young stems

Rhubarb can be harvested until mid summer, after which the stems become rather tough, stringy and

---

EATING ARTICHOKES

Many gardeners are not sure how to prepare artichokes for eating, but they are well worth any trouble!

Cut the stem off with a sharp knife, just below the lower scales. Remove any brown or damaged scales at the base. Using a pair of scissors, cut off the tips of each scale – they carry a thorny point, which can be very sharp. Wash under running water, opening the scales out slightly to allow the water into the centre. Boil the entire head in a large saucepan of water until a scale near the base of the stem comes away easily when pulled – this usually takes 30–40 minutes depending on size. Remove from the pan and turn upside down to drain for a few minutes.

Eat the artichoke by pulling away scales, starting from the outside; dip the base of each scale in butter and scrape off the fleshy portion with your teeth. Continue until you reach the papery inner leaves and remove these to expose the 'choke' – the fuzzy, hairy centre of the flower. Remove and discard these silky fibres, carefully using a teaspoon to scrape them off the base and reveal the flat green 'heart', which is the tastiest part.

green. Stopping in mid summer also allows the plant to produce sufficient foliage to build up food reserves for a good crop next year. Remove no more than half the stalks at one time, harvesting as soon as the leaves open fully. To remove a stalk, hold it at the base, pull down and twist.

A CROP OF YOUNG BEETROOT *should be harvested by easing a fork or trowel under the soil, enabling you to lift the swollen roots gently out of the ground.*

TO PULL RHUBARB *(top), grab the stem at its base, close to the crown of the plant, and pull it down with a slight twist. Stems come away easily. Remove no more than half the stalks at one time.*

GROW RHUBARB *(above) in a sunny position and in well-drained, moisture-retentive fertile soil that has been prepared with lots of organic matter. Harvest as soon as the leaves open fully.*

ROOT AND STEM VEGETABLES

Beetroot

Harvest roots when young

For the best flavour and texture, pull roots when they reach tennis-ball size; any larger and they develop an unpleasant woody texture. Succulent and tender baby beets can be harvested as soon as they are large enough to eat, usually around golf-ball size. Before lifting, use a garden fork to loosen the soil beneath, but take care not to damage the roots, particularly if they are intended for storage.

Carrots

Lift baby roots

Carrots are ready for harvesting about 12–16 weeks after sowing, although the timing depends on whether you prefer tender baby carrots or larger roots. In light soils young carrots can be pulled up carefully by hand, but in heavy clay or when roots are larger, they are best lifted by gently easing them up with a fork to avoid damaging or breaking the roots.

It is impossible to avoid bruising the foliage when lifting carrots and this gives off a scent that attracts carrot root fly. Pull carrots in the evening to give the insects minimum time to home in on the scent before darkness stops them flying.

Florence fennel

Weed and water bulbs

Keep fennel well watered during dry spells. Weed the crop regularly, hoeing between the rows and handweeding close to the plants. As the bulbs start to swell, use a hoe or trowel to pile up the soil around the roots to make them whiter and sweeter.

Potatoes

Finish earthing up

Spring-planted potato tubers should be earthed up for the last time over the next few weeks, leaving them in a rounded ridge around 30cm (12in) high.

Check early varieties

Early-planted potatoes may be producing tubers of a usable size already. Once the plants have started flowering, you can scrape some of the soil away and check to see how big the tubers are; usually you are looking for potatoes the size of an egg. With care, you

THE CULINARY USES OF BASIL *are many and it's easy to keep your kitchen stocked up with your own fresh supply. Sow indoors now in a greenhouse and pot up individually when large enough to handle.*

can take enough tubers for an early meal without disturbing the plants. Lift just a few tubers from each plant and return the soil so the rest of the crop can carry on growing. The first meal of home-grown new potatoes is always an eagerly anticipated treat.

Turnips

Encourage steady growth

Water the developing plants every 5–10 days in dry spells to avoid irregular growth, which can lead to splitting roots. Hoe or handweed around the plants frequently to keep them growing at their best.

SALADS

Cucumbers

Sow or plant ridge varieties outdoors

Ridge varieties bear short, rather stumpy but tasty cucumbers and are not difficult to grow. Choose a sheltered position and add plenty of well-rotted organic matter to the planting site to help retain moisture and supply nutrients to the plants. The cucumbers can be sown direct into the ground now, or young plants can be obtained from garden centres.

Look for varieties such as 'Marketmore', 'Long Green Ridge' and 'Burpless Tasty Green'. When the plants have six sets of leaves on the main stem, pinch out the tip; this helps to encourage plenty of fruit.

Herbs

Sow basil indoors

Basil likes warm conditions and will grow well in a greenhouse alongside tomatoes. Sow seeds in a 9cm (3½in) pot of sowing compost now, covering them lightly. Prick off the seedlings into individual pots as they become large enough to handle.

There are many different varieties and flavours of basil, including lettuce leaf basil, cinnamon basil, lemon basil, Thai basil and Genovese basil. All of them go well with tomatoes and as part of a mixed salad. It is also believed that having basil growing beside tomatoes helps to keep whitefly at bay, though it's not a proven control.

'LOLLO' LETTUCE AND CURLY ENDIVE *make a striking pattern, grown in interweaving bands. Cut off lettuce close to ground level and it may sprout fresh leaves if conditions are right.*

Lettuces

Cut mature heads

Harvest lettuces by cutting rather than pulling – the stems will often sprout fresh leaves if cut off close to ground level, provided conditions are not too hot and dry. Loose-leaf types are particularly good at this, and leaving a few of the outer leaves will help the plant to re-establish itself. Cut-and-come-again crops (see page 120) should be harvested when about 10cm (4in) high.

In hot weather, harvest in the morning, putting small leaves of a cut-and-come-again salad straight into a bucket of clean water to prevent wilting. Many varieties will store well in the fridge for at least a couple of days in a polythene bag, if wetted first, but wash the leaves again before use.

Tomatoes

Feed and water regularly

Tomatoes are thirsty and hungry plants, and the soil should be kept evenly moist. Avoid fluctuations between wet and dry conditions, which can result in the fruit splitting. Allowing the soil to dry out can cause blossom end rot (pictured above right). Feed tomatoes regularly using a specific tomato fertiliser that contains high levels of potash to encourage good fruiting. Always use according to the manufacturer's instructions.

Bush and trailing tomatoes need little attention, but vine types need to be tied in regularly. Snap or cut off

BLOSSOM END ROT *on tomatoes can be identified by the dry, black or brown discoloration at the base of the fruit and a sunken, shrivelled appearance. Control watering carefully to prevent the disorder.*

sideshoots, as this concentrates the plants' energy on the fruits that grow from the main stem. Remove any yellowing lower leaves as they appear.

Avoid blossom end rot

Never letting plants go short of water is the key to avoiding this damaging disorder. If plants are allowed to wilt while they are flowering, it is almost inevitable that the fruits that were forming at this time will be affected.

Blossom end rot causes the base of the tomato opposite the stalk to become sunken and shrivelled, with a dry, black or very dark brown discoloration. The top part of the fruit may still be edible, but the rot usually extends into the centre of the tomato.

Tomatoes in growing bags are particularly prone to drying out because of the shallow depth of soil around the roots, so make sure you water frequently on hot days. Occasionally add a handful of garden lime to a full watering can of water as a lack of calcium contributes to the problem and this will help.

Spinach

Keep the soil moist

Keep spinach well watered at all times, as hot, dry conditions lead to the plants bolting to seed at the expense of growing leaves. Once a plant has bolted, there isn't much you can do except pull it up – a real waste of your time and trouble, and of space in the vegetable garden!

Remove weeds regularly and apply a mulch on moist soil to lock the moisture in the ground. If the vigour of the plants seems to be failing, apply a nitrogen-rich fertiliser following the manufacturer's instructions. Where birds are a problem, you may have to grow spinach under netting to save your crop.

Spinach is the gourmet plant of the leaf crops, producing delicately flavoured, soft-textured leaves that are particularly good in salads. They are also delicious when lightly cooked. Whatever size of leaves you harvest, pick them straight into a plastic bag to keep them fresh and succulent. Store in the fridge as soon as possible until you need them. Spinach can also be successfully frozen, either cooked or raw.

Courgettes, marrows and summer squashes

Train trailing plants

Check the spread of trailing types by pinning down the growth in a circle or training them over a support, tying plants in regularly as they grow. This is important where space is limited, as they can quickly romp over a huge area of ground and smother other crops if left alone.

Hand-pollinate flowers

Sometimes the earliest flowers do not set fruit well, but this can be avoided by hand-pollinating. Female flowers have a round swelling at the base, while the male ones have a straight stem. Pick off a male flower and carefully remove or fold back the petals, then push it gently into the female one so that the pollen is transferred.

Feed and water as fruits develop

As the fruit starts to form, give plants a liquid fertiliser every week or two, or sprinkle general-purpose fertiliser near the base and water in. Watering is most important

COURGETTES ARE FORMIDABLE GUZZLERS *in hot weather, and should never be allowed to dry out in summer when new fruit is developing. Regular drinks guarantee quality fruit.*

FEED SQUASHES WITH A LIQUID FERTILISER *every couple of weeks as fruit starts to form. Given the right care, this new bud and growth (above) will grow into an impressive pumpkin.*

TO GROW LARGE PUMPKINS or squashes, leave one fruit on each plant and give it extra water and feed. They are by far the most impressive vegetables you'll ever grow.

as the fruit is developing; the more the plants get at this time, the better quality the fruit will be. Water generously every 10 days in dry spells, soaking the soil well. Keeping the roots moist also helps to prevent powdery mildew.

Winter squashes and pumpkins

Feed plants regularly
Apply liquid fertiliser every couple of weeks, or scatter general fertiliser pellets around the plant shortly after planting. It should be necessary to water only during particularly hot and dry spells.

Aim for large fruits
If you are growing large cultivars, remove the growing tip of the main stem once three fruits have set, since limiting the number of fruits gives them a better chance of reaching a large size. If your main aim is to grow the largest possible pumpkin or squash, leave one fruit on each plant and give it extra water and fertiliser. As the fruit swells, place it on pieces of wood or brick to keep it off the wet soil and avoid it rotting or being attacked by pests such as slugs.

Sweetcorn

Transplant young plants
Choose a sheltered, sunny site for planting. Sweetcorn is not fussy about soil and will grow well provided it is well

drained and has average fertility. If in doubt, dress with a general fertiliser. When transplanting, the spacing of young plants is crucial to achieve good pollination; only pollinated kernels will swell to fill the cobs. They are most successful when grown in blocks because the pollen is less likely to be blown away from its target. Make blocks at least four plants deep and wide, with each plant 38–45cm (15–18in) apart. Keep the soil moist while plants are establishing, and later when the kernels are swelling.

Sow outside in warm areas
For a successful crop in warm areas, sow the seeds now directly where they are to grow. Space them at 38–45cm (15–18in) square in blocks, as above.

SWEETCORN POLLINATION

Sweetcorn is unusual among vegetables because it is pollinated by wind rather than by insects. The male flowers are called tassels and appear in a tuft at the top of the stem. The female flowers are held in rows in the developing cob, and each has a slender strand called a silk that emerges out of the end of the cob. The pollen from the tassels is shed in the wind and drifts down to land on the silks of the female flowers. Growing the plants in a block ensures that the pollen is more likely to come into contact with the female flowers than if they were growing in rows, where it could be blown away without reaching them. You can help the pollination process along by giving the stems a gentle shake on a still day to help release the pollen.

YOUNG OKRA PLANTS *can reach quite a size, about 1.2m (4ft) high, and need plenty of space, so don't be fooled. Position them carefully when growing your own.*

TENDER VEGETABLES

General

Ventilate greenhouses as the weather warms up

Increase the ventilation of greenhouses on warm sunny days. An automatic vent opener, which controls the vents according to the temperature, is a great help in achieving a good growing atmosphere if you are out all day and cannot adjust the ventilation yourself.

Aubergines

Plant out young plants

If you have not raised your own plants from seed, young plants are usually available from garden centres. Pinch out the growing tips (see right) once they reach 30cm (12in) to encourage them to become stocky and stable. Plant out when the first flowers form, two or three per standard-sized growing bag or one per 30cm (12in) pot, and grow on at 16–18°C (60–64°F). In warm areas they can be planted outside in the open ground, 60cm (24in) apart in a sheltered spot, using black plastic mulches to warm the soil.

Okra

Plant out under cover

Okra needs a humid environment with soil temperatures of 22–30°C (71–86°F) to crop well, so is best grown in a greenhouse or polytunnel. When young plants are 30cm (12in) tall, pinch out the growing tips and plant in growing bags, 30cm (12in) pots of multipurpose compost, or in a greenhouse border in soil improved with organic matter. The plants are self-fertile, so damp down periodically to create the humid conditions needed for pollination.

Alternatively, try okra under tall cloches or in frames in the sunniest site. Lay black plastic sheets two weeks before planting to warm the soil and plant through slits. Support indoor and outdoor plants with bamboo canes. Keep well watered and fed with a tomato fertiliser.

Peppers and chillies

Plant out indoors or outside

Plants growing outside or in a greenhouse bed need a well-drained, moisture-retentive soil, so dig in plenty of well-rotted organic matter before planting. Sweet and chilli peppers like similar conditions to tomatoes – sunshine and high temperatures – so are best grown in a polytunnel, greenhouse, large frame or fleece tent. They do well in pots of multipurpose compost or growing bags. When growing in a garden, choose a warm site such as a sheltered raised bed or against a sunny wall that will radiate the sun's heat back on to the ripening fruit.

BIOLOGICAL CONTROL

Plants growing under glass are susceptible to whitefly and red spider mite. Whitefly initially looks like airborne specks of dust, but close inspection under the leaves and a quick tap, sending scores flying away, immediately indicates the problem. The biological control *Encarsia formosa*, a tiny parasitic wasp, is available to use against whitefly.

Red spider mite can be spotted when the leaves develop a silvery sheen and fine, white silky webs appear at the tips of the leaves and stems. If you look closely, tiny reddish brown mites can be seen scuttling about on the webbing. The biological control for red spider mite is *Phytoseiulus persimilis*, a predatory mite.

Order biological controls when the pests are seen to be building up and introduce them to your plants according to the manufacturers' instructions. They are a natural way of keeping pest numbers down and limiting the amount of damage that they do.

| Grow your own salad leaves

The days when lettuce was the only leafy salad vegetable are long gone – now we enjoy a whole mix of different colours, tastes and textures in our salads. For some time, supermarkets have been selling bags of mixed salad leaves at a premium price, but growing your own could hardly be easier.

Salad leaves can be grown in the open ground or in pots or growing bags. They are very quick to crop, being ready to harvest within a few weeks of sowing, and because they are eaten so young they hardly have time to fall prey to any pests or diseases. Simply sow short rows of seeds in well-prepared soil and keep them moist. Make several sowings for a long succession of baby leaves.

When the plants have made sufficient growth, harvest them by either picking a few leaves at a time, or simply cut the entire crop, leaving a short stump from each plant in the ground. Keep the soil moist and these stumps will resprout to give a further harvest. The process can often be repeated for a further cut.

Because salad leaves are so quick to mature, they are very useful for sowing as a catch crop to make use of ground that is vacant for a short time between other crops. When sowing a very slow-germinating crop such as parsnip, sow pinches of salad leaves down the row between each sowing station; not only will they make use of the space, they will germinate quickly to mark out the row for you, making weeding between the rows easier.

To enjoy fresh salad in early spring and again in late autumn and into the winter, leaves can be grown under glass in a pot, growing bag or direct in the greenhouse border (they don't need much heat, just keep frost-free).

MANY LETTUCE AND SALAD LEAVES, *all different colours and textures, look as good in the garden as they do on the plate.*

Recommended salad leaves

Seed companies sell a range of salad leaves, either separately or as preselected mixtures, often with a spicy, Oriental or Continental theme. Colourful, interestingly shaped lettuce varieties feature strongly, but there are plenty of other types of leaves to try.

Amaranth

Similar to spinach, with a sharp bite to the leaves and attractive red-veined foliage.

Beetroot

A mild, earthy, sweet-flavoured leaf. 'Bull's Blood' (below) has burgundy red foliage for impact on the plate.

Buckler-leaved sorrel

Bright green, shield-shaped leaves (below) with a sharp lemony flavour. Also known as French sorrel, it has a variegated form called 'Silver Shield'.

Corn salad

Also known as lamb's lettuce (below). Forms rosettes of small, bright green, succulent leaves; very hardy and can withstand frost, so a good source of salad over winter and in early spring.

Greek cress

Quick-growing cress with a lovely peppery tang. For a less spicy taste, cut the leaves young, as they get hotter with age.

Kale

Full-flavoured and full of vitamins and antioxidants (below). Try dark-leaved 'Nero di Toscana', feathery 'Red Russian' or deep purple 'Redbor'.

Mustard

Spicy leaves that become hotter as they get larger. 'Red Giant' has purple-tinged, rough-textured leaves.

Pak choi

Thick, deep-green leaves, tender and succulent with a mild flavour. 'Hanaken' is a good variety for salads.

Red orach

Arrowhead-shaped leaves of deep maroon-red (below). Make a number of successional sowings because the young leaves are the most tender and have the best colour.

Rocket

Distinctive peppery-tasting leaves (below). In the height of summer it will bolt rapidly, becoming tough. Turkish and wild rocket are more bolt-resistant than leaf rocket, with a different flavour but still delicious.

Spinach

Deep green, soft-textured foliage with a subtle flavour (below). Keep the soil moist to avoid bolting.

fruit | GENERAL ADVICE

Feed pot-grown trees | This is the time to change the balanced fertiliser for pot-grown fruit trees to one that is high in potash. It is one of the three main plant nutrients: nitrogen promotes leafy growth, phosphorus promotes root growth and potash is particularly important for flowering and fruiting. High-potash fertilisers include rose and tomato fertilisers, both of which can be used on fruit trees.

Continue training fans | Continue tying in suitably placed shoots on fan-trained trees.

Continue trapping codling moth | Monitor codling moth traps and replace them if necessary. If there are a lot of moths on the wing, the sticky surface of the trap sometimes becomes covered with insects and loses its effectiveness.

Water fruit where necessary | Make sure fruits aren't drought-stressed at this time of year, especially those that are newly planted or growing in pots or against a wall.

Keep weeding | Continue to weed regularly round all tree and soft fruit to prevent competition for water and nutrients. Where trees or bushes are growing in a lawn, maintain a circle of bare soil extending some 30cm (12in) from the main stem to prevent competition from the grass.

FIGS AND OTHER TREE FRUIT *will benefit from regular weeding at this time of year. Give figs plenty of water throughout summer.*

fruit | WHAT TO DO NOW

TREE FRUIT

Apples and pears

Train fan-trained trees

If you are training a fan from a feathered maiden, the branches that were selected in winter (see page 253) should now have developed sideshoots of their own. Select two or three of these sideshoots and spread them equally on the wire system and tie them with string – ideally two above the branch and one to train downwards. On more established fans, remove any sideshoots that are making vigorous upright growth from the first tier of branches. Encourage weaker stems as these will be more fruitful.

Thin fruits

At the beginning of early summer there will be a natural shedding of fruitlets known as the 'June drop'. This is the tree's way of making sure it doesn't carry more fruits than it can manage to ripen satisfactorily. However, to obtain large fruits, you may need to thin them out some more to leave well-placed fruits that can develop fully. Wait until the June drop has taken place before doing so.

Apricots

Thin crowded fruits

If there is a heavy crop, thin the fruit to about 8cm (3½in) apart when the fruits are the size of hazelnuts.

Water trees where necessary

Water newly planted trees frequently as they establish. More settled trees need watering only during dry spells.

Cherries

Net against birds

Erect netting to deter birds before fruits start to show some colour – trees will be stripped if left unprotected.

JUST BEFORE CHERRIES START TO RIPEN (top), erect some netting over the fruits to protect against birds. A frame is best as netting can be kept taut; this stops the birds getting caught up in it.

TREE FRUITLETS (above), such as these young apricots, are vulnerable to late frost damage in early summer, so do not remove the netting until the fruits are more mature (see page 50).

Check early varieties

Pick early cherries as soon as they start to ripen. The earliest varieties in sheltered areas will start cropping soon. Pick fruits during dry weather, by the stalks rather than the body of the fruits, which bruise easily.

Cover trees to prevent skin splitting

Cherries are among several fruits where the skin will split if the trees are subject to fluctuating moisture levels, particularly if they suddenly receive a large amount of water. To prevent this, erect polythene covers over the trees as the fruit is ripening to protect them from excess rain. Try to keep fruits dry and pick over trees regularly.

Prune fan-trained trees

Shorten all new growth to roughly 7.5cm (3in) long to encourage sunlight to ripen the developing fruits. Also remove shoots growing directly into or away from the wall or fence, and prune out a proportion of old or unproductive twiggy growth, tying in well-placed replacement shoots.

Prune acid cherries

Because of their different cropping habit, acid cherries need heavier pruning than sweet cherries to keep them productive. Each summer, prune out a proportion of the older stems of both fans and freestanding trees, training in new replacement growth, which will then bear the crop the following summer.

Citrus

Move trees outside

Move citrus trees outside for the summer months, placing them in as sunny a spot as possible.

Summer prune new growth

Pinch out the tips of new shoots to promote bushiness. Stop pinching out in late summer, to give the new growth time to mature and harden up before winter.

Thin fruits

Thin out citrus fruits to leave the strongest dozen or so on an established tree. Not all the fruit that sets will reach a good size or ripen properly if it is allowed to remain.

CITRUS PLANTS *can produce lots of vigorous vertical growth. Remove the tips of these shoots to control height and encourage side branching.*

Figs

Water frequently and start feeding

Give figs plenty of water – watering will probably be necessary each day during summer. Apply a high-potash feed such as tomato fertiliser every two weeks until the figs start to ripen. One of the advantages of figs is that you don't have to worry about pollination; the fruit are seedless and develop without the need for fertilisation.

Pinch back new shoots

Pinch back new growth to five or six leaves to stimulate the formation of embryonic figs in the tips of the shoots. These will develop into fruit that will ripen next year.

PINCH BACK THE TIPS OF FIG BRANCHES *in early summer to produce compact growth and encourage a good crop next year.*

Peaches and nectarines

Thin fruit

Thin the fruitlets out to 10cm (4in) apart when they are hazelnut size, and to 20cm (8in) when walnut size. This allows them to mature to their full size and obtain maximum sugar levels. Aim to have the fruits spaced equally over the plant, removing ones that will become trapped and bruised against the wall or fence when ripe.

Train fans

On young trees, tie in the shoots that are growing at the tip of each rib to extend their length. Select three or four new shoots that have branched out along the ribs and cut the others back to one bud or leaf. One shoot can be tied downwards and a couple upwards. On established fans, tie in the new shoots as they grow. Pinch back all secondary shoots to one leaf, and to about six leaves on shoots that were left in early spring.

Pick up fallen leaves

Leaves that have been affected by peach leaf curl and have fallen from the trees should be picked up and destroyed. This helps to prevent the spores remaining near the tree to infect the following year's growth.

Plums, damsons and gages

Train fans

Remove the central leader from a tree to be fan-trained in its first summer; tie canes to the horizontal wire supports and the remaining sideshoots to the canes. Tie in new shoots that develop from these stems to fill any gaps.

Look out for the first signs of 'shothole'

Shothole can affect all stone fruits. Small circular patches on the leaves start to develop now, and by the end of the season the patches will have turned brown and fallen out, leaving the foliage peppered with tiny holes. This is often a sign that the tree is suffering from bacterial canker or powdery mildew, or is under some other form of stress.

Thin plums

Thin out plum fruitlets where necessary to obtain a satisfactory crop (see apples and pears, page 123).

Quinces

Water in dry spells

Water in periods of drought, even when well established. Quince is relatively low-maintenance but requires moist soils, and supplementary watering is often necessary.

THIN PEACHES and nectarines. If it proves difficult without damaging neighbouring fruit, slice the unwanted one in half; it will soon wither.

PEACH LEAF CURL is likely to be a problem if trees are not given adequate protection from wind and rain, which spreads the spores.

Raspberries

Remove suckers
Pull up suckers between the rows of summer raspberries and thin autumn raspberries to 10cm (4in) apart.

Pick early varieties
The first summer raspberries should be ready to pick (see left); do it on a dry day as they deteriorate when wet. Best eaten fresh, they can be frozen or made into preserves.

Blackberries and hybrid berries

Water in dry spells
Water young plants during dry spells. While mature plants shouldn't need extra irrigation, their fruit size will benefit from watering if the weather is particularly dry.

Tie in new canes
Tie newly produced canes to their supports to prevent them from being damaged by wind.

Gooseberries

Remove suckers
Remove suckers around the base of the plant as they appear throughout summer. Pull them by hand if you can as gooseberries are prone to regenerate from pruning cuts.

Water in dry spells
Container-grown gooseberries in particular often struggle in dry conditions, so monitor their watering requirements carefully.

Prune established plants
Shorten the shoots back to five leaves when the plant has produced 8–10 leaves. Like red and white currants, gooseberries fruit on old wood.

Pick fruit for cooking
Harvest gooseberries in two main pickings. A few weeks before the gooseberries are fully ripe, pick every other fruit and use to make pies, tarts and sauces. The

TIE NEW BLACKBERRY CANES (top) *carefully into position along the wires where the fruited one-year-old canes had been. Use a figure-of-eight knot and space them out well.*

FROM A HEALTHY MATURE BUSH *you can expect 3.5kg (8lb) of gooseberries (above) each season; from a cordon about 1kg (2lb). Pick the fruit with its stalk to prevent the skin tearing.*

gooseberries that are left to ripen and develop their full sweetness can be enjoyed raw.

Look out for mildew
American gooseberry mildew first appears as a powdery grey coating on leaves, stems and fruit. As it progresses, it often forms a thick, brown, furry coating over fruit; this can be rubbed off so that the gooseberries can still be eaten, but it is a laborious task.

Spray bushes with a fungicide containing myclobutanil at the first signs of the disease. Varieties such as 'Invicta' and 'Greenfinch' have some resistance to American gooseberry mildew.

Black currants

Water in dry spells

Black currants should be watered during dry periods throughout the growing season.

Blueberries, cranberries and lingonberries

Water during dry spells, using rainwater where possible, especially in hard-water areas.

Red and white currants

Support cropping plants

Tie the plants to canes using twine to stop the branches flopping onto the ground from the weight of the fruit.

Protect against birds

Net bushes tightly against birds before the fruit starts to ripen. Some people find white currants easier as they are not as attractive to birds as the bright red varieties.

Water when necessary

Red and white currants will benefit from extra watering during the growing season if it is particularly dry.

Prune established bushes

Prune new growth back to five leaves. Red and white currants fruit on old wood, so this summer pruning encourages small fruiting spurs to develop on the branches.

Harvest when ripe

When the fruit first turns red it is not yet fully ripe, so harvest only once it has sweetened. It is simplest to cut the strigs (bunches of fruit) using scissors. Fruit can be stored in a fridge for a week or two after picking.

Strawberries

Straw around plants

If you have not already done so, place straw around strawberry plants to keep the fruits clear of the soil.

Pick early fruits

Early strawberries outdoors will be starting to ripen now. Strawberries have a short but heavy cropping period over two or three weeks; there are early, mid- and late-fruiting varieties cropping from now to mid summer.

Perpetual strawberry varieties – sometimes called everbearers – produce small flushes of fruit from now to early autumn and are useful for a prolonged season of picking. The crops aren't as heavy as the summer-fruiting varieties and the fruit is smaller, with the plants less likely to produce runners. Pick strawberries when they are bright red all over, ideally during the warmest part of the day as this is when they are at their juiciest and tastiest.

Remove mouldy fruit

Any strawberries affected by grey mould disease (botrytis) should be removed promptly to avoid it spreading. It is common in wet weather.

De-blossom perpetual varieties for a late crop

To extend the season and concentrate strawberry production in late summer and early autumn, remove the early summer flowers from perpetual varieties.

Start picking alpine varieties

Alpine strawberries produce tiny fruits from now until late autumn. They are usually red but some varieties are white or yellow. They are very sweet, aromatic, and have superb flavour, but are not as juicy as the perpetuals and summer-fruiting varieties.

PRUNE RED AND WHITE CURRANTS' NEW GROWTH *of that year to five leaves in summer, to encourage the formation of small fruiting spurs on the main branches.*

ROOTING STRAWBERRY RUNNERS

GROW ON NEW STRAWBERRY PLANTS *from the old ones by planting up runners, which usually arise in prolific numbers from the main plant.*

PEG DOWN A YOUNG PLANTLET *into a small container of fresh potting compost. Use a wire hoop as a peg to keep the runner in direct contact with the soil.*

CUT THE RUNNER *from the main plant after a few weeks, when the plantlet has taken root. Grow on the plantlet as a separate plant.*

Remove runners

Unless they are wanted for propagation, remove strawberry runners with secateurs. Runners – long stems with baby plants attached to them – compete for water and nutrients and crowd out the main plant. They also make it difficult to keep the strawberry bed tidy and weed-free as they grow in the pathways. If you need to increase your plants, some of the runners can be retained and rooted (see above).

Remove cloches from protected plants

Once protected strawberries have finished cropping you can remove the cloches. Plants that have been forced in the greenhouse should also be moved outside now.

EARLY SUMMER *is the season every strawberry grower longs for – when they finally get to sample their delicious fruit. Strawberries are at their best when eaten immediately after picking.*

VINE FRUIT

Grapes

Prune guyot-trained vines

Remove buds or stems that appear low down on the trunk of grapevines trained by the guyot system (see page 259). This process is called 'bud rubbing' and is important as these water shoots will deprive the plant of necessary nutrients and water.

Between now and mid summer, pinch out the growing tips (or on long rows use a hedge trimmer) on the tops of the vines to prevent them getting too high and shading neighbouring rows.

Train cordon vines

Tie in the leading shoot to its vertical cane with soft twine and shorten the main other shoots to five or six leaves. Prune back any sideshoots on these main shoots to one leaf.

Care for young plants

In their first year after planting, water grapevines during dry periods. Once fully established, those in cool-temperate regions shouldn't need watering because their deep-rooting system makes them tolerant to drought.

Remove all flowers for the first couple of years after planting to prevent overcropping on young vines. Allow about three bunches of grapes on a three-year-old vine and about five on a five-year-old vine – a few more if it's growing well.

Mulch to retain moisture

Suppress weeds and retain moisture by placing stones or gravel around the base of the plants. White gravel is useful because it reflects sunlight back into the canopy of the grapevine, while black gravel or recycled slate is also suitable as it absorbs the heat from the sunlight, helping to warm up the soil. Avoid mulching around the vines with manure because this encourages surface rooting and contributes to luxuriant vegetative growth.

Foliar feed where necessary

Grapevines can be prone to magnesium deficiency, which can be treated with a foliar feed of Epsom salts or a fertiliser containing trace elements. Symptoms of magnesium deficiency are yellowing between the leaf veins (interveinal chlorosis) while the margin of the leaf remains green. Later in the season the edges of the leaves turn brown or rust coloured. Magnesium deficiency is particularly common on chalky soils.

Thin dessert fruits

Thin out individual dessert grapes to allow the berries to ripen fully and to improve air circulation. Use scissors with long thin blades to snip off berries when they are small, removing about one in three per bunch.

Kiwifruit

Water young plants

During their first two growing seasons, young plants need regular watering. More established plants require less watering but yields will be significantly increased if plants are watered thoroughly during dry spells.

Train plants to their supports

When the central shoot of a young plant reaches the top of its support, train it along the horizontal wire, removing the tip when it reaches the end. Allow the central shoot to develop sideshoots along the horizontal wires, thinning these out to 50cm (20in) apart. Train the sideshoots to the outer wires, then remove their tips.

TUCK OR TIE IN ALL NEW GROWTH *on a grapevine (top) to the parallel fixed wires. Remove any buds or shoots that develop low down on the trunk.*

REMOVE ALL NEW GROWTH *on a grapevine (above) that appears above the top wire. Shorten any sideshoots that grow from the new branches to one leaf.*

NUTRIENT DEFICIENCIES

Plants usually get all the nutrients they need from the soil, but in some cases they are not able to do this. This is often because the soil is chalky, as lime 'locks up' certain nutrients so that even though they are present in the soil, they become unavailable to plants.

The main nutrients needed by plants are nitrogen, phosphorus and potassium, but there is a whole range of other elements required in only tiny amounts. These include iron, magnesium, manganese, boron and copper, among others. These are known as trace elements and their shortage often shows as yellowing or browning of leaf edges, or between the leaf veins.

One way to remedy trace element deficiencies is to apply them as a foliar feed, as leaves will absorb them even when the roots are unable to do so. Look for a trace element fertiliser that has been specially formulated for foliar application, otherwise it could scorch the leaves.

These sideshoots will form permanent fruiting arms. Pinch back any shoots that arise from them to four or five leaves. These will flower and fruit in subsequent years.

Summer prune established vines

Shorten shoots with fruits developing at their bases to five or six leaves past the last fruit. This will divert energy into the developing fruits. Once harvested, cut this fruited shoot back to 5–7.5cm (2–3in) to develop a spur system.

Melons

Plant outdoors

Plant fully hardened-off melons in their final positions, setting each one so the top of its rootball is just below soil level – do not plant too deeply as this encourages rotting. Space plants 60cm (24in) apart. Choose a warm sunny spot in humus-rich, well-drained soil. It must be light, as heavy soils remain too cool, and deeply cultivated to allow roots to grow down for moisture. On heavier soil, use raised beds filled with free-draining soil that will warm up more quickly. For best results, warm up the site by covering with cloches or black plastic before planting.

Plant greenhouse varieties

Water the compost the day before transplanting into pots or growing bags in a greenhouse, and leave it in the sun to warm up. Set two plants in each standard-sized growing bag or one plant per 30cm (12in) pot filled with multipurpose compost. In the very sunniest weather, shade indoor crops with netting or a whitewash on the glass. Keep well watered at all times and feed with tomato fertiliser at

ONCE KIWI VINES BEGIN TO BEAR FRUIT, *cut back the fruiting shoots to five or six leaves to divert energy into fruit production and allow sunlight to penetrate the canopy at this critical stage.*

weekly intervals. Pinch out the growing tips to encourage the sideshoots, which will bear the fruiting flowers. Melon needs warm, humid conditions and is usually far more successful in a greenhouse than when grown outdoors.

NUTS

Almonds

Prune fan-trained trees

Pinch back all secondary shoots to one leaf, and to about six leaves on shoots that were left in early spring.

Remove diseased leaves

Almonds can suffer from peach leaf curl. Pick up and burn any fallen diseased leaves to prevent it spreading.

CULTIVATING MELONS

PLANT FULLY HARDENED-OFF MELONS *in their final positions outside in a warm, sunny spot, in humus-rich, well-drained soil. Don't plant too deeply as this encourages rotting.*

GROWING BAGS ARE IDEAL *for the cultivation of melons. Plant no more than two plants per bag, and in a greenhouse tie their stems onto bamboo canes for support.*

GIVE WATER TO MELONS OFTEN *and feed them weekly with tomato fertiliser when they are in growth. This encourages strong growth that is more resistant to pests and diseases.*

| Grow your own superfoods

All sorts of foods have been hailed as 'superfoods' in recent times and fruit is no exception. There is no strict definition of what makes a superfood, but it is generally held to be a food that is very dense in nutrients, with some special property that helps to protect us from disease and enables us to live healthier lives.

Various foods have been claimed to lower cholesterol, improve eyesight, reduce the risk of cancer and heart disease and even prevent Alzheimer's disease. 'Free radicals' are unstable molecules that occur naturally in our bodies and cause cell damage, which can lead to cancer and other diseases. They can be stabilised by substances known as antioxidants, and these are especially abundant in a number of fruits.

While scientists are sceptical about many of the more outlandish claims that are made about superfoods, nobody disputes that simply eating more fresh fruit and vegetables can only improve our general health. Growing your own fruit is a major advantage, because eating fruit absolutely fresh ensures that the nutrient levels remain at their peak – you can also make sure you pick the fruit when it is in perfect condition and not overripe. Plus, of course, there are benefits to be had from the physical exercise involved in gardening itself.

One group of antioxidants consists of substances called anthocyanins, which are pigments that give plants red and purple colours. Many berries are rich in anthocyanins, and the stronger their colour, the more anthocyanins they contain. Purple grapes, blueberries, black currants, redcurrants and cherries are rich in anthocyanins, while pale fruits such as white currants and green gooseberries contain much less.

RASPBERRIES AND BLUEBERRIES (above) both contain high levels of vitamins and antioxidants, which can help fight against diseases.

Popular superfruit

Black currants

The Scottish Crop Research Institute put black currants at the top of their league of 20 types of fruit tested for their vitamin, mineral and antioxidant content, making them potentially useful in fighting cancer, heart disease and neurodegenerative diseases such as Alzheimer's. They also contain anthocyanins that are thought to have some effect in preventing diabetes.

Cranberries

Cranberries have similar properties to blueberries, although they are not as high in most nutrients. However, they have been found to have effective anti-bacterial properties that make them particularly useful in preventing urinary complaints. They may also offer protection against gum disease and stomach ulcers. Cranberries have long been recognised as a good source of vitamin C.

Lycium barbarum, and the berries follow lavender-coloured flowers. Goji berries are something of an acquired taste.

Raspberries

Raspberries contain relatively high amounts of fibre, vitamins, calcium and iron, plus moderate amounts of potassium. They also have higher levels of zinc than most fruits and are thought to benefit allergy and diabetes sufferers, among others.

Blueberries

Perhaps the first superfruit to come to public attention, blueberries have been called the 'ultimate superfood' and are claimed to slow down mental ageing, protect against cancer and heart disease and lower cholesterol.

Goji berries

One of the latest 'miracle foods', goji berries have high levels of vitamins, iron and beta-carotene, which is the precursor of vitamin A and has antioxidant properties. They are grown on a sprawling shrub,

Plums

One of the latest crops to be awarded superfruit status, plums have high levels of antioxidants. As they tend to be eaten in larger amounts than others, it's easier to get the required levels of nutrients from a serving.

mid summer

This is the time when we start to really enjoy the fruits of our labours. Soft fruit, plums and cherries, peas and French beans, crisp-hearted summer cabbages, baby new potatoes, salads and summer squashes are all there to be picked, and if we've timed our sowings right, there are plenty more crops to come.

Weed growth slows down a little after the frantic pace of early summer, but we still need to keep weeding constantly and to watch out for pests and diseases, too. Take action at the first sign of trouble and you may prevent real problems developing. Plenty of watering will be needed in all areas of the garden; if you added lots of organic matter to the soil earlier in the season this is the time you will see the benefit, as it clings on to soil moisture instead of letting it drain away.

It may be high summer, but it is also time to start thinking ahead and plant out winter crops such as kale, winter cabbages and Brussels sprouts.

vegetables | GENERAL ADVICE

Stake tall crops | Canes and stakes should be inserted in good time to support taller crops such as runner beans and tomatoes.

Feed greedy crops | Plants of the cabbage family, beetroot, celery, celeriac and leeks are all hungry feeders that will benefit from supplementary fertilisers. Container-grown vegetables also benefit from regular liquid feeds.

Look out for pests | Many crops are targeted by pests at this time of year. Erect netting to protect peas and cabbage-family crops against hungry pigeons, and use collars to fend off cabbage root fly and netting as a precaution against carrot fly. Insect pests, including blackfly, caterpillars, greenfly and leaf-mining insects, are beginning to cause serious damage. Red spider mite thrives in hot dry conditions, causing leaf loss on French beans, runner beans and crops under glass. Act promptly to prevent significant damage.

Act against diseases | During summer, blight on potatoes and tomatoes is a constant menace and fungicide sprays may be necessary. In dry seasons, powdery mildew on courgettes, cucumbers, peas, pumpkins and swedes can be a problem. Careful watering to keep the soil moist can limit damage.

Continue sowing | Continue making successional sowings of lettuce, spinach, turnips, radish, French beans, beetroot, carrots, kohlrabi and spring onions.

TALLER CROPS, SUCH AS THESE RUNNER BEANS, *will need supporting and can be made into a natural and practical centrepiece.*

vegetable | WHAT TO DO NOW

ONION FAMILY

Leeks

Keep crops moist and weed-free
Weed leeks regularly, preferably using a hoe. During long, dry spells, water thoroughly but sparingly – a good soaking every 10 days will do.

Continue to blanch stems
Continue drawing soil up around the stems of leeks to increase the length of the blanched portion. This is not essential, and deep-planted leeks will have a good length of white stem anyway.

Onions and shallots

Begin harvesting
Both onions and shallots are ready to harvest when the leaves begin to yellow; the exact time will depend on the sowing or planting time. You can take one or two shallot bulbs out while they are in growth to use fresh, without disturbing the rest. For the general harvest, use a fork to

HOE YOUR LEEK BED *regularly to keep weeds at bay, being careful not to damage the plants, and water them thoroughly but sparingly every 10 days during long dry stints of weather.*

loosen the bulbs from the soil then spread them out in the sun to dry, ideally on wire mesh above the ground so the air can circulate around them. Separate shallots into individual bulbs first.

Once the bulbs are thoroughly dry, gently knock off any loose soil and leaves, then store them in a net bag and keep in a cool, dry shed or garage. The skins are brown and papery, and the remnants of stems and leaves make a convenient tool for bunching or plaiting them together and hanging them ready for use.

HARVESTING ONIONS AND SHALLOTS

ONIONS AND SHALLOTS *can be lifted as soon as you need them, although they store better if allowed to die back first.*

PUSH A GARDEN FORK *under the plants and lever the soil up as you pull the bulb out of the ground by its neck.*

BULBS CAN EITHER BE LEFT *to dry out in the sun or taken directly to the kitchen for immediate use.*

CABBAGE FAMILY

Cabbages

Sow spring cabbage

Sow spring cabbages from now until late summer for cropping next year, in rows 30cm (12in) apart. The distance you thin the seedlings to depends on the type of crop you want. For leafy greens, thin plants to 15cm (6in) apart; for hearted cabbages, thin to 25cm (10in). By thinning in stages, it is possible to take a proportion of the plants to use as leafy greens, leaving the rest to heart up later. Good varieties include 'First Early Market', 'Pixie', 'Hispi' and 'Durham Elf'.

Plant out winter varieties

Set out young cabbage plants for winter cropping into prepared, firmed soil. Space the rows 45–60cm (18–24in) apart, with the plants 45cm (18in) within the row. Plants that were sown direct where they are to grow should be thinned out to this spacing now. Winter cabbages include some quite ornamental varieties, useful for livening up the bare winter garden.

Feed cabbages planted earlier

Cabbages planted out over the last few weeks can be given an application of high-nitrogen fertiliser to boost their growth.

Cauliflowers

Transplant seedlings

Transplant seedbed-raised seedlings as soon as they are large enough to handle, ideally at around six weeks old. Water them shortly before you begin. Replant the slow-maturing winter varieties 76cm (30in) apart – they are more widely spaced than earlier maturing types. Ensure that the soil is kept moist at all times during the growing season.

Kale

Transplant to growing positions

Transplant young kale to its final position 6–8 weeks after sowing. Water the plants thoroughly before moving and 'puddle' them in with copious watering after planting (see page 108). The seedlings should be set 45cm (18in) apart and planted to the depth of the first set of true leaves. Keep watered during dry spells. As they grow, support stems using a stout wooden stake, especially on exposed sites.

Kohlrabi

Sow seeds now

Kohlrabi is a quick-growing brassica with a swollen stem that has a very pleasant flavour if it is harvested while still young. Sow in rows 30cm (12in) apart and thin

KEEP BRASSICAS FREE OF COMPETING WEEDS *by regular hoeing and handweeding. Remove any root collars that have been put in place and take care not to damage the vulnerable stems.*

BIRD-PROOF NETTING *should be put in place if pigeons are known to be a problem. Watering can be done in the usual way, but weeding is made more difficult as the nets will need to be removed.*

seedlings to 15–23cm (6–9in) apart. Keep the soil moist. Pull the stems for eating when they reach the size of golf balls; do not let them grow much above tennis-ball size or they may be woody and fibrous. They reach a usable size in about seven weeks from sowing.

BEANS AND PEAS

French beans

Start picking
Harvest pods as soon as they are large enough. Pods that snap crisply in half are at their peak; flabby pods that don't break cleanly or are stringy are past their best. Harvest beans regularly to prolong cropping. Coloured varieties of beans such as 'Purple Queen' or yellow 'Valdor' have pods that are easy to spot among the green foliage, making picking easier.

Runner beans

Sow now for a late crop
Sow a batch of seeds now for a crop of tender young beans in autumn, after the current crop has finished.

Water plants for good flower setting
Weed around the plants regularly and water thoroughly in dry weather, particularly once the flowers begin to form. Sufficient water at the roots is essential to get the flowers to set a good crop of pods; dryness at flowering time is the prime cause of poor yields. A thick mulch around the base of the plants is a good way of keeping the soil moist as well as the weeds down.

Pollinators may fail to do their job if the weather is too cold or windy. There is little that can be done about this, but make sure you choose a sheltered spot for runner beans in future years.

Pick beans as they become large enough
Start harvesting runner beans as soon as they reach a usable size. It is important to keep picking regularly once cropping has started to encourage a prolonged season.

Pinch out growing tips
Once the beans reach the top of their supports, pinch out the growing tips. This prevents them becoming top heavy.

Peas

Harvest frequently
Pick peas regularly to ensure they are at the peak of freshness. Even if some pods are clearly past their prime, take them off anyway to leave more resources for the remaining pods. Start picking pods from the bottom of the plant and work your way up. Eat or freeze the peas as

PICK FRENCH BEANS *once the plants start cropping in summer. The young pods will be sweetest, and regular picking will stimulate the growth of more beans.*

PICK PEAS REGULARLY *to enjoy them at their freshest. The shoots and sideshoots of pea plants can also be eaten and make excellent additions to a salad. Use before the leaves have opened out.*

soon as possible after harvesting to retain the maximum flavour and nutrients.

Cut down cropped plants

After the harvest, do not pull up the spent crops but cut off the stems at ground level. This is because the clusters of small white nodules found on the roots are full of nitrogen-fixing bacteria. If left in the ground, these nodules will rot down, releasing the nitrogen they have taken from the air back into the soil for the next crop to use.

PERENNIAL VEGETABLES

Asparagus

Keep weeding beds

Remove weeds from the beds and give a topdressing of general fertiliser if you have not already done so.

Support tall ferns

The ferns of asparagus should be allowed to develop fully to build up the plants' resources for future crops. In windy positions in the garden, stake the ferns with canes as they are brittle and can be easily snapped off at the base.

Continue to remove asparagus beetle

Keep picking off and destroying any adult asparagus beetles found near the crop and their larvae.

Globe artichokes

Water young plants

Weed and water well plants in their first year. Though mature plants are drought-tolerant, better yields can be obtained if they are watered during dry spells, especially during the period when flower buds are forming.

Harvest small heads

On established plants, small secondary heads develop in the sideshoots of the main stem, below the main head. These will not be as large as the main head, but they make a useful second crop and can be picked as soon as they are big enough, before the sepals start to open.

Jerusalem artichokes

Stake stems on windy sites

The stems of Jerusalem artichokes are very tall and can be easily blown over in exposed positions. Stake the plants now if necessary, or cut back the stems to 1.5m (5ft) high.

JERUSALEM ARTICHOKES *are tall plants that may need staking or cutting back in height to stop them blowing over. Use as a windbreak for garden boundaries or as a great focal feature, as pictured above.*

GLOBE ARTICHOKES *are regal-looking plants and every ornamental vegetable garden should have at least one. If one large head is required, remove the sideshoots on each flower stem.*

ROOTS AND STEMS

Beetroot

Sow now for overwintering
In mild areas, you can try your luck by sowing an over-wintered crop from now to late summer to mature the following spring. The foliage of some beetroot varieties becomes a beautiful dark red in cold weather.

Celeriac

Water in dry spells
Water plants every 5–10 days if no rain falls. Remove the lower leaves to expose more of the crown; also remove any blistered leaves, which may be a sign of attack by the celery leaf miner larvae.

Potatoes

Guard against blight
In warm, wet weather, potato blight is common and can devastate a crop. Spraying plants with mancozeb or

copper fungicide helps to protect against the disease and is worth carrying out in wet seasons. Affected leaves develop brown or black blotches, sometimes with white mould growth, and the topgrowth very quickly turns yellow, wilts and dies. Rain washes spores off the foliage down into the soil to affect the tubers, which also rot.

If the topgrowth is cut off and removed as soon as the first symptoms are seen, the crop can sometimes be saved if the tubers are large enough to use. They will need eating quickly, however, as they are likely to rot if stored.

Swedes

Keep plants growing strongly
Keep the crop well weeded to avoid competition for water and nutrients. Take precautions against pests such as cabbage root fly and flea beetle by covering the crop with fleece or finely meshed netting.

An irregular water supply can lead to poor growth and to the roots splitting, so water the developing plants every 5–10 days in dry spells. This also helps to prevent powdery mildew from forming on the leaves.

SALADS

Chicory

Water and feed plants
Water plants during dry weather and apply a nitrogen-rich fertiliser if growth begins to flag.

Continue sowing
Continue to sow radicchio and sugar loaf chicory right through the summer.

Blanch leafy varieties
The bitter taste of chicory is sometimes welcome in salads, but it can be removed by blanching, where light is excluded from parts of the plant. On open-hearted types, the best method is to cover the entire centre of the plant with a plate, which allows some light to reach the outer leaves and leads to an attractive gradation in colour from green to white. To blanch the whole plant, cover it with a bucket, which will exclude all light completely and turn the entire plant white in colour.

THOROUGHLY WATER EMERGING CELERIAC *every 5–10 days during dry spells, adding a high-nitrogen fertiliser if growth is poor. Cut off the lower leaves on the plants to expose more of the crown.*

SUGAR LOAF CHICORY *forms a dense heart and is naturally self-blanching, but tying the leaves together will enhance this blanching further. Do not tie the leaves too tightly.*

AFTER ABOUT TEN DAYS, *the plant can be harvested, and will have a creamy yellow, blanched heart, which will be tender and less bitter than the leaves on an unblanched plant.*

Red radicchio and sugar loaf varieties of chicory both usually form hearts of leaves, although a proportion of any crop will always fail to do so. Because of this heart-forming habit, they tend to be naturally self-blanching; to enhance this, tie the leaves together. Blanch only as many plants as you are likely to need, as they will deteriorate if left covered or tied for too long. It should take about 10 days for blanching to take place.

Cucumbers

Feed and water plants regularly

Water cucumbers regularly and, once the crop starts to swell, feed weekly with a high-potash feed such as tomato fertiliser. Where cucumbers are growing under cover, spray the ground with water on hot days to boost humidity. This also helps to keep down red spider mite.

Tomatoes

Continue training plants

Continue to remove sideshoots from cordon-trained plants and to tie the main stems to their supports or twist them around strings in the greenhouse. Bush varieties do not need their sideshoots removing.

Pinch out cordons

Outdoor tomatoes being grown as cordons (on a single stem) should have their growing points pinched out once there are four or five trusses of fruits forming. This concentrates the plants' energies into ripening the fruit.

PINCH OUT SIDESHOOTS *on cordon-trained tomatoes in order to concentrate all the plants' energies into ripening the fruit, rather than making leafy growth.*

Watch out for blight

Blight is a fungus disease that attacks potatoes and tomatoes in warm, wet conditions. Outdoor tomatoes are particularly prone, but in bad years greenhouse tomatoes can be affected, too. Brown spots appear on the leaves, which quickly yellow and wilt, and brown rotten patches spread rapidly to the fruit. Remove and burn affected plants as soon as symptoms are seen. Spraying plants with mancozeb or copper fungicides has some protective effect and is worth undertaking in wet summers.

Pick fruits as they ripen

Pick tomatoes when fully ripe and evenly coloured, but don't leave mature fruit on the plant for long or it will soften and split.

SPINACH AND CHARD

Spinach

Make summer sowings

Choose a shaded or partly shaded spot for sowing at this time of year, and make sure the soil is moisture retentive. Sow in rows 30cm (12in) apart and thin plants to 15cm (6in). Keep the drills well watered during germination and

WHEN HARVESTING CHARD, use sharp secateurs to snip away the leaves, being careful not to cut too close to the plant. When harvesting the whole plant, make the cut 5cm (2in) up the stem.

while the seedlings are growing; in hot weather spinach will quickly bolt if it is allowed to become dry at the roots.

Swiss chard

Weed and water

Weed and keep the soil moist during dry weather for the best leaves, but established plants will withstand some drought. Swiss chard is very easy to grow; with any amount of neglect it still looks good and produces leaves.

Keep harvesting leaves

Harvest large leaves for cooking individually as you need them, but do not cut too close to the plant. You can cut the whole plant for cooking but make it 5cm (2in) up the stem so the stump can resprout.

Cut back bolted plants

Plants may bolt in hot weather or if they are not regularly cut, but they are so vigorous they can be chopped back and will soon start producing good, tasty leaves again.

SQUASHES, MARROWS, PUMPKINS AND SWEETCORN

Courgettes, marrows and summer squashes

Harvest regularly

Always use a sharp knife to cut courgettes and summer squashes cleanly from the plant. If you are tempted to

THE TASTIEST COURGETTES are picked when young and thin. Slice them off using a sharp kitchen knife. Never try the twist-and-pull approach as it will damage the plant.

try to twist or pull the fruit off, you will invariably damage the plant or the fruit.

Cut courgettes when they are young and tender; they quickly grow larger, becoming less well flavoured and more watery as they do so. Try to cut the fruit before the flower has fallen off. It is important to pick the courgettes frequently to encourage more fruit to be formed. Marrow size is less critical to flavour. As a rule, marrows are ready when about 20–30cm (8–12in) long, or they can be left to mature for winter use.

Many courgettes and squashes have very prickly stems and it is a good idea to wear long sleeves when picking the crop to avoid scratches and skin irritation.

Keep plants well watered

Courgettes, marrows and summer squashes need watering frequently in dry spells to keep the plants growing and cropping well. Sink a plant pot into the soil near the crown of the plant and pour water into that; it helps to make sure the water penetrates to the roots where it is needed rather than running off the surface.

ADD SOME MORE EARTH AROUND THE SWEETCORN PLANTS (top), as well as mulching them.

GENTLY SCOOP THE NEW EARTH AROUND THE BASE of each sweetcorn plant (above), protecting them from wind damage and encouraging the growth of adventitious roots.

EATING COURGETTE FLOWERS

Courgette plants often produce an abundance of male flowers, but these need not go to waste. Pick them when they are just opened and wash them if necessary (sometimes all that is needed is to brush the inside of the flower to get rid of insects). The flowers can then be stuffed; feta cheese and mint is a traditional filling, but cooked rice, grated cheese and herbs also works well. Do not over fill the flowers, and twist the petals gently to close. Dip them in a light batter and fry until golden.

Winter squashes and pumpkins

Support developing fruit

As the fruits swell, place a piece of wood or tile beneath them to keep them off the wet soil and away from slugs. Give regular liquid feeds if your aim is to grow giant fruit.

Sweetcorn

Provide supports

On windy sites, sweetcorn may start to rock, which loosens the roots and hinders growth. Earth up the bases to foster the growth of stabilising adventitious roots, or supply plants with a stake.

Keep the soil moist

Water sweetcorn plants during dry spells, especially while they are flowering.

TENDER VEGETABLES

Aubergines

Thin out fruits

Pinch out the first fruit to form on large-fruited varieties such as 'Moneymaker' and 'Black Beauty' and thin subsequent fruit to leave three to five per plant. Water and feed regularly with a high-potash liquid feed, and damp down to aid pollination and deter red spider mite.

Okra

Harvest pods regularly

Cut okra pods when bright green, firm and 5–8cm (2–3in) long. They can become stringy quickly so eat when young.

Peppers and chillies

Train plants and feed regularly

Train sweet peppers up stout canes or loops of string, especially if carrying a heavy crop. Chilli peppers usually form compact plants but some may need supports. Push canes round the edge of the container and loop twine around them to keep the plants in shape. Feed both with tomato fertiliser while flowering and fruiting. If growth flags, use a balanced liquid feed to boost the plants.

PREPARING OKRA FOR COOKING

Okra is a popular and traditional vegetable in Africa and also features widely in the cuisine of Asia, the southern United States and eastern Mediterranean countries. The pods have a glutinous texture used to thicken soups and casseroles and are a vital ingredient of gumbo. They are usually covered with fine hairs, but 'Clemson's Spineless' has smooth skin. Inside, there are creamy white edible seeds.

The pods should be washed only if necessary and dried before cooking. They can be used whole or sliced and added to soups and stews, stir-fried with other vegetables or tossed in seasoned flour and fried. Some people don't like the characteristic slimy texture; to reduce this, use very young pods and stir-fry them whole.

HOW HOT IS A CHILLI PEPPER?

Chilli peppers can range from relatively mild to searingly hot – it all depends on the variety. The fieriness of chillies is measured on a scale known as the Scoville Heat Scale, which measures the amount of capsaicin present – this is the substance that gives peppers their heat.

Sweet peppers register zero on the scale, while Scotch Bonnet types are between 100,000 and 325,000 units and habaneros around 500,000 units. The naga chilli is probably the hottest and has registered nearly 900,000 Scoville heat units. Very hot chillies must be handled with great care as they burn sensitive skin; never touch your eyes, nose or lips during or after handling raw chillies and use gloves to protect your hands. The pain of chilli burns can be reduced by the application of olive oil and lemon juice.

| Plot to plate: the tastiest lettuces

Look at any seed catalogue and you will discover a surprising range of lettuces in a wide variety of colours and forms – certainly plenty more than can be found on the supermarket shelf! Lettuces can be divided into two main kinds. Loose-leaf types have an open arrangement of leaves from which you can harvest just a few leaves at a time on a cut-and-come-again basis. The more traditional hearting types form a dense, firm centre and are generally harvested whole.

Among the hearting varieties there are butterhead types, with soft, tender leaves; Cos, with upright leaves that add a refreshing crunch to salads; and crisphead, also known as iceberg, with wavy outer leaves and crisp, pale hearts. Loose-leaf lettuces often have highly decorative leaves, including curled and frilly leaved varieties and striking oak-leaf-shaped types. There are also many beautiful red-leaved varieties, some of which have a slightly bitter taste.

In warm weather, cut lettuces early in the day when they are fully charged with moisture and move them to a cool place straight away. Loose-leaf types are picked as soon as they are large enough, either picking a few leaves at a time or cutting the whole plant, leaving enough of a stump for it to resprout.

Hearting lettuce varieties should be picked when they have formed a tight, dense heart. Test the state of the heart by pressing the centre of the lettuce gently with the back of your hand; this doesn't bruise the foliage like poking or pinching it does.

LETTUCES VARY GREATLY *in leaf shape and colour. They are ideal for creating mixed salads that look good on the plate and taste great.*

Recommended varieties

'Little Gem' AGM

A variety of Cos lettuce with small solid heads of mid green, medium-blistered leaves. It has a sweet, crisp heart. Resistant to root aphid.

'Bijou' AGM

A leafy Batavian lettuce with attractive red glossy leaves that add impact to the plate and have a good flavour. The plants are uniform with a fairly small frame.

'Tom Thumb'

A small and solid lettuce of the butterhead type, with soft leaves and a mild taste. This variety crops early and is suitable for growing in restricted spaces.

'Sangria' AGM

A butterhead variety for summer cropping with soft, pale green, pink-tipped leaves. It is slow to mature and resistant to bolting.

'Lobjoit's Green Cos' AGM

A large Cos variety with an open head and relatively smooth mid-green leaves. It has crisp, flavoursome leaves.

'Lollo Rossa Assor' AGM

A hardy, slow-to-bolt leafy lettuce variety with attractive, pale green, red-tipped leaves. It has a distinctive peppery taste.

'Clarion' AGM

A fairly open-headed butterhead lettuce that can be grown for spring or autumn cropping under protection. Good quality with some mildew resistance.

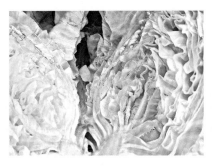

'Little Leprechaun'

A dwarf semi-Cos or romaine variety with striking mottled red and green leaves. It tolerates hot weather well and is slow to bolt, making a dense, crisp heart.

'Set' AGM

A crisphead variety, this lettuce is easy to grow and slow to bolt. 'Set' is medium to large in size, solid and heavy to the touch with crisp green leaves.

fruit | GENERAL ADVICE

Feed trees in pots | Liquid feed fruit trees in containers with a high-potash fertiliser such as tomato feed.

Check tree ties | As tree trunk girth increases tree ties may start to restrict growth so adjust where necessary.

Control weeds | All fruit trees grow better if they are kept free from competing weeds around the base. Handweeding and hoeing are the most effective non-chemical method of controlling weeds, along with mulching around the trunk. Avoid strimming near the base of trees because it can rip the bark and in extreme cases kill the tree – in the commercial world strimmers are known as mechanical rabbits because of the damage they can cause. Weedkillers are also effective methods of weed control provided they are used safely.

Water trees thoroughly | In dry weather, don't let fruit trees suffer before you start watering. The canopy of the tree in full leaf will prevent the full amount of any rain reaching the roots. Give trees a thorough soaking so the water penetrates down to the roots. Light watering does more harm than good by encouraging roots to grow in the upper layer of soil, which is most prone to drying out.

Check for pests | Holes in the leaves of fruit trees can be caused by a number of pests such as pear and cherry slugworm, capsids, winter moth and various caterpillars. Often the damage isn't serious, but keep an eye on the situation so you can take early action when necessary.

CHERRIES *are one of the earliest tree fruit to ripen and their flavour is delicious. Keep an eye on pests nibbling holes in the leaves.*

fruit | WHAT TO DO NOW

Apples and pears

Thin fruits

In a good year, apples and pears can set a lot of fruit. Unless the crop is already very small, which can be due to late frosts, the fruit on apple and pear trees will need thinning if it is going to ripen fully, and if biennial cropping and broken branches from heavy yields are to be avoided. Thinning on both trees should therefore be carried out now.

When thinning apple trees, remove the king fruit, which is the apple at the centre of the cluster of fruit and is generally misshapen. Thin dessert apples to leave one or two fruit every 10–12cm (4–5in), and cooking apples to leave one fruit every 15–20cm (6–8in). On freestanding pear trees, thin the fruit out to two every 10–12cm (4–5in), and on restricted forms such as cordons and espaliers to one fruit every 10–12cm (4–5in).

THIN APPLES *in mid summer if fruit is to ripen fully. It also prevents biennial cropping and broken branches from heavy yields.*

MAYPOLING

Trees heavily laden with fruit may require support as the fruit swells and develops. Maypoling is a popular method with spindle trees, whereby strings are looped around the centre of the branches and tied upwards to the top of each tree's post. Alternatively, stake individual branches if they look as though they may break.

Water in dry weather

Water apples and pears during dry spells and from the time the fruit starts to swell, particularly if they are newly planted or on restricted rootstocks. The most effective method of doing this for rows of fruit trees is to place a drip line or seep hose under the trees. Large established trees will be more resistant to periods of drought so require less watering.

Control bitter pit on apples

If bitter pit has been a problem in past years, spray apple trees with calcium to help prevent the issue recurring. The disorder shows later in the summer as sunken brown pits on the surface of the apples, which extend into the flesh. It is a similar problem to blossom end rot on tomatoes (see page 115), being caused by a shortage of calcium. It is usually due to a lack of water interfering with the distribution of calcium within the plant, so maintaining a regular water supply to your apple trees is of key importance.

Apricots

Start picking fruit

Like peaches, apricots are likely to be ready for picking between now and late summer. The fruit is ready when it feels soft and parts easily from the tree. Apricots can only be stored for a few days so are best consumed right away. Alternatively, they can be dried or made into preserves.

Cherries

Harvest fruit
The majority of sweet cherry varieties are ripening now. Handle the ripe fruit by its stalk, as cherries are easily bruised. They are best eaten shortly after picking, but can be frozen or made into preserves. Acid or cooking cherries ripen later in the summer.

Citrus

Keep containers well watered
Do not allow container-grown citrus trees to dry out, as this can cause them to shed their leaves and their crop. Keep the compost moist at all times and keep the plants protected from strong winds.

Foliar feed where necessary
If citrus plants show yellowing of the leaves, particularly between the veins, they should be given a foliar feed containing trace elements.

Figs

Protect fruit from birds
Cover figs with a net as harvest time approaches or the birds will harvest the crop before you have a chance to.

Feed container-grown trees
Figs in containers can be given a balanced liquid fertiliser every 10 days or so during the summer.

REMOVE SUCKERS ON MEDLARS, *as these trees are often grafted onto rootstocks. Ideally pull them off at the base, but if this proves impractical cut them off at ground level using secateurs.*

SWEET CHERRIES *are ripe and ready for harvesting by mid summer. Pick them by their stalks to avoid bruising the fruit and eat fresh soon after picking to enjoy them at their best.*

Medlars

Remove suckers
A medlar that has been grafted onto a quince or hawthorn rootstock may occasionally produce suckers during summer. Remove these from the parent plant while they are still small by pulling, rather than cutting them, if possible, which removes dormant buds at the sucker's base. If the suckers are numerous they can, as a second choice, be cut out.

Peaches and nectarines

Harvest ripe fruits
Most peaches and nectarines grown outside will be ready now or in late summer, though the exact harvest time is dependent on individual varieties and weather conditions. The fruit is suitable for picking when it has fully coloured and the flesh near the stalk feels soft. To pick the fruit, cup it in the palm of your hand and gently lift – it should come away easily from the tree. The tree will require regular visits for picking as the fruit will not ripen all at once.

Peaches and nectarines are best eaten directly after being plucked from the tree. Alternatively, they can be stored in a cool place for a few days after picking. Fruit harvested just before ripening will last longer and can be left to mature in the fruit bowl, but they are unlikely to achieve their full potential in terms of juiciness and flavour. Expect 9–12kg (20–27lb) of fruit from a mature,

WHEN PEACHES ARE RIPE *and ready to harvest, you should be able to pick them by simply cupping the fruit in your hand and gently lifting, and it will come away easily from the tree.*

PLUM VARIETIES *that crop heavily benefit from having their fruit thinned out in mid summer. This will boost fruit size, reduce biennial bearing and avoid branches snapping under the weight.*

healthy fan that hasn't been affected by frosts or peach leaf curl. A freestanding bush will produce as much as 20kg (44lb) of fruit.

Trap wasps

Wasps are strongly attracted to ripening peaches and nectarines, so hanging wasp traps around the branches may help to keep down the damage. Remove any damaged fruit promptly as this will attract even more wasps to the tree and the fruit will suffer further.

Feed wall-trained fruit

Trees trained against a wall will usually benefit from an application of high-potash liquid fertiliser every 10 days or so during the time the fruits are forming and ripening.

Plums, damsons and gages

Thin fruits and support branches

Fruits may require thinning to ease congestion and weight in the canopy, as well as to boost fruit size. It is often essential to prop up branches in mid-to-late summer, as the weight of fruit can otherwise snap them.

Water trees

If the weather is dry, water trees from now right through until the fruit is harvested. Keeping the soil evenly moist will allow the fruits to reach a good size and help to prevent them splitting.

Pick plums as they ripen

Early plum varieties such as 'Early Laxton' should be ripening now. If they are to be eaten raw, pick the fruits when they are fully ripe for the sweetest flavour. You do not need to be quite so fussy about the ripeness of plums that will be used for cooking.

Remove branches affected by silver leaf

Silver leaf is a fungal disease that affects many members of the plum family and causes branches and eventually the whole tree to die off. Unfortunately there is no cure for this disease and it can become a serious problem if left unchecked, but cutting out affected branches can sometimes halt or at least slow down its progress, and this should be completed as soon as possible.

The foliage of plums affected by silver leaf disease has a distinctive silvery appearance and the wood of the branch shows a brown stain in the centre. Prune out all affected branches, cutting the branch back to a point that no longer shows the brown stain. Pruning cuts should be painted over with a sealing compound. The branches that have been removed, plus any fallen branches, should then be disposed of by burning to prevent the disease spreading.

Blackberries and hybrid berries

Pick ripe berries

Pick hybrid berries such as tayberry and loganberry as they ripen. Blackberries tend to be a little later, ripening in late summer and early autumn.

Black currants

Pick fruits as they ripen

Harvest the fruit on modern varieties such as the 'Ben' series by cutting the strigs (or bunches of fruit) as they turn black. Older types of black currant varieties ripen at different times, with the currants at the top of the strig ripening first. The fruit should therefore be painstakingly picked individually. Protect from birds.

Blueberries

Protect plants from birds

Cover fruiting blueberry bushes with nets to keep birds at bay. They pick the fruit off well before it is ripe, leaving you with nothing to harvest.

Harvest ripe fruits

Pick blueberries once the colour changes from green to dusky blue. Pick over the plant several times as not all the fruit ripens at once. Eat fresh or they can be dried, frozen, made into preserves or used in cooking. They are rich in antioxidants and vitamins so have many health benefits.

Cranberries and lingonberries

Keep the soil moist

Water these plants to keep the roots moist at all times, preferably with rainwater to maintain the acid conditions they need. The fruits will not be ripe until early to mid autumn, but the bushes can be netted against birds now.

Gooseberries

Allow fruit to ripen fully

Leave the remaining fruit to ripen in the summer sun until the sugars and flavours have fully matured. If time

HARVEST BLACK CURRANTS *from mid summer onwards, but remember to net the crop if you don't want to share a good proportion of it with the birds in your garden.*

permits, do this second picking gradually over a few days, harvesting as and when the fruits are wanted.

Raspberries

Gather fruits and cut out old canes

Continue to harvest raspberries as they ripen. The canes that have borne fruit will be cut down to soil level in autumn and canes that have grown this season will be used to replace them. Select the best of the canes that are growing now and tie them into the supports; those that are coming up in the pathways or are weak and spindly should be cut off at ground level.

Red and white currants

Pick fruit by the strig

Harvest the fruit by cutting the whole strig (bunch) as soon as most of the currants on it are ripe (see right). It is difficult to pick currants individually because they are more delicate than black currants and easily squashed.

Strawberries

Propagate plants from runners

If more strawberry plants are required, they are easy to propagate from the runners that are freely produced by the plants (see page 129). Continue to cut off runners that are not needed for propagation.

Choose runners from healthy vigorous plants, selecting a maximum of three or four from each. Pinch off the tip of the runner just beyond the first plantlet – the one nearest the parent. Peg the plantlet down either directly into the soil, or preferably into a small pot filled with soil or potting compost that has been plunged into the soil. Keep the base of the plantlet in close contact with the soil by pinning it down firmly with a piece of bent wire. Keep the pot watered through the rest of the summer so the plantlet can form a good root system.

Strawberry plants deteriorate after a few years, so it is a good idea to root runners to provide replacement plants on a regular basis.

Shear off leaves after harvest

Once all the fruit has been picked, and provided none of the plants are being used for propagation, the strawberry bed can be cleared. Remove any straw used around the plants and cut off the strawberry leaves with shears, taking care not to damage the crowns, which will soon produce new growth. Rake up all the old straw and foliage and burn it to help control diseases such as mildew.

PINCH OUT THE GROWING TIPS on guyot-trained grapevines to prevent the rows getting too high, and let more sunlight into the canopy by shortening the sideshoots back to one leaf.

ON CORDON VINES, allow just one bunch of grapes to develop on each lateral branch. Remove all the others using secateurs so that the vine concentrates its energy into those remaining.

VINE FRUIT

Grapes

Prune sideshoots

On guyot-trained vines (see page 259), pinch out the growing tips at the top to prevent the rows becoming too high and shading others. Shorten sideshoots (produced in the leaf axils of the fruiting arms) back to one leaf to get more sunlight into the canopy and improve air circulation.

Feed nutrient-deficient vines

Apply a foliar feed containing trace elements to vines with signs of nutrient deficiency, particularly yellowing between the leaf veins, often seen on chalky soils.

Remove grapes that will not ripen

If the vine is carrying immature bunches of grapes that it is clear will not have time to develop and ripen for the autumn harvest, remove these to allow the plant to put its energy into the fruit that will be able to ripen.

Kiwifruit

Continue summer pruning

If not already done, shorten fruiting shoots to five leaves past the last fruit to divert energy into the developing ones. After harvesting in autumn, this fruited shoot will be cut back to 5–7.5cm (2–3in), to develop a spur system.

Train shoots to their wires
Continue to train main shoots along the horizontal wire supports and pinch back any shoots that arise from them to four or five leaves.

Melons

Shade greenhouse crops
In the very sunniest weather, shade indoor crops with netting or a whitewash on the glass to prevent scorching.

Feed and water crops
Keep the soil moist around the roots at all times. A regular water supply is very important for successful crops, but don't allow the soil to become waterlogged. Plants in containers, especially growing bags with a shallow compost depth, may need watering several times a day. Apply a high-potash liquid feed every 10–14 days.

Pollinate flowers
Wait until the plants have five or six flowers open before opening up greenhouses, cloches and frames to allow in

MELON FLOWERS *ideally need to be pollinated all at the same time. Open up greenhouses to allow pollinating insects in, or lend a hand by picking a male flower and pushing it into the centre of a female one.*

pollinating insects. The setting of the first fruit inhibits fertilisation of the remaining flowers, so the aim is to get the flowers all pollinated at the same time.

A surer method, particularly in a greenhouse, is to pollinate the flowers yourself. Once sufficient female flowers are open, remove a male flower, fold back the petals and push it into the centre of the female flower. (Female flowers can be identified by the swelling of the developing fruit immediately behind the flower.)

Pinch back sideshoots
Once it is clear that flowers have been pollinated and the fruit begins to swell, pinch out the sideshoots at one or two leaves past the pollinated flower.

Thin fruits
Melon plants will not be able to ripen a large number of fruit. Once they reach golf-ball size, thin the fruit to leave three or four per plant that are in the best positions.

Damp down greenhouses
Greenhouse-grown melons enjoy a humid atmosphere, so the floor and staging should be damped down on hot days. This will also help to deter red spider mite.

Order biological controls where necessary
Greenhouse melons are very prone to attack by red spider mite. If plants do not seem to be thriving, inspect the leaves closely, especially the ends of the shoots. Affected plants have dry-looking white-speckled leaves, and on the undersides tiny reddish-brown or yellowish mites may be seen running over the surface. These pests are very small and you often need a hand lens to spot them clearly. Strands of webbing may also be evident.

The biological control *Phytoseiulus persimilis* is a predatory mite that feeds on eggs and adults of red spider mite. Order the control as soon as the pest is seen, and as soon as it arrives, release the predatory mites on to the leaves of affected plants. They work best at temperatures of around 20°C (68°F) and in humid conditions.

Look out for mildew
Powdery mildew forms a white coating over leaves, especially at the shoot tips. Remove any affected leaves promptly and destroy them. Increase the ventilation and humidity in greenhouses where mildew is a problem.

| Grow your own currant crops

Currants are not difficult to grow. The glossy fruits of black currants carried in bunches known as 'strigs' are very well known and loved; they are bursting with flavour and have a powerful fragrance. Red and white currants are rather less well known, but deserve to be more widely grown. The dangling chains of bright crimson or pearl-coloured berries are very attractive in summer gardens. Although closely related, black currants fruit on young wood; the branches are cut out at the end of the season while strong young stems are retained for the following year's crop. Red and white currants fruit on old wood and are pruned to encourage a more permanent framework.

SOME VARIETIES OF CURRANT *(above) are sweet enough to eat off the bush, otherwise they are used in cooking. They are rich in vitamin C.*

AS WELL AS DELICIOUS BERRIES, *currants bear dainty flowers (right) that rely on bees and other insects for pollination.*

Recommended black currants

'Ben Sarek'

A good choice for the small garden as this is a compact, high-yielding black currant bush growing only to about 1.2m (4ft) high. It offers resistance to mildew and frost. 'Ben Sarek' produces large, glossy round berries (below) that are easily picked from short strigs.

'Ben Hope'

An excellent grower with heavy yields of delicious medium-sized currants. It is resistant to mildew, leaf spot and gall midge. 'Boskoop Giant' is also recommended but makes a bigger plant so is best for larger gardens.

'Ben Lomond'

An upright black currant with some frost resistance because of its late flowering. Produces heavy yields of large, short-stalked berries (below), which are ready to harvest in late summer.

'Ben Gairn'

This compact variety, with large, juicy fruit, is good for small gardens. It is also one of the earliest to come into fruit. Resistant to reversion disease.

'Ben Connan'

A compact plant suitable for a small garden. It has resistance to mildew, frost and gall midge. The berries are large with good flavour (below).

Jostaberry

A popular black currant x gooseberry hybrid. It is very vigorous, thornless, and has good resistance to mildew, fungal leaf spot and big bud mite. The gooseberry-sized fruits have a black currant taste.

Recommended red currants

'Jonkheer van Tets'

One of the earliest varieties of red currant bearing heavy crops of large berries (below) with an excellent flavour.

'Stanza'

This heavy cropping late variety has a superb flavour. The berries are much darker than most other varieties once fully ripened. Compact growth, so good for a small garden.

'Red Lake'

A mid-season variety producing heavy yields (below). It has long strigs that are easy to pick.

Recommended white currants

'Versailles Blanche' (syn. 'White Versailles')

Bearing fruit in mid summer, this early variety of white currant produces heavy, regular yields of large, pale white berries.

'White Grape'

An early white currant variety with an upright habit. The pure white, large berries (below) have a better, sweeter flavour than 'Versailles Blanche'.

late summer

The harvest continues, sometimes threatening to swamp the kitchen with its overflowing bounty. Later-maturing crops such as sweetcorn and the first winter squashes join the rest of the summer crops; tomatoes, peppers and aubergines from the greenhouse and outdoors add to the haul. You may be tiring of endless runner beans and courgettes now, but they will be welcome through the winter months so fill your freezer with the surplus.

As the earlier crops finish, their remains must quickly be cleared to make way for the next plantings and sowings. Autumn and winter crops need nurturing to bring them on, watering and feeding them where necessary.

Soft fruits are still going strong, with autumn-fruiting varieties of raspberry and strawberries extending their season; there are luscious plums to pick, and both acid and sweet cherries. Apples and pears will start ripening now, too, and the early varieties may be ready to pick and enjoy straight off the tree.

vegetables | GENERAL ADVICE

Tidy after harvest | Clear spent crops promptly to eliminate pests and diseases and expose weeds.

Sow green manures | If you have spare time and space and the soil is sufficiently moist, sow green manures to improve soil fertility and the workability of stiff ground. Fodder radish and mustard are good for sowing now.

Keep harvesting | The more you pick fruiting crops such as courgettes, beans and tomatoes, the more will be produced. Allowing crops such as beans to develop a few mature pods provides a signal to the plant that its job, which is to produce seeds for next year, is achieved and it will cease production. Even if you have a surplus of produce at present, keep picking to ensure a supply later, when it will be more welcome.

Sow extra crops | As soil becomes free, sow quick-growing crops of beetroot, French beans, kohlrabi, radishes, winter salad leaves and turnips.

Look out for slugs and snails | When plant growth is lush and there are plenty of hiding places during the day, slugs and snails continue to be a nuisance at this time of year. Keep weed growth down and remove spent crops and debris promptly to help keep them at bay. The bases of hedges must be kept clear, too, especially when they border the vegetable garden because these provide a favourite home for slugs and snails.

Water when necessary | There can be heavy downpours in late summer, but long, hot, dry spells are not uncommon. Keep vegetables growing strongly and crops tender by watering when necessary. Seep hose is often the most economical way to water; it applies moisture near the plants' roots and little is wasted by evaporation.

Remove diseased leaves | Clear away leaves affected by fungal diseases such as blight and mildew promptly. It is

IMPROVE SOIL WITH GREEN MANURES

Green manures are fast-growing crops that are sown specifically to improve the soil. The plants are usually cut down while they are still young and incorporated back into the soil where they rot down and release their nutrients.

Broadcast the seed of a green manure crop over a piece of spare ground. When the plants have reached about 20cm (8in) tall, and before they flower or the stems have become woody, cut them down to ground level using shears or a nylon line trimmer. Allow them to wilt for a few days, then turn them into the soil with a spade or rotary cultivator. Suitable plants to grow include lupins, clover, rape, mustard, vetches and fodder radish.

Alternatively, some types of crops can be sown in late summer or autumn and left in the ground over winter before being dug in during spring. These help to prevent nutrients being washed away by winter rains. Rye, Italian ryegrass and field beans are suitable for overwintering.

better not to compost diseased material; if the compost heap reaches high enough temperatures the spores will be killed, but not all parts of the heap will heat up sufficiently to ensure this.

Pot up herbs for winter | Although herbs dry successfully, fresh ones have a much better flavour. If you want to be able to pick a few sprigs through the winter months, this is a good time to pot up some herb plants. In early to mid autumn they can be moved into a bright spot in the home and can be picked sparingly through winter. Rosemary, parsley, thyme, marjoram, mint and summer savory are among those that can be potted up now.

A GOOD GREEN MANURE is Phacelia tanacetifolia; *it adds nutrients and humus to the soil when dug in and looks beautiful when growing.*

vegetables | WHAT TO DO NOW

ONION FAMILY

Garlic

Harvest as soon as crops are ready

These crops are ready to harvest once the leaves have turned yellow and toppled. While some varieties are ready earlier, most mature around now.

Choose a spell when the weather looks settled and dry for a few days. Loosen the bulbs by inserting a fork under the roots and lifting slightly; after a day or two, lift the bulbs completely and spread them out to dry. Ideally raise them off the ground on wire mesh for air to circulate freely. Bulbs that are not properly dried will rot in store.

Once the bulbs are thoroughly dry, gently rub off any loose soil and leaves and inspect them for damage. Any that are damaged or those with soft necks should be put to one side for immediate use. Firm, sound bulbs can be stored in net bags in a cool, dry shed or garage, preferably hanging up for good air circulation. They can also be plaited together in ropes, but though these look attractive enough to hang in the kitchen, this is not a good place to store them as it's too warm and humid.

MAKE A GARLIC ROPE

Choose firm, dry bulbs with a good length of stem. They can be plaited together, but it's easier to use a piece of strong twine, about 1.2m (4ft) long, and doubled into a loop. Twist the end of the loop around the neck of a large bulb and feed the rest of it through to form a secure noose; this will make the base of the rope. Hang the twine up and twist the neck of the next bulb around several times so it lays close against the twine and the rest of the neck lies along it. Continue adding bulbs to make an evenly filled rope.

LIFT GARLIC BULBS *gradually over a couple of days then leave them to dry out thoroughly. Cut off the stems of the bulbs, unless you plan to plait them together.*

ONCE THE GARLIC BULBS HAVE DRIED OUT, *you can gently split some of the individual cloves apart for planting your next crop. Keep these in a cool shed or garage for planting in the autumn.*

Leeks

Harvest baby leeks
Young leeks are particularly sweet and tender, and baby leeks can be pulled for use as soon as they are large enough. However, it is more usual to wait for the stems to thicken to ensure a harvest of good-sized plants from late summer right through the winter, for soups, casseroles and other dishes.

Onions and shallots

Sow overwintering varieties
Sow a suitable variety for overwintering in rows 30cm (12in) apart and thin to 2.5cm (1in) apart in autumn. Overwintered onions are only worth growing in mild areas and some losses can be expected, but they will give a very early crop next year where they are successful. The final thinning to 8–10cm (3–4in) apart is not made until late winter or early spring. 'Senshyu Yellow Globe' is the most popular variety for overwintering.

CABBAGE FAMILY

General

Stake tall crops
Stake or earth up tall winter crops such as Brussels sprouts and purple sprouting broccoli to secure them against autumn gales.

Broccoli and calabrese

Pick summer-sprouting broccoli
Most sprouting broccoli varieties need a spell of cold weather to initiate flowering and cropping, so are not available to harvest until spring. Summer-cropping types, however, do not need this cold stimulus and some may be ready to cut now, although often you will have to wait until autumn for a good flush of heads to be produced. 'Bordeaux' and 'Summer Purple' are two good varieties.

Pick calabrese
Calabrese, sometimes called green sprouting broccoli, is ready any time between now and early winter according to variety and sowing time. Cut the large central head

CALABRESE *is ready to harvest any time between late summer and early winter according to variety and sowing time. Cut the florets from the plant using a sharp knife, cutting the central spear first.*

first; smaller heads will then develop from the leaf axils for a second harvest later on.

Cabbage

Sow spring greens
Make another sowing of cabbages such as 'Spring Hero' to be grown as spring greens.

Harvest firm heads
Cut summer cabbages as they become large enough to use. Do not leave them to stand too long or you risk the heads splitting.

Oriental vegetables

Sow seed now
Oriental greens are good for sowing in late summer; they often bolt if sown earlier. Chinese cabbage, choy sum, pak choi and mustard greens all make an interesting change from more familiar leafy crops. Sow in rows 45cm (18in) apart and space plants 15–30cm (6–12in) according to variety. Keep the young plants watered regularly.

| Grow your own tasty tomatoes

A summer salad is somehow incomplete without the splash of colour and the intense sweet flavour and aroma of ripe tomatoes – preferably picked sun-warmed and taken straight from the plant to the plate.

The multitude of tomato varieties on offer in seed catalogues is almost overwhelming. There are tomatoes of all shapes and sizes, from tiny currant-sized ones to huge beefsteaks; from ones shaped like plums to those that are more like bananas. And even their colour provides us with a choice; as well as the normal pillar-box red there are yellow, orange, pink, mahogany and even striped varieties to choose from.

While all the major seed companies offer a wide range of different tomato varieties, you can get even more choice, including long-established heirloom varieties and some extraordinary shapes and colours, from specialist suppliers. Tomatoes are either vine type, which have

their sideshoots removed and require training up canes or strings, or bush types, which are left more to their own devices.

Make sure you pick the right variety of tomato for your conditions. If you don't have a greenhouse, you must take care to choose one that is suitable for growing outdoors. If you are really short of space, look out for tomatoes that have been specially bred for growing in pots, windowboxes and even hanging baskets. You should be able to find something suitable and enjoy growing and eating your own tomatoes no matter how big or small your garden is.

CHERRY TOMATOES *(above) bear small round fruit, which make a tasty addition to summer salads and pasta dishes.*

Recommended varieties

'Sungold'

An exceptionally sweet, orange-red cherry tomato that does best if given some protection. The growth is vine type and has some virus resistance.

'Tornado' AGM

This tomato has a bushy habit and does well when grown in containers and in the ground. It can be supported with short stakes or allowed to sprawl.

'Olivade' AGM

The large, dark-red plum tomatoes are very early to mature and are borne in profusion on the vine-type growth. They are juicy and fruity with a good flavour. For outdoors or under glass.

'Gold Nugget' AGM

A very tasty cherry tomato of bush habit. The fruit is a shade of golden yellow and is early to crop with good yields.

'Outdoor Girl' AGM

An early ripening variety that will grow well outdoors. The vine-type growth produces classic round red tomatoes that have a good flavour.

'Summer Sweet' AGM

Expect heavy crops of attractive, small, juicy, red plum tomatoes. They are very early to mature and grow outdoors or under glass.

'Golden Sunrise' AGM

These unusual, yellow, medium-sized tomatoes are borne on vine-type plants. They make colourful additions to summer salads and have a nice fruity flavour.

'Gardener's Delight' AGM

A vine-type cherry tomato with an exceptionally sweet flavour. The plants bear long trusses of fruit and will grow either under glass or outside in a warm spot.

'Marmande'

A popular beefsteak variety with large, ribbed, sweetly flavoured fruit that are particularly good for cooking. Grows outdoors in a warm, sunny position and needs staking.

BEANS AND PEAS

French beans

Keep harvesting

Keep picking beans as soon as they are ready, before they become stringy. Try to keep the beans off the soil, where they are liable to be eaten by slugs; use twiggy sticks or canes and string to hold the plants up if necessary. If you don't want to use a knife, use two hands to pick the beans, holding the stem with one hand while you pull the bean with the other. If you tug at a bean with only one hand you can easily uproot the plant.

Runner beans

Keep harvesting

Pick beans while they are young, before there is any hint of swelling seeds within the pods. Bean pods that are too old become stringy and are not worth eating; remove these unless you intend to save the seed to use next year. Try snapping the pods in two if you are unsure about them – as long as they snap cleanly, with no stringiness, they should be fine to eat.

Once the beans start coming, it is sometimes not easy to pick them fast enough. If any pods have been missed and are past their best, these should be picked if only to throw them away. If you leave them on the plants it will slow down the production of new pods. You can expect up to 1kg (2lb) of beans from a single plant.

Peas

Support young plants

Peas sown in early summer will need to be provided with supports as they grow. Keep the plants well watered in dry spells.

Harvest and clear crops

Continue harvesting peas. Clear away the topgrowth once all the crop has been gathered, cutting the haulms down to ground level.

Pick mangetout and sugar snap varieties

These varieties are eaten complete with their pods. Mangetout, such as 'Delikata', are picked at a very young stage when the pods are still flat and the young peas are only just starting to form. Sugar snap types give a much bigger crop because they can be left on the plant longer until the peas inside are larger. The pods are much fleshier than those of mangetout peas and remain sweet and crisp for far longer. 'Sugar Ann' and 'Sugar Bon' are reliable varieties.

AVOIDING PEA MOTH

Pea moths lay their eggs on the foliage of pea plants at flowering time. The caterpillars hatch out and bore their way into the young pea pods then feed on the developing peas inside, where they are hidden and safe from predators. Usually they are only discovered after harvest when the peas are being shelled. They cause a lot of damage, both by eating peas and spoiling others with their frass or excrement.

Because the moth carries out its activity while the peas are flowering, it is difficult to treat them with insecticides without potentially harming pollinating insects. The best way to avoid damage is to time sowings so that the peas will flower outside the peak time that pea moths are on the wing, which is from early to mid summer. This means sowing early maturing varieties either early or late; avoid sowing in early to mid spring.

Pea moth traps, which are baited with pheromones to attract and trap the male moths, are available from some biological-control suppliers and help cut down the amount of damage. You can also cover the crop with fleece during flowering time to prevent the moths' access to the plants.

PERENNIAL VEGETABLES

Asparagus

Keep weeding

Keep asparagus beds free of weeds. It is important that they are kept under control because they can quickly get out of hand and are then very difficult to eradicate.

Jerusalem artichokes

Cut back plants

Reduce the height of the plants in windy sites if you have not already done so. Earth up the stem bases or provide stakes where necessary.

ROOTS AND STEMS

Florence fennel

Harvest bulbs when large enough

Harvest from now to mid autumn, as soon as the bulbs are sufficiently large, using a fork to loosen the roots carefully before lifting. When harvesting, cut the bulb off just above ground level and leave the stump in the ground. Young feathery shoots will soon appear and these can also be used in the kitchen.

Potatoes

Start lifting maincrops

Once the early potatoes are finished you can start lifting the second earlies, or even the maincrops when they are large enough. Only dig as many as you want to use immediately – maincrop potatoes intended for storing should be left in the soil for a while yet.

Carefully dig the potatoes up with a garden fork, taking care not to spear the tubers. Any mildly damaged potatoes should be eaten promptly. Throw out any that have gone green through exposure to light because these are potentially poisonous.

Deal with scab

Potatoes affected by common scab, a fungal disease, have corky, raised brown patches on the skins. This is

FLATTISH FENNEL BULBS *are nearly as rewarding as rounded ones and can be harvested for the table as soon as they are ready. The foliage can be used as a herb dressing.*

LIFT POTATOES *as soon as they are ready if your garden suffers badly from slugs. Soil-dwelling slugs are a nuisance as they eat and burrow into the tubers.*

not a serious problem and the affected potatoes can still be eaten – they just need to be peeled more deeply than usual to remove the scabs. If the whole crop is affected, however, you may want to select a resistant variety to grow next year.

'Accent', 'Arran Pilot', 'King Edward' and 'Pentland Crown' are among potato varieties with reasonable resistance to the disease. 'Desiree', 'Foremost', 'Majestic' and 'Maris Piper', on the other hand, are particularly susceptible to scab and should be avoided.

SALADS

Chicory

Harvest blanched plants

Cut blanched plants immediately once the cover is removed, as they will soon start to revert to their dark-green colouring and bitter taste. Stored in a cool place, the cut leaves have better keeping properties than lettuce.

Cucumbers

Pick early in the day

Once the cucumbers are sufficiently large, cut them off using a sharp knife and pick before the strongest heat of the day for maximum crispness. Harvest regularly, because leaving mature cucumbers on the plant will stop the development of new ones.

Lettuces

Sow outside for autumn crops

Sow varieties that are suitable for cropping in autumn. They can be protected with fleece or cloches as the weather cools later in the season for a prolonged harvest. 'Winter Density', 'Tom Thumb' and 'Little Gem' are all suitable for sowing now. Water the drill before sowing to cool the soil because lettuce seed becomes dormant if temperatures are too high.

Sow mixed leaves

Continue sowing seed mixtures for baby salad leaves. Make your own mix from several varieties of lettuce, spinach and herbs, or use one of the commercial packets that are already mixed for you.

Radishes

Sow for succession

Sow further short rows outside for succession. Keep the seedlings well watered to avoid them becoming woody and over hot due to dry conditions.

Sow winter radish

Winter radishes are hardier than the summer varieties and are generally larger with thicker skins. Sowings are

HARVEST CUCUMBERS *when the fruit tips are rounded with parallel sides and no longer pointed. Cut them off using a sharp knife and do so before the strongest heat of the day to pick them at their crispiest.*

best made now, as plants sown earlier than this are more likely to bolt. Grown in well-drained soil in a reasonably sheltered site, they can be left in the ground through the winter and pulled as required. Sow in rows 25cm (10in) apart and thin to 10cm (4in) apart in the row.

There are several varieties of winter radish available. 'Round Black Spanish' forms a large, round, black-skinned root and has peppery white flesh, 'Mantanghong' is round with a white skin and deep-rose flesh, while long-rooted 'China Rose' has rose-pink skin and white flesh. Mooli is another type of radish, with long, white, tapering roots that are crisp textured with a mild flavour. Some mooli radishes, such as 'Long White Icicle', can also be eaten when immature as a summer radish.

Tomatoes

Watch for blight

Blight becomes more of a possibility as the summer progresses; it is at its worst in wet seasons. Keep an eye on tomatoes and remove affected plants promptly, spraying the remaining plants with mancozeb or copper fungicide as a preventive. Blight is much more likely on outdoor tomatoes, but it can affect greenhouse ones, too.

Keep harvesting fruits

Pick tomatoes as soon as they are fully ripe. Try to break the fruit off complete with the green calyx attached, as they keep better like this. Water the plants regularly;

PICK TOMATOES *as required as soon as they are fully ripe. Try to break each fruit off complete with its green calyx attached, as this makes the tomatoes keep better once harvested.*

sudden watering after a dry spell can result in the fruit splitting. Cut down on the watering slightly while the fruit is ripening, as this produces a sweeter flavour.

SPINACH AND CHARD

Spinach

Keep plants watered
Water spinach regularly in dry spells to ensure that fresh young leaves continue to be produced.

Control downy mildew
Yellow patches on leaves, which may be slightly furry underneath, are a sign of downy mildew. This is common on spinach, especially late in the season. Remove the affected leaves immediately and thin out plants if necessary to provide better air circulation.

Sow Oriental spinach
Oriental spinach has large, dark-green pointed leaves on long stems that are tinged pink at the base and look attractive in the vegetable garden. It is particularly good for sowing now in late summer because of its resistance to bolting and downy mildew. Sow in rows 30cm (12in) apart and thin seedlings to 5–8cm (2–3in) in the row. Varieties of Oriental spinach include 'Oriento', 'Koto' and 'Mikado'.

Swiss chard

Make another sowing
Although earlier sowings will often carry on producing well into winter, a further sowing of Swiss chard made now will produce a good crop for winter and early spring.

Clear bolted crops
Plants that have been productive through the summer will often bolt to seed over the next few weeks. It is best to pull these plants up and compost them now, and let new sowings take over.

EVERY SPINACH LOVER'S NIGHTMARE *(top) – a spinach bed that has bolted or gone to seed, resulting in wasted plants that are only good for the compost heap.*

THE GLOSSY TEXTURE OF SWISS CHARD *(above) is enhanced by the glowing colour of the leaves and stems, giving them an ornamental value in the vegetable garden. They remain productive for many weeks.*

SQUASHES, MARROWS, PUMPKINS
AND SWEETCORN

Courgettes, marrows and summer squashes

Continue harvesting

Keep cutting courgettes frequently, so that the plants continue to produce more. Marrows can be cut as soon as they reach a usable size. They are usually more tender and tastier to eat if they aren't allowed to grow too large – the flesh of very large marrows can become fibrous and stringy.

If you want some marrows to store over winter, however, leave the fruit on the plant until it is ripe and the skin is firm – you should not be able to puncture it with a fingernail. These marrows can then be cut and stored in a cool place.

Winter squashes and pumpkins

Prepare for stored fruits

Fruit for eating fresh can be cut off the plant as required, but to store well over winter it must be fully ripened and cured. Leave fruits that are to be stored on the plant for as long as possible so that they can ripen fully and develop a tough skin.

Sweetcorn

Test cobs for ripeness

Once the tassels on the ends of the cobs turn brown you can start testing for maturity. Peel back the husk to check the corn; it will be pale yellow when ready to be picked. Prick a kernel with your thumbnail; a milky liquid should ooze out if the cob is ready. If the liquid is thin and watery it is too early, and if it is thick and pasty the cob is past its best.

It is vital to harvest the cobs at just the right stage if they are to be at their sweetest and best. As soon as the cob is picked, the sugar in the kernels starts to change to starch, so for the very best flavour you should cook and eat – or freeze – the sweetcorn within minutes of picking. If not eaten right away, sweetcorn will remain fresh for a few days if kept refrigerated.

MAKING MARROW RUM

Brewing your own marrow rum is a traditional and resourceful way of dealing with a monster marrow that nobody wants to eat. To make it, first cut the stem end off the marrow and scoop out as many of the seeds as possible while leaving the flesh intact. Be careful not to puncture the skin. Pack the hollowed-out marrow with brown sugar –some people add a little powdered ginger or orange zest, and some add winemaking yeast – then replace the stem end on top.

Place the marrow in a nylon stocking and hang it over a bowl or large jug to catch the liquid that will drip from the base. Leave it for two or three weeks; at the end of that time, make a hole in the base of the marrow if the liquid hasn't already leaked out. Continue to ferment the liquor in a glass jar fitted with an airlock or bottle it straight away. Store for several months before drinking – at your own risk!

HARVEST SWEETCORN *in late summer, testing the cobs for maturity once the tassels turn brown. Pick only what you want to eat that day, preferably as close to cooking time as possible.*

HOW TO GROW BABY CORN

Baby corn is a relatively new concept; it is simply corn cobs that are picked at a very early stage, before the kernels are mature. Grow the plants as you would for normal sweetcorn, but harvest the cobs within one or two days of the silks emerging from the end of the cob. At this stage the whole cob is sweet and crunchy. Remove the green sheaf and cook the cob, either whole or sliced according to size, by quickly stir-frying, or serve it raw in salads. Fresh-picked baby cobs are much sweeter and tastier than the tinned varieties we are more used to.

TENDER VEGETABLES

Aubergines

Harvest ripe fruit
Pick aubergines as soon as they are full size and develop their full colour; for most varieties the skin is glossy purple-black, but there are also red, white and striped ones. Don't allow the fruit to dull on the plant; this is a sign of over-maturity and it will be leathery and dry.

Control red spider mite
Biological controls should be keeping red spider mite under control. Increase the humidity by misting plants regularly, as red spider mite dislikes humid conditions.

Okra

Continue picking pods
Okra pods can quickly become stringy and tough, so pick frequently. They take three to five days to develop after flowering and grow 5–7.5cm (3–4in) long. Harvest with a sharp knife when pods are bright green, firm and dry, and handle carefully because they bruise easily, which affects their shelf-life. Dull and yellowing fruit are past their best but must be picked to encourage continued cropping.

Peppers and chillies

Pick sweet peppers as required
Peppers can be picked while still green and immature, or left to change colour on the plant. The flavour of ripe

AUBERGINES *(top) make a lively, surprising addition to the container garden, and they are not all black or purple. There are also white, red or striped ones. They make a nice feature grown in a well-cleaned olive can.*

PICK OKRA PODS *(above) quickly to avoid them becoming tough and stringy. Ideally, okra should be eaten as soon as it is harvested because it doesn't store particularly well. Very young pods can be eaten raw.*

peppers is fuller and sweeter, but leaving the fruit to mature on the plant does reduce yield.

Harvest chillies
Like sweet peppers, chillies can be harvested green or left to ripen. This doesn't only affect their flavour, but also their heat. Handle hot varieties with care as the juice can burn your skin. Discard the seeds for a milder flavour.

| Grow your own edible flowers

It may be a surprise to discover that many flowers can be used in the kitchen. Some petals have a strong peppery or fruity taste while others impart more subtle aromas and flavours. Flowers wilt quickly, especially in hot weather, so pick in the morning if possible and move to a cool place indoors for preparing. Spread them on a piece of kitchen towel so any small black pollen beetles can be removed.

In most species, the flowers are too tough to eat whole, so place the removed petals in a small polythene bag and seal with a little air inside to stop them getting squashed. The petals should keep like this in the fridge for several hours. Avoid washing flowers to avoid damage, but if they're wilting, place in a bowl of water to revive them.

BORAGE AND CALENDULA *(above) grace the garden in summer, but their petals can also be picked for the plate.*

EDIBLE FLOWERS AND LEAVES *(right) give a salad an extra peppery, fruity, nutty taste – and it looks beautiful, too.*

Recommended edible flowers

Calendula (*Calendula officinalis*)

A hardy annual with double and single varieties in shades of orange. Deadhead to prolong flowering or use successional sowings. Petals add colour to salads.

Tagetes (*Tagetes tenuifolia*)

Bush marigolds (such as varieties 'Lemon Gem' and 'Tangerine Gem') are very easy to raise from seed and young plants are readily available from garden centres. The petals have a distinctive zesty flavour and add a splash of sunshine-yellow to salads.

Clary sage (*Salvia sclarea*)

Strictly speaking it is not the flowers that are of interest here but the purple and pink bracts. Select the younger ones as these are brighter and will not yet have become papery. Their flavour is negligible but they make a decorative garnish.

Nasturtium (*Tropaeolum majus*)

A wonderful flower for use in the kitchen as both the leaves and petals of nasturtium have a strong peppery taste, which takes a few seconds to develop on the tongue. The flower colour can vary from deep red to butter yellow. The seedheads can also be collected and pickled to use as a substitute for capers – pick while green and fresh.

Heartsease (*Viola tricolor*)

This delicate wildflower is small enough to use whole. Just snip as much of the calyx off as is possible without causing it to fall apart. It is pretty frozen in ice cubes and used in summer drinks. Cultivated violas and pansies can also be used but are best bought as bedding plants. Winter-flowering pansies will offer a supply of petals when little else is available.

Borage (*Borago officinalis*)

A tall bushy plant and apt to flop without support, so ensure you allow enough room for it. The starry blue flowers are easily detached from the calyx by gently pulling at the centre. They look beautiful in ice cubes or mixed with dark-leafed lettuce. The young leaves have a cucumber-like flavour and can be chopped and added to summer drinks.

fruit | GENERAL ADVICE

Feed trees in pots | Continue giving a high-potash fertiliser to fruit trees growing in pots.

Deal with wasps | Hang wasp traps on the branches of trees bearing ripening fruit. Wasps will damage ripe fruit and make it inedible, and there is also the risk of being stung if you unsuspectingly pick fruit with wasps inside. Remove any damaged and overripe fruit promptly, as these help to attract wasps.

MAKE A WASP TRAP

Take an empty plastic 2-litre fizzy drink bottle and cut the top off at the shoulder, discarding the cap. Put the top to one side. Place something sweet to attract the wasps in the base of the bottle; sugary fruit juice works well. Position the top of the bottle back on the base, but turning it upside down to form a funnel. If you want to hang the trap in a tree, make three holes in the sides of the bottle, below the level of the funnel, and thread string through to form a hanging loop. Seal the edges of the top and base with tape if necessary, and place the trap where wasps are a problem. They will have no trouble entering the bottle through the funnel, but it will be almost impossible for them to find their way back out again.

Deal with brown rot | Fruits affected by brown rot turn soft, brown and wrinkled, eventually with creamy white raised pustules on the surface. The fungus gains entry at a point of damage, so promptly remove all damaged fruit (such as those that have been attacked by birds or wasps). Remove fruit affected by brown rot, including those that have fallen, and destroy them.

RIPENING APPLES *and other fruit will be attractive to wasps and birds, so take the necessary action to avoid damaged crops.*

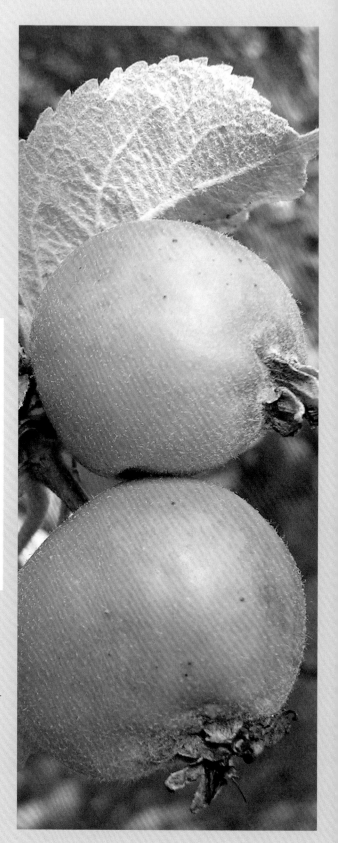

fruit | WHAT TO DO NOW

TREE FRUIT

Apples and pears

Summer prune restricted forms

Cordons, fans and espaliers are usually pruned in late summer as their growth slows down for dormancy during winter. Pruning at this time of year allows sunlight to get into what would otherwise be a crowded and congested canopy. This helps the wood to ripen and to initiate the development of fruit buds for next year.

Cordons: A cordon has a trunk that is straight or, if it is an oblique cordon, one that is angled at 30–45 degrees. They are trained against horizontal supporting wires and the leader should be tied to a cane fixed to these. If the leader has reached the required height, prune it back now. Prune sideshoots back to one or two buds past the basal cluster (the group of leaves at the base of the stem).

On an established cordon, prune most of the new growth back to one or two buds past the basal cluster, using a pair of sharp secateurs. Ensure that the wood has ripened and is no longer green. If growth is less than 20cm (8in) long, leave it to develop further, then prune it in autumn or winter. Shorten any shoot that has developed directly from the main stem, cutting it back to three or four buds above the basal cluster to encourage a system of fruiting spurs to develop. Prune any weak or wispy growth to just one leaf past the basal cluster.

Espaliers: Trees being trained as espaliers should have two shoots being trained against canes at a 45 degree angle; these canes can now be lowered to the horizontal. Prune the tip only if the shoot has reached the end of the

RESTRICTED FORMS *like a cordon apple tree benefit from summer pruning. Vigorous trees put on less growth when pruned at this time of year and it helps prevent biennial fruiting.*

PRUNE THE SIDESHOOTS *back to one or two buds past the basal cluster using sharp secateurs. Ensure that the wood has ripened and is no longer green.*

PRUNING IN SUMMER *allows sunlight to get into what would otherwise be a crowded and congested canopy, which helps the ripening of the wood and development of fruit buds.*

wire. On an established espalier, prune sideshoots of more than 25cm (10in) that have formed from existing spurs back to one bud past the basal cluster. Shorten new growth directly from the horizontal branch tiers to three or four buds above the basal cluster. Remove spurs or shoots on the central trunk.

Fans: Prune new growth back to a couple of buds above the basal cluster. Remove any dominant shoots that are attempting to take over as the central leader. If the tree is predominantly a spur bearer, shorten some sideshoots to one or two buds past the basal cluster. Fill empty spaces by tying in other sideshoots and pruning back the tips.

Pyramid: A feathered maiden being trained as a pyramid should have the leader and lateral branches shortened by two thirds to downward-facing buds. On established trees, maintain the shape by removing vertical growth and keeping growth at the apex short. On lateral branches, cut back new growth to 20cm (8in) to a downward-facing bud.

Summer prune over-vigorous trees

Unrestricted trees such as bushes and standards have a more open branch structure than restricted forms, meaning sunlight can enter the canopy allowing the fruit buds to develop without summer pruning. However, trees that are making lots of unwanted, vigorous growth are pruned now, as winter pruning will only encourage further vegetative growth.

Pick apples as they are ready

To pick an apple, cup it lightly in your hand, lift gently and give it a slight twist. The fruit should come away in your hand with the stalk intact. If it doesn't, then it isn't ready for picking. Never pull at the fruit because this can break the fruiting spurs. Place the apples gently into a box or bucket, being careful not to drop or bruise them. Specially designed buckets that hang from the shoulders are useful if lots of apples are to be harvested.

Harvest pears

Pick pears just before they are fully ripened. They should be firm and swollen, with a subtle colour change to their

---

WHEN IS AN APPLE READY FOR PICKING?

With most fruit, the obvious method of testing whether it's ready for picking is to taste it. This is certainly possible with some of the early apples such as 'Discovery', which can be eaten fresh off the tree. However, some later-maturing apples require a period of storage before being ready for eating – a bit like a fine wine – and therefore other methods of identifying their readiness for harvesting are required.

The tell-tale sign of an apple being ready for picking is a few windfalls lying beneath the tree. The fruit should have swelled to a good size and have started to colour up. Cut the apple in half and look at the pips; if they have changed from white to brown then the apple is close to harvest time.

HOW TO STORE APPLES FOR A LATER DATE

A LINED FRUIT BUCKET is the ideal tool for collecting an apple and pear harvest. Discard rotting and damaged fruit as you go along to make sure you collect the best pickings.

WRAP APPLES in paper or perforated freezer bags, or lie each of the fruit unwrapped on a tray away from the others. Make sure you keep all the stalks intact.

PLACE THE WRAPPED APPLES and pears in a crate or pallet and store them in a cool, dark place. Inspect the fruit regularly and remove any rotting fruit immediately.

skin. Test early varieties by tasting one of the fruit for sweetness, yet firmness. Later varieties should part easily from the tree when lifted and gently twisted. Check picked pears daily to see if they are ready for eating. They quickly become overripe with unpleasantly soft flesh.

Apricots

Keep picking fruit

Continue harvesting apricots as they ripen, when they feel soft and part easily from the tree with a gentle lift.

Cherries

Carry out any pruning necessary

Once a basic framework is established, an open-centred sweet cherry tree needs simply to have dead, diseased and damaged growth, as well as congested and crossing branches, removed annually after harvest.

Citrus

Water and feed trees

Keep the compost for citrus just moist at all times. Continue feeding with a high-nitrogen fertiliser; it will shortly be time to switch to a winter-feeding regime.

Deal with scale insects

Citrus are particularly prone to attack by scale insects. These appear mainly on the undersides of leaves and on the stems, and are brown and flat with no recognisable head or legs. They are up to 6mm (¼in) long. Only the young insects are mobile; once they have found a good feeding location they secrete a waxy shell that covers their bodies and glues them permanently in place. This makes it very difficult to treat them with insecticides, but the mobile stages are vulnerable to soft soap, fatty acids or plant oils. They also secrete sticky honeydew, which attracts sooty mould. This forms a black, soot-like deposit on the leaves and can be wiped off with a damp cloth.

Figs

Harvest ripe fruit

Figs are ready for harvesting when the skin is soft, sometimes split, and hanging limply from the branch.

CHERRIES ARE VULNERABLE *to silver leaf and bacterial canker infections, so to minimise the risk, prune in the summer months (top) when cuts heal quickly.*

PINCH OUT WAYWARD GROWTH *regularly on cherry trees trained as fans (above) and tie in well-placed shoots to keep the restricted shape.*

Occasionally a sugary liquid is secreted from the eye of the fig. In this condition, pick and eat raw straight away.

Select next year's fruit

It is important to understand how a fig tree produces fruit, as this affects how it is pruned. Figs grown in cool-temperate climates are usually borne in the tips of wood produced the previous season. Embryonic figs – about pea size – appear at this time of year in the growing tips of shoots. They should overwinter on the tree (although they may be damaged by harsh frosts and cold winters) and ripen into figs ready for harvesting this time next year. The tree will also be carrying larger, unripened figs that formed in spring. These won't ripen before the onset of winter and also won't overwinter successfully as they are too prone to cold damage, so remove them now.

Medlars

Leave fruits on the tree

The hard fruit of medlars should be left on the tree as long as possible; picked now, they will be very astringent. The flesh needs to break down and soften before they are palatable. Known as 'bletting', this occurs when the fruit is frosted, or has been stored for several weeks (see page 196).

Mulberries

Harvest ripe fruit

Mulberries flower mainly on older wood so trees can take four or five years to begin cropping. Ripe fruit will soon fall from the tree and can be a nuisance underfoot. Spread an old sheet on the ground below the tree and shake the branches; the fruit stains bright red so take care!

Peaches and nectarines

Prune fan-trained trees

After harvesting, prune out some of the older wood and shoots that fruited last year. Tie in some new growth from the current year as replacements, as these will be the branches that produce next year's crop. Remove shoots that are overcrowding the fan and any diseased wood.

Plums, damsons and gages

Harvest fruits when ripe

Pick the fruit carefully so as not to bruise them, then eat fresh, destone and freeze them, or make into preserves. Damsons and bullaces can also be steeped in alcohol to make a liquor similar to sloe gin.

Quinces

Leave fruit to ripen

Quinces need a long, hot summer to ripen well. They should not be harvested yet but left to hang on the tree as long as possible, picking them just before the first frosts.

General

Harvest currants and berries

Continue to pick fruit of black currants, red and white currants and gooseberries as it ripens. Blackberries and hybrid berries are best eaten fresh shortly after picking but also make good preserves. Blackberries are great for cooking, traditionally teamed with apples for desserts.

Blueberries

Pick fruits as they ripen

Pick blueberries, handling them gently so as not to spoil the greyish 'bloom' on the fruits' surface. Cover

THE SOFT FRUITS OF RIPE MULBERRIES *(top) can easily bruise and stain skin and clothing with their rich juice. Take care when harvesting.*

BLUEBERRIES *(above) are just bursting with goodness. It's so simple for gardeners to grow them at home and pick them fresh off the bush as they ripen. Do so with care to avoid spoiling their greyish bloom.*

the bushes tightly against birds, or there will be no crop left for you to pick.

Water plants

Continue to water blueberry plants, preferably with rainwater. Keep the soil moist at all times.

Cranberries and lingonberries

Keep soil moist

Continue to water cranberries and lingonberries with rainwater to keep the compost moist at all times. The fruit will normally start ripening shortly.

Raspberries

Tidy canes

Cut out fruited summer canes once they have finished cropping and tie in new canes to the supporting wires, thinning them to 10cm (4in) apart.

Pick autumn-fruiting varieties

Pick fruits as they ripen. Autumn-fruiting raspberries carry their fruit on the current season's canes, instead of last year's growth like summer-fruiting types. Varieties include 'Autumn Bliss', yellow 'Allgold' and 'Polka'.

Strawberries

Clean up beds

If you have not already done so, clear away straw and old foliage from fruited strawberry beds.

Order new plants

Order strawberry plants from specialist suppliers so they can be planted in the next few weeks. Strawberry plants deteriorate markedly after a few years. Aim to replace one third of your strawberry bed each year, that way you will always have a crop and your plants will be replaced before they become worn out.

Prepare beds for planting

Dig over the planting site, adding well-rotted organic matter, removing weeds and breaking the soil down to a reasonably fine tilth. Rake in a dressing of balanced fertiliser and tread over the site to firm the soil.

Plant rooted runners

If you have rooted strawberry runners, these can now be lifted and planted in their permanent positions. Runners that were pegged down into pots sunk into the soil will transplant more readily than those lifted from the open ground, as they suffer much less root disturbance.

CUT OUT ALL ONE-YEAR-OLD RASPBERRY CANES *using sharp secateurs after they have fruited. They are easy to recognise as they are brown at the base – the current year's canes are green.*

TIE IN THE NEW CANES OF SUMMER-FRUITING RASPBERRIES *to the sturdy wire supports as soon as the fruited canes have been pruned out, spacing them evenly or wrapping into bundles.*

Pick perpetual strawberries

Continue to pick fruits of perpetual or autumn-fruiting varieties as they ripen and remove damaged or mouldy fruit promptly. Perpetual strawberries can carry on cropping until mid or late autumn if conditions are right; cover the plants with cloches as the weather deteriorates. Good varieties include 'Flamenco', 'Tango' and 'Aromel'.

VINE FRUIT

Grapes

Harvest fruit as it ripens

Grapes are ready for picking when they feel soft to the touch and taste sugary. The skins on white grapes often change from deep green to a translucent yellow and they become much thinner. The best way for an amateur to tell when wine grapes are ripe is by tasting them – only when they are at their sweetest, containing maximum sugar, will they be ready. Cut them in bunches with each stalk still attached.

Protect fruit from wasps

Ripe grapes are very attractive to wasps. Use wasp traps (see page 174) or cover the vine with netting to keep them at bay. Netting also helps to stop birds getting at the fruit.

Melons

Support ripening fruit

Once greenhouse melons have reached grapefruit size, support them with nets so that their weight doesn't break the stem of the plant. Place outdoor fruits on blocks of wood to lift them off the soil.

Check fruit for ripeness

It is sometimes difficult to tell when a melon is ready for harvest. Many varieties start to crack and soften around the stalk when they are ripe, but the best test is usually smell. A ripe melon emits a strong, aromatic scent, which is particularly noticeable in a greenhouse.

Thin fruit

Reduce the crop on outdoor and greenhouse-grown melons to four fruits per plant.

SUPPORT MELON FRUIT IN A NET *made from recycled materials, such as an old sack, bag or tights, once it is grapefruit size (top), to stop it breaking the lateral branches.*

LATER VARIETIES OF MELON *(above) will be ripening now – they emit a strong scent, and start to crack and soften around the stalk when ready for harvesting. Remove the support net to check for ripeness.*

COBNUTS ARE READY TO HARVEST *just when the nuts and husks begin to turn yellow in late summer, but do not pick too early or the unripe nuts will shrivel in storage.*

PICK ALMONDS *and remove the outer husks, which crack open when the nuts are ready to harvest. Make sure you store them in a building that is free of rodents or you may end up with nothing.*

Remove mildewed leaves

Pick off leaves affected with powdery mildew as soon as they are noticed. Keep the plants moist at the roots, but avoid watering over the foliage.

NUTS

Almonds

Harvest ripe nuts

Almonds are ripe when the outer husks crack open. Pick the crop and remove the outer husks. Lay the nuts in a sunny, dry place for a few days, then store them in a rodent-proof shed until required.

Cobnuts and filberts

'Brut' trees

Break some new shoots in half and leave hanging on the tree to encourage flower buds to form in autumn. In winter, shorten these 'brutted' stems to 10–12cm (4–5in).

Harvest nuts

Pick cobnuts and filberts just as the nuts and husks begin to turn yellow in late summer. If left on the tree after that

they will often be stolen by squirrels, yet if picked too early the unripe nuts will shrivel in storage.

Once harvested, lay the nuts out on a rack in a sunny, dry spot for two weeks until the husks turn brown and papery. At this point, pick over the nuts and discard any that are showing signs of nut weevil attack (the grubs' round exit holes can be seen on the shells), or any other evidence of damage. Place the remaining nuts on slatted trays or in net bags and store them in a cool, dry, rodent-free building.

STRONG NEW SHOOTS OF COBNUTS AND FILBERTS *can be broken – but not detached – halfway along their length in late summer. Such 'brutting' encourages flowers and suppresses vigorous growth.*

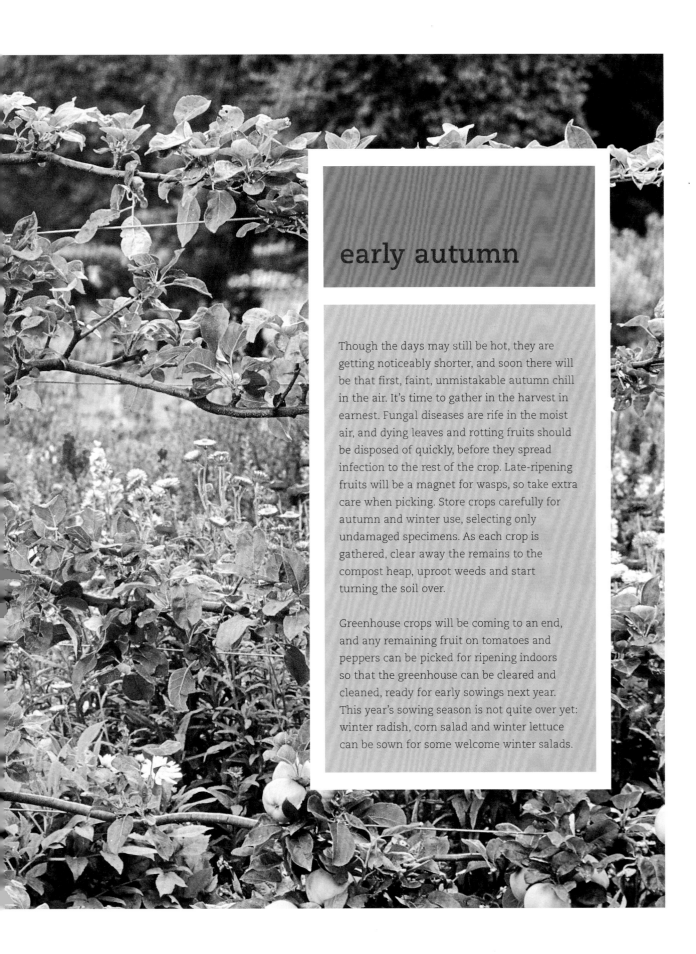

early autumn

Though the days may still be hot, they are getting noticeably shorter, and soon there will be that first, faint, unmistakable autumn chill in the air. It's time to gather in the harvest in earnest. Fungal diseases are rife in the moist air, and dying leaves and rotting fruits should be disposed of quickly, before they spread infection to the rest of the crop. Late-ripening fruits will be a magnet for wasps, so take extra care when picking. Store crops carefully for autumn and winter use, selecting only undamaged specimens. As each crop is gathered, clear away the remains to the compost heap, uproot weeds and start turning the soil over.

Greenhouse crops will be coming to an end, and any remaining fruit on tomatoes and peppers can be picked for ripening indoors so that the greenhouse can be cleared and cleaned, ready for early sowings next year. This year's sowing season is not quite over yet: winter radish, corn salad and winter lettuce can be sown for some welcome winter salads.

vegetables | WHAT TO DO NOW

ONION FAMILY

Garlic

Plant cloves

Because warmth is needed to ripen the bulbs, garlic must be grown in a sunny site, in rich soil that is moisture-retentive but with good drainage. Avoid planting on freshly manured ground, which could cause rotting.

Just before planting, thoroughly rake the top few centimetres of soil and incorporate a general fertiliser. Split garlic bulbs into individual cloves and plant each one with the pointed end uppermost, spacing them 10cm (4in) apart with 23–30cm (9–12in) between the rows. The tips of the cloves should be hidden just below the surface.

Leeks

Harvest leeks as required

Continue to harvest leeks as required, as soon as they are large enough. Since these are hardy vegetables that are available throughout the harshest winter weather, most gardeners leave their leeks to be enjoyed during the winter months rather than eating them now, when there are plenty of alternative crops on offer.

Onions and shallots

Plant onion sets and shallots

Autumn-planted onion sets will give an early crop next year, but are not suitable for soils that are prone to waterlogging in winter. Choose a suitable hardy variety: 'Senshyu', 'Shakespeare', 'Electric', 'Radar' and 'Silvermoon' can all be planted now.

Prepare the soil thoroughly and rake in a dressing of general fertiliser. Plant in rows 30cm (12in) apart, spacing the sets 5–8cm (2–3in) apart in the row. Make a shallow drill, deep enough for the tips of the sets to show just above the soil, and push the sets lightly into the base of

the drill before drawing the soil back around them with a trowel and firming them in. If the weather is very dry, water the sets after planting.

Plant shallots in the same way as onions, but spacing them 10–15cm (4–6in) apart in the row. 'Escalote Grise' and 'Jermor' are good varieties for autumn planting.

BIRD PROBLEMS

Blackbirds as well as other garden birds can sometimes pull newly planted onion and shallot sets out of the soil after planting. Taking off the loose, papery skin at the top of the set can help to prevent this, as the birds grab hold of this skin to tug at the bulbs. Check the beds shortly after planting and replant and refirm any sets that have been pulled up. If the problem persists, cover the newly planted bed with fleece or netting while the roots get established.

LEEKS ARE SIMPLE TO HARVEST: *using a garden fork, just lift them as required when the stems are sufficiently thick. Then rub off the surplus soil and trim the leaves and roots.*

CABBAGE FAMILY

Broccoli and calabrese

Harvest regularly

All types of broccoli should be picked when the flower shoots are well developed, but before the flowers actually open. Slice the florets from the plant using a sharp knife, cutting the central spear first. Picking regularly and early will encourage sideshoot formation for further harvests.

Calabrese is available to harvest until mid autumn, depending on the variety. Most sprouting broccoli varieties such as 'Early Purple Sprouting' are not ready until late winter or early spring, but one or two varieties such as 'Summer Purple' and 'Extra Early Rudolph' may be producing spears now.

Cabbages

Transplant spring cabbages

Continue to transplant spring cabbages to their final positions. Firm the young plants in well, especially on light soils, treading round the plant stem with boots.

Harvest autumn cabbage

Cut autumn cabbages as required. Protect the crop from pigeons where necessary.

Prepare for winter

Some cabbages – red, white and some green varieties – are prone to winter damage. These should be harvested and stored before the first frosts. Remove some of the outer leaves, and store the heads in straw-lined boxes in a cool, dry place, where they will last until early spring.

To provide additional protection from wind and frost for the cabbages left in the ground, pile up soil around the base of each plant before the first heavy frosts. Such 'earthing up' protects the plant stem.

Cauliflowers

Harvest as required

The autumn varieties that were sown in summer are ready to harvest between now and late autumn. They range from large-headed varieties to the more compact Australian-bred types.

BROCCOLI HEADS *(top) are ready to cut when the buds are well developed but before the flowers actually open. Regular picking of heads encourages more cropping.*

HARVEST CAULIFLOWER *(above) while the heads are still firm and small, and before the curds have started to separate, to ensure that the crop lasts for a longer period.*

BEANS AND PEAS

Broad beans

Prepare for autumn sowing

In sheltered districts with well-drained soil, it is worth trying an autumn sowing of broad beans for an early crop the following year. Prepare the ground now, clearing debris and weeds from the site, digging the soil thoroughly and then raking it to a fine tilth. Cover the cultivated area with cloches or plastic sheeting to protect the soil from excess rain and to keep it in good condition for seed sowing.

Wait until next month before actually sowing the broad bean seeds. For an overwintered crop you need to choose a hardy variety, such as 'Aquadulce Claudia' or 'The Sutton', so check your supplies of them now.

Runner beans

Continue picking
Most runner beans will still be producing a crop, though beans from the earlier sowings are likely to gradually become coarse. If a late sowing of runner beans was made in midsummer, these will provide a welcome picking of fresh, young, tender beans in autumn, until the arrival of the first frosts.

Clear spent crops
Once the runner bean crop is finished, clear away the plants. Consign the above-ground growth to the compost heap, and remove, clean and store the cane supports.

Peas

Prepare for sowing hardy varieties
Like broad beans, peas can be sown soon in sheltered gardens and in free-draining soil in order to obtain an early crop. Choose a hardy variety such as 'Feltham First', 'Kelvedon Wonder', 'Avola' or 'Meteor'. Most peas for autumn sowing are round-seeded. These are not as sweet as wrinkled-seeded varieties, but wrinkled seeds are more prone to rotting in the cool weather of autumn, because the wrinkles hold on to soil moisture.

Prepare the soil for peas in exactly the same way as for broad beans (see page 185).

PERENNIAL VEGETABLES

Asparagus

Cut back yellowed ferns
As soon as the foliage of asparagus turns yellow, it should be cut back to ground level. Depending on the weather it may still be green for some weeks, in which case it should be left to allow it to build up the plants for next year.

Globe artichokes

Cut down stems
Once the foliage of globe artichokes has turned yellow, cut the stems down to ground level. Before the first frosts, cover the crowns with some insulating material such as chipped bark, straw or dry leaves.

SAVE YOUR OWN RUNNER BEAN SEED

At the end of the season, allow some pods to remain on the plants to ripen their seeds. Leave the pods on the plants for as long as possible, until they become dry and crisp. The seeds can then be shelled out; reject any damaged, very small or non-typical seed and store the rest in a cool, dry place for sowing next spring. You can store them in a paper bag, or in a lidded jar with a silica sachet to absorb any moisture. If your bean variety was an F1 hybrid, the beans grown from the seed will not be true to type; open-pollinated varieties may also have cross-pollinated with nearby varieties to produce variations.

ROOTS AND STEMS

Beetroot

Lift roots for storing
In light, free-draining soils, beetroot can be left in the ground over winter, but many gardeners find it more convenient to lift the roots over the next few weeks and store them. Prise the roots up carefully with a fork and gently knock off surplus soil. Inspect the roots for damage and select only sound ones for storage. Twist off the leaves several centimetres from the top of the root, wearing rubber gloves to avoid staining your hands. Then carefully place the roots, not touching each other, in boxes of dry sand or coir compost. Store in a cool shed or garage. Damaged roots should be used up straight away.

HARVEST BEETROOT *when the roots reach tennis-ball size for the best flavour. If they are allowed to grow any larger, they may develop an unpleasant, woody texture.*

Celeriac

Earth up plants

Draw soil around the swollen stem-bases of celeriac to keep the flesh white.

Potatoes

Continue lifting maincrops

Carefully dig up maincrop potatoes for storage in dry spells. The tubers will continue to increase in size all the time the weather is good, so you will get a heavier crop by leaving them in the ground as long as possible. However, the longer they stay in the soil, the more liable they are to become diseased or damaged by slugs and other pests.

Swedes

Harvest roots

Swede roots can be harvested as soon as they are large enough to use. This may be as early as late summer, but since the plants take quite a long season to mature – up

LIFT POTATOES (top) *as soon as they are ready if your garden suffers badly from slugs. Store only undamaged potatoes with any loose soil removed, and check them regularly for signs of rot.*

TURNIPS CAN BE STORED (above) *in a cool, frost-free cellar or garage. They will last longer when stored if they are placed in a shallow box and covered with moist peat, coir compost or sand.*

to seven or eight months – the majority of roots are ready for use only over the autumn and winter periods. Much depends on growing conditions, the variety grown and the time of sowing.

Harvest the roots as required, carefully pulling or lifting them from the soil. Unless you have very light soil, a fork will probably be necessary.

Swedes can be left in the ground for pulling as they are needed throughout the winter, but if you lift a few roots and store them in wooden boxes of moist peat, coir compost or sand you will have some available for use when the ground is frozen solid and cannot be dug.

Some varieties can become woody if left in the ground beyond early winter, and should be lifted for storage before then. Before you buy the seed it's a good idea to check when the optimum harvest time is.

Turnips

Store lifted roots

Lift turnips throughout autumn for storage. Brush away wet soil; place the roots in a shallow wooden box and cover with moist peat, coir compost or sand, like swedes. Store in a cool, frost-free place. Use up damaged roots straight away, as they will not store well.

SALADS

Chicory

Harvest plants

Chicory and endive are ready for cutting now. Continue to blanch plants to remove excessive bitterness. When forced, the deep roots of witloof chicory produce chicons.

To force plants outdoors without having to dig up the roots, cut off the leafy head to leave a 5cm (2in) stub. Use a hoe to draw soil over these stubs, and within a few weeks chicons will form under the soil, particularly if a cloche is used to provide extra warmth.

Better results are often achieved by forcing indoors, where plants are lifted and planted in a box of moist peat or peat substitute, with the leaves trimmed to 1cm (½in) from the roots. Cover the roots with 23cm (9in) more peat and put the box in a warm, dark place. Modern witloof varieties may need darkness only to form chicons.

Cucumbers

Continue picking

As in summer, harvest cucumbers as they are ready, under glass and outdoors. In the greenhouse, take care with ventilation as the weather starts to cool down. Although the weather in early autumn can still be hot, the days are shortening and the nights becoming cooler. Cool, damp conditions favour the spread of some fungal diseases, so pick off dead or dying plant tissue promptly and remove it from the greenhouse.

Lettuces

Harvest heads as soon as they are ready

Keep cutting lettuces and picking leaves from cut-and-come-again crops. Remove damaged or dying outside leaves from plants as soon as they are seen, in order to prevent the rest of the plant succumbing to fungal diseases. Remove and compost plants that bolt, or start to go to seed. They are not worth eating as the leaves become very bitter once flowering has initiated.

Sow varieties for overwintering

In mild areas, hardy varieties of lettuce are worth trying outside in a sheltered spot. Suitable varieties for overwintering include 'Winter Density', 'May King', 'Rouge d'Hiver' and 'Valdor'. Prepare the soil thoroughly and rake it to a fine tilth before sowing. Sow in drills spaced 30cm (12in) apart. Thin the seedlings in stages to leave them 15–20cm (6–8in) apart. Cloches or fleece will help the plants to come through the winter well, and give an even earlier crop. Depending on conditions, lettuces should be ready for cutting from early spring onwards.

Sow greenhouse crops

Sow suitable lettuce varieties in modules or pots for transplanting into the greenhouse border once the summer crops have been cleared. In a frost-free greenhouse these will produce a welcome winter crop when salads are very scarce; they will not heart up but the leaves are crisp and tasty. 'Kweik', 'Kloek' and 'Dandie' are good varieties for winter forcing.

In an unheated greenhouse or cold frame, lettuce varieties suitable for overwintering outside can be grown. Even without the assistance of artificial heat, they will be earlier than the outdoor crops.

SPICY GREENS *(top) have an especially fine flavour when you grow them yourself and they are eaten within hours of harvesting. They are available in a range of colours, leaf types and tastes.*

CUT-AND-COME-AGAIN LETTUCE *(above) offers delicious leaves over a period of months and constantly picking leaves, rather than lifting the whole plant, keeps them immature and tender.*

Radishes

Continue sowing

Although it is early autumn you can continue to sow summer radishes. Also make a sowing of a winter radish variety for use later in autumn and through the winter.

Tomatoes

Pick remaining fruits

Outdoor tomatoes will soon be finished. Use your judgement to decide when it is time to consign the haulms to the compost bin; a lot depends on the weather conditions. At the end of the season, both outdoor and unheated greenhouse plants are likely to be left with lots of green fruit. This can be left on the plant for as long as the weather is good enough; otherwise it can be picked and ripened indoors on a sunny windowsill, or in a drawer along with a couple of ripe apples or bananas. These give off the gas ethylene, which is responsible for starting off the ripening process.

Once you have disposed of outdoor tomato plants, remove, clean and store their cane supports.

PICK TOMATOES (top) when fully ripe and evenly coloured, but don't leave them too long or the skins will split. You can ripen green fruit on a windowsill or in a drawer alongside apples or bananas.

GROWING MARIGOLDS (above) with tomatoes is thought by some to repel pests such as whitefly and aphids. The strong scent of the marigold plants is said to be disliked by the pests and may keep them away.

SPINACH AND CHARD

General

Sow winter varieties
Sow in drills 30cm (12in) apart and thin the seedlings to 23cm (9in) apart in the row.

SQUASHES, MARROWS, PUMPKINS AND SWEETCORN

Courgettes, marrows and summer squashes

Continue picking crops
Keep picking until either the plants are exhausted and cease to crop, or the first frosts kill them off. Mildew is common late in the season; badly mildewed plants are not worth saving and should be dug up.

COURGETTE FLOWERS are quite delicious and need to be picked just as they are starting to open. Take them straight to the kitchen. They can be stuffed and fried in batter.

PUMPKINS FOR STORING *need special treatment: leave them on the plants for as long as possible, ideally in a polytunnel or greenhouse. They should have a firm, hard skin, and they should sound hollow when tapped. Leave them to cure in a protected environment for a week or two.*

Winter squashes and pumpkins

Start harvesting

Fruit for immediate use in the kitchen can be cut off the plant as required, but if it's to store well over winter it must be fully ripened and cured. After cutting those to be stored for winter, they should be 'cured' by leaving them in a warm, sunny place for a week or two; a greenhouse or sunroom is idea. After curing, store them in a cooler, dry, frost-free place. Depending on the variety, fruit that has been fully cured should last for up to six months.

TENDER VEGETABLES

Aubergines

Encourage fruit ripening

Remove any fruit that forms after late summer, because it's unlikely to mature. This will channel the plant's energy into ripening the larger fruit. Cover plants, even those under cover, with a double layer of horticultural fleece on autumn nights; this will also help with ripening.

Harvest the fruit as soon as it reaches full size and develops its particular skin colour (see right).

Okra

Continue harvesting

Continue to pick okra pods as soon as they reach a suitable size, before they become stringy. Once the plants have finished cropping, pull them up and put them on the compost heap.

Peppers and chillies

Ripen and harvest fruit

Cover outdoor plants with fleece to help them ripen their remaining fruits at the end of the season. Chilli plants can also be uprooted and hung upside down in a greenhouse or dry shed.

| Grow your own herbs

No garden is complete without herbs. They add flavour to so many dishes, and their wonderful fragrances can be appreciated when you brush past their foliage, or squeeze their leaves between your fingers in passing. Most herbs are very easy to grow, and are undemanding – in fact, many herbs have better flavours and more powerful aromas when they are growing in poor soil conditions. Moist, fertile soils promote lots of lush, leafy growth, but this has lower concentrations of the oils that give herbs their flavour than growth produced in leaner conditions.

The majority of culinary herbs come from Mediterranean regions, and like a warm, open, free-draining position in full sun.

MANY HERBS (above) are not only a source of nourishment but also provide decorative interest in the garden for much of the year.

HERB POTS (right) can be stuffed full of your favourite herbs and then positioned in a handy spot for quick and convenient harvesting.

Recommended herbs

Basil
Basil needs a sheltered, sunny spot. Sow seed under cover in mid spring and set plants outside only after all risk of frost is over. All varieties of basil are treated as annuals.

Marjoram
Pot marjoram (or oregano) is a perennial, while the closely related sweet marjoram is grown as an annual. Both like an open, sunny site. Sow sweet marjoram under cover and plant out in late spring.

Sage
Sage has a characteristic strong aroma, and its spikes of blue flowers are popular with bees. Grow in an open position in free-draining soil and replace plants when they become leggy. Perennial shrub.

Chives
These have a mild onion flavour and attractive flowerheads of papery purple blooms, which are also edible. Sow seed in mid spring, or divide clumps in early autumn. Perennial.

Parsley
Sow the slow-germinating seed under cover in early spring and plant out in mid to late spring. Plants left to overwinter will quickly run to flower in their second year. Biennial.

Thyme
Creeping or low-growing bushy perennial with flowers that are alive with bees in summer. Thyme likes well-drained soil and a sunny spot; propagate by cuttings or division.

Fennel
The seeds can be used as well as the leaves. Fennel prefers moist, fertile soil. Sow seeds *in situ*. Perennial.

Rosemary
This evergreen shrub likes a warm, sheltered site. Is usually propagated by cuttings; can be raised from seed.

Coriander
An annual with pungent leaves and seeds. Sow seeds *in situ* and keep plants moist. Will stand light shade.

fruit | GENERAL ADVICE

Prepare for fruit storage | Ready your fruit store for fruit crops to be kept through the autumn.

Deal with wasps | Hang wasp traps round trees with ripening fruit. Wasps tend to become more of a nuisance as the season progresses, until the first frosts.

Control disease | Remove rotting and damaged fruits promptly to prevent the spread of disease.

Order new stock | Research and purchase new, certified nuts, fruit trees, canes and bushes.

ESPALIERED APPLE TREES *are not only productive but they also look decorative, especially when grown against a wall with bricks that complement the colour of the fruit.*

fruit | WHAT TO DO NOW

TREE FRUIT

Apples and pears

Harvest fruit

Pick apples and pears as they ripen, and before autumn gales bring them down as windfalls. Handle the fruit carefully, cupping it in your palm rather than grasping it, and lift it off the tree with the stalk intact. If the stalk remains on the tree, the fruit isn't ready for picking. Never pull at the fruit, because this can break the fruiting spurs. Some varieties need eating within one or two days of picking, while some of the later fruits can last for months and so are suitable for long-term storage.

APPLES ARE READY FOR PICKING *when there are a few windfalls lying beneath the tree. The fruit should have swelled up to a good size and have started to colour up. The pips should be brown.*

STORING FRUIT

Fruit such as apples, pears and quinces store best in a well-ventilated, airy place that has an even temperature, preferably 3–7°C (37–45°F), but certainly frost-free. A shed or garage is often ideal. Only store perfectly sound fruit.

There are two main methods of storage. The traditional one is to wrap individual fruits in tissue paper, newspaper or waxed paper, and place them in a single layer in a shallow tray. Trays can be stacked on top of one another if there is a gap between them to allow air to circulate.

A more modern method is to place around half-a-dozen apples in a polythene bag, seal the end with a twist-tie, and make several holes in the bag with the tip of a ballpoint pen, allowing one hole for every 500g (1lb) of fruit approximately. This method prevents the fruit shrivelling but fruits may rot more easily.

All stored fruit needs to be checked regularly and any showing signs of rot must be removed at once.

Pears are frequently stored unwrapped because they need to be carefully examined frequently to ensure they are eaten as soon as they are perfectly ripe; they quickly go past their optimum condition.

Citrus

Move trees under cover

Citrus plants that have been spending the summer out of doors should be moved back under cover well before the first frosts. Established plants will usually survive a slight frost, but they need temperatures above 13°C (55°F) to ripen their fruits. These fruits take almost a year to ripen.

Medlars

Harvest and store fruits

Pick medlars as late as possible but before the first frosts. The fruits are hard and extremely astringent when they are picked, which should be as late as possible but before the first frosts. To make them palatable, the fruits should be stored before being eaten.

To store medlars, lay fruits that are unblemished in a wooden or cardboard box and place this in a dark, cool but frost-free shed or garage for a few weeks. The fruits will gradually turn from light to dark brown and their texture will become much softer. This process is known as 'bletting'. Medlars can then be eaten raw; they are often also used to make a perfumed, amber jelly for game and other meats.

Peaches and nectarines

Pick indoor fruits

The season for outdoor peaches is over or coming to an end now, but those being grown under glass are still ripening their fruits. Late-ripening varieties include the peach 'Bellegarde' as well as 'Elruge', 'Madame Blanchete' and 'Pineapple' (all nectarines).

The fruit is suitable for harvesting when it has fully coloured and the flesh near the stalk feels soft. Handle the fruit very carefully when picking. Cup it in the palm of your hand and lift it to see whether it separates easily from the tree. The tree will require regular visits for picking as the fruit will not ripen all at once.

Plums, damsons and gages

Harvest fruit

Continue to pick fruits as they ripen. Some varieties of plum ripen much earlier, in summer, but there are others that are not ready until early autumn. 'Cambridge Gage',

MEDLARS (top) *are closely related to apples, but their distinctive fruits can't be eaten until they have been stored for many weeks while their texture softens and their skin matures to dark brown.*

LATE-RIPENING NECTARINE 'PINEAPPLE' (above) *should be ready for picking by now. Its skin should have turned red and its flesh golden-yellow. It is best eaten directly after being picked from the tree.*

'Edwards' and 'Marjorie's Seedling' are all late varieties that carry on the season after the early plums are over. Damsons are also usually not ready until now.

Finish pruning

This is the last chance to prune trees; they should never be pruned in the dormant season because this will make them more prone to bacterial canker and silver leaf infection. Remove congested growth as well as dead, diseased or damaged stems.

QUINCES *are a delicious and useful fruit. Their aromatic flavour is excellent when cooked with stewed apples, and their high levels of pectin make them indispensable for the setting of jams and fruit jellies.*

FORAGING FOR BLACKBERRIES *is one of the great pleasures of early autumn. It is a wonderful activity that shouldn't be rushed, especially as you will want to sample the produce fresh off the canes.*

Quinces

Harvest fruits before the frost

Although quinces ripen well in hot, sunny summers they are very unlikely to produce fruits that are edible straight off the tree. Leave the fruits to hang on the tree as long as possible, but harvest them before the first frosts. Cook the quinces before consuming them.

One of the quince's assets is that the fruits can be stored up until mid or late winter before they will spoil, so their season of use is much extended. Leave them on slatted trays or in cardboards boxes in a cool, dark but frost-free location.

Quinces are strongly aromatic and if stored near other produce their perfume may taint it. If you do not want this, store them in a separate place.

SOFT FRUIT

Blackberries and hybrid berries

Continue harvesting fruit

Carry on picking fruit as it ripens. Blackberries can be picked up until the first frosts, but hybrid berries such as loganberries and tayberries usually finish cropping

earlier. The fruit is more prone to developing moulds in damp, cool weather, so remove diseased fruit on sight.

Eat the good-quality fruit fresh; alternatively cook it, freeze it or make it into jams or jellies.

Prune after harvest

Once all the fruit has been picked, remove the one-year-old canes of black- and hybrid berries. Do this by cutting these fruited canes in sections so as not to damage the new growth. Tie in the new canes, or bundle them together over winter.

Black, red and white currants

Prepare for planting

Prepare the site now so it is ready for planting new bushes in late autumn. Dig the soil over well, adding plenty of well-rotted organic matter.

Prune black currants

Cut out about one third of the older stems, removing them right down to ground level. Also remove any weak, damaged or diseased shoots. The aim is to encourage strong new growths that will bear fruit in future years. Pruning can be carried out from now until late winter.

Blueberries

Continue harvesting

Blueberries may still be producing ripe fruits, provided they are protected from birds. Keep the plants well watered, and when the soil is thoroughly moist apply a mulch over the roots. Chipped bark or leafmould are suitable mulches for these acid-loving plants; do not use mushroom compost as it contains lime.

Cranberries and lingonberries

Harvest fruits

Cranberries and lingonberries take longer to mature than blueberries. Their first fruits should be ripening now, and you can continue picking until mid autumn. The fruit stores well in a polythene bag in the bottom of the refrigerator, but make sure the fruit is dry and that all damaged fruit is removed.

CRANBERRIES *make good subjects for containers where garden soil doesn't have a sufficiently low pH or where it is not boggy enough to satisfy their cultivation needs.*

Raspberries

Pick autumn-fruiting varieties

Harvest autumn raspberries from now until the first frosts. In colder areas it is worth covering the plants with fleece to extend the cropping season.

Strawberries

Plan for an early indoor harvest

Plant healthy strawberry plants – and runners that were rooted in early summer (see page 129) – in 13cm (5in) pots and bury the pots almost to their rims in soil in a sheltered place. Keep the plants well watered. This is the best time of year to plant strawberries.

These containerised strawberries will need to be moved into a greenhouse in late winter for an early crop. In an unheated greenhouse, you should be picking the first fruits 10–14 days before outside crops are ready. In a heated greenhouse or conservatory, it is possible to bring forward their cropping by several weeks, so long as the temperature does not go above 16°C (61°F), because this will inhibit flowering.

Strawberry plants can also successfully be grown under a tunnel cloche to produce a crop 7–10 days earlier than outside. The plants will need to be covered with cloches or fleece in early spring.

LINGONBERRIES *bear clusters of spherical, red berries. They naturally occur in very boggy, acidic sites but, with care, the gardener can replicate such an environment at home.*

Plant new outdoor beds

Strawberries are so versatile they can be widely planted outside the fruit garden – in the vegetable garden or among ornamental plants – provided they have sun, shelter and fertile, well-drained soil. Avoid areas prone to frost (because strawberries are low growing) as well as windy sites (which will prevent pollinating insects from reaching the flowers). Also avoid sites that have previously grown potatoes, chrysanthemums or tomatoes because they are all prone to the disease verticillium wilt. In poor soils grow in raised beds, which improves drainage.

Dig the planting site to a depth of one spade blade. Remove perennial weeds, then add well-rotted manure. Level the soil and rake it to a fine tilth.

Dig out a hole large enough to accommodate the strawberry plant. Trim the roots lightly to 10cm (4in) if necessary, then spread them out in the hole. Ensure that the base of the crown rests lightly on the surface. Planting at the correct depth is important: if the crown is planted too deeply it will rot; if it is planted too shallowly the plants will dry out and die. Once the plant is at the correct depth, backfill the soil, keeping it off the crown and firming it around the plant using finger tips. Set plants 35cm (14in) apart. If planting another row, place it 75cm (30in) away – closer if in a raised bed. Water the plants well. To exclude weeds, a fibre mat can be placed around each plant, or you can plant through black plastic.

Pick perpetual strawberries

Continue harvesting late varieties as the fruits ripen. They become more prone to rotting as the season progresses, so pick the strawberry beds over frequently and remove all affected fruits.

VINE FRUIT

Grapes

Protect fruit from wasps

Continue to protect the ripening fruit from wasps by using wasp traps or by covering the vines.

Harvest bunches when ripe

Pick bunches of grapes only when they are fully ripe, so that they achieve maximum sweetness.

Kiwifruit

Harvest fruits

Pick kiwifruit just as they start to soften. Hard fruits can be allowed to ripen in the home; storing them with ripe fruit like apples and bananas will encourage ripening.

Melons

Protect plants from cold weather

Late varieties of melon may need protecting with fleece during the first cool nights of autumn, while they finish ripening during the warmer daytime.

NUTS

General

Continue to harvest almonds, cobnuts and filberts and store them in a dry, cool, rodent-free shed or garage.

Almonds

Prune where necessary

On established almonds remove any dead, diseased or badly placed branches immediately after harvest.

PRUNE ALMONDS *now, in order to avoid potential infection by silver leaf fungus and bacterial canker – this will be your last chance until next spring. Established almonds usually need minimal pruning.*

| Grow your own unusual fruits

There are numerous plants that are a source for edible but unusual fruits. Some are quite exotic but others can be found growing wild in hedgerows. (Make sure you have identified wild fruits properly before you eat them.)

If you are short of room in your garden, it is an excellent idea to plant hedges that will provide you with the bonus of edible fruits – for example, roses for hips, or sloes and elder for their berries. Plants such as sea buckthorn and passion flower also play a dual role, being highly ornamental as well as productive. Even if you have plenty of room for a conventional fruit garden, the addition of these crops will provide a more diverse and interesting harvest.

THE PASSION FRUIT *(above) grown as an edible fruit is Passiflora edulis. It requires a minimum temperature of 16°C (61°F).*

ELDER BLOSSOM *(right) can easily be confused with similar flowers on other hedgerow plants so check its identity accurately before picking.*

Recommended unusual fruits

Cape gooseberry

Tender perennial with a bitter-sweet flavour. Grow from seed in a polytunnel or greenhouse for harvest in late summer and early autumn.

Elderberry

Pick the creamy flowerheads of this hedgerow plant to create elderflower fritters, champagne and cordial. Harvest the fruits in late summer, to make preserves and wine.

Goji berry, wolfberry

This hardy, deciduous shrub, with self-fertile flowers, can be grown in a wide range of soils in a sunny site.

Huckleberry

This tender annual is easily raised from seed, but always purchase from a reputable source because the plant looks very similar (and is related) to the poisonous deadly nightshade. Harvest the fruits from late summer.

Passion fruit

An attractive perennial climber for a greenhouse or a warm, sunny spot. Harvest the egg-shaped, purple fruits when they begin to shrivel on the plant, from late summer onwards.

Rosehips

The best roses to grow for their hips are *Rosa rugosa* and *R. canina*. Harvest the hips in autumn before the frosts.

Sea buckthorn

A large, thorny shrub tolerant of salt-laden winds. Both male and female plants are needed to obtain the fruits which are high in vitamin C and antioxidants. They can be cooked and used as a flavouring with other fruits.

Sloes

A large, thorny, wild hedgerow shrub bearing round, very astringent fruits. Pick them in autumn, add gin and some sugar to taste and allow to steep for delicious sloe gin.

Saskatoon berry, June berry

The berries of this medium shrub or small tree have a mild, sweet flavour. Netting against birds is essential.

mid autumn

It's time to start winter digging, a job that's best done little by little to protect your back muscles. The earlier soil can be turned over, and left exposed to autumn and winter frosts, the better, but it is unwise to wear yourself out by digging the whole plot in one go.

The harvest of winter vegetables now starts to replace the summer crops, with stout leeks, fat winter cabbages and chunky roots ready to be gathered. There are still apples, pears, medlars and quinces to be picked and stored away; remember to keep an eye on all your stored produce, looking out for rotting or mice-nibbled specimens and removing them quickly.

All tender plants should be protected or moved back under cover before the first frosts strike, which is usually before the end of mid autumn. The weather is unpredictable at this time of year – you may have a glorious Indian summer or you may have gloom, chill and rain. Best be prepared for anything.

vegetables | GENERAL ADVICE

Clear up the vegetable garden | Remove spent stems and debris to avoid harbouring pests and diseases, and to expose slugs and other pests to the birds and the changeable weather conditions of autumn.

Sow green manures | There is still time to sow green manures, including Italian ryegrass, grazing rye and vetches. These establish in autumn, survive the winter and are ready for digging in early next spring.

Start winter digging | The earlier you can start digging the better, as this gives the soil plenty of time to be broken down by winter frosts to a good crumbly texture for spring sowings. As digging is strenuous work, it is also a good idea to undertake it in small batches, especially if you are not used to heavy exercise. Dig vacant soil over as soon as crops are cleared. Incorporate well-rotted bulky organic matter such as farmyard manure or garden compost if you can – but not where you intend to grow root vegetables next year as it causes misshapen, forked roots.

EVEN IN AUTUMN, *the kitchen garden can still remain an attractive feature, with late-flowering marigolds, ornamental planters and rhubarb pots, and late fruit.*

vegetables | WHAT TO DO NOW

Garlic

Plant garlic cloves

Garlic can be planted from now to late winter, but the best yields are obtained if planting is completed before Christmas. On heavy ground that could become waterlogged, plant on a raised ridge or start off cloves in a frame or greenhouse for planting outside in late winter.

PLANT EACH GARLIC CLOVE *(top) in the ground with its pointed tip uppermost and about 2.5cm (1in) below the surface. Plant the cloves in a greenhouse if you have soil that may become waterlogged over winter.*

DIG UP LEEKS AS REQUIRED *(above), trying to avoid scattering soil over the remaining plants. Leeks are difficult to clean, and the cleaner they are in the garden, the simpler their preparation will be in the kitchen.*

Leeks

Harvest as required

Lift leeks as they are needed, prising the roots up gently with a garden fork.

Onions and shallots

Check stored crops

Look at onions and shallots in store often and remove any rotting bulbs before they have a chance to infect the rest.

Finish planting onion sets

There is still just time to plant autumn onion sets for an early crop next summer.

General

When preparing the soil for any cabbage family crop, dig the ground over deeply, incorporating plenty of well-rotted organic matter. Digging in autumn gives the soil time to consolidate over winter. Check the soil pH; the ideal range for brassicas is 6–7.5. If the pH is too low, you may need to apply lime, which will help to deter club root.

Practise crop rotation (see also page 262)

Plant cabbage family crops on different ground each year; avoid the same piece of ground within two years. This minimises the build-up of soil-borne diseases and prevents the soil there becoming starved of nutrients.

Broccoli and calabrese

Sow calabrese

Sow seeds in modules in the greenhouse. Transplant the seedlings to a cold frame in early winter for a crop in spring, when fresh vegetables are in short supply.

BRUSSELS SPROUTS *should be harvested when they are about the size of a walnut. Snap them off or remove with a sharp knife and pick only firm sprouts. Start from the bottom and work upwards.*

KALE LEAVES *will be ready to harvest from mid autumn to mid spring. Remove them when the foliage is still young and tender and this will encourage more sideshoots to develop.*

Brussels sprouts

Stake where necessary

On exposed sites or in windy weather, this top-heavy crop may be blown over. If in doubt, support plants with a 5 x 2.5cm (2 x 1in) stake to keep them upright. Tread round the bases of the plants to ensure they are firm, in case any have been loosened in the soil by wind rock.

Harvest from the base up

Depending on the variety, Brussels sprouts may be ready to pick now. Start harvesting at the base of the stalk, where the sprouts are largest, and work your way up.

Leave tops in place

Sprout tops make a good leafy vegetable, but they should be left on the plants over winter, to provide some protection for the sprouts.

Cabbages

Continue harvesting

Keep on cutting heads as required. To produce sound, large heads of crispy leaves, cabbages need a sunny site and firm soil. If your results are disappointing, make sure you choose a better site next year.

Protect spring cabbages

Place netting over the plants if pigeons are a problem. In cold weather they can decimate crops.

Cauliflower

Sow summer varieties in a cold frame

Sow seeds in pots and keep the young plants growing on steadily in the cold frame until they are ready for hardening off for planting out in early spring. Many modern varieties are extremely hardy and will withstand severe winter weather, so are ideal in very cold districts.

Cauliflowers require a sunny site with deep, firm, moisture-retentive soil. Prepare the site where they are to be planted now, by digging in plenty of well-rotted organic matter such as farmyard manure or garden compost to improve the soil's moisture-holding capacity, so that the soil has plenty of time to settle and consolidate over winter. Early digging also avoids poorly formed curds.

Protect curds

Cold weather may cause browning of the curds and leaves, although this can also be caused by boron deficiency. To prevent the curds being discoloured by a severe frost followed by a rapid thaw, or by direct sunlight, bend one of the uppermost leaves over the developing curd to protect it.

Colourful cauliflowers

If you fancy a change from pure white cauliflowers, 'Purple Graffiti' and 'Sunset' are two varieties to look out for. As its name implies, 'Purple Graffiti' has rich purple heads, while 'Sunset' has curds of a warm salmon pink. They will be particularly popular with children.

Kale

Start harvesting

Kale can be harvested from now on. This is one of the hardiest of winter vegetables, and leaves will be available right through the winter, even in the harshest weather.

BEANS AND PEAS

General

Sow hardy peas and broad beans

Hardy pea and broad bean cultivars can be sown in the ground in sheltered districts with well-drained soil. Protect sowings with cloches if there is a particularly cold spell during the winter.

Clear spent crops

Tidy away the haulms of all pea and bean plants once the crop has finished. Leaving the top growth in place encourages the growth of weeds and provides hiding places for slugs and other pests. Put the top growth on the compost heap; dig the roots into the soil as they will help enrich it with nitrogen.

PERENNIAL VEGETABLES

Asparagus

Cut down ferns

Cut asparagus foliage down to the base as soon as it turns completely yellow. Remove weeds, preferably by hand; hoeing can be difficult because the plants are shallow-rooted, and the roots are easily damaged. Once all the weeds have been cleared, apply a layer of mulch to help prevent any more weeds from appearing.

Prepare new beds

If you intend to plant asparagus next spring, start preparing the bed now. This is a long-lived crop, so make sure you do the job properly. Dig the soil deeply, adding plenty of well-rotted organic matter. If the drainage needs improving, dig in some grit; asparagus will not thrive in waterlogged soil. On heavy, clay soils, asparagus will do better in a raised bed.

ASPARAGUS FOLIAGE *(top) turns completely yellow in autumn – when this happens, cut it down to the base. By then it will have done its essential job of building up the plant's food reserves for future crops.*

INCORPORATE PLENTY OF ORGANIC MATTER *(above) when digging a new asparagus bed, to improve the soil structure. The fleshy crowns of asparagus hate a waterlogged site, so ensure the soil is well drained.*

Globe artichokes

Mulch crowns

Apply a mulch of straw or bracken over the root area if you have not already done so. In particularly cold spells, cover the mulch with horticultural fleece.

Jerusalem artichokes

Cut back stems

Once the foliage has turned yellow, cut back the stems of Jerusalem artichokes to about 10cm (4in) above soil level.

Lift roots as required

The tubers can be harvested as they are needed; a covering of straw or dry leaves along the row will protect the soil from freezing so that roots can be lifted more easily in cold weather. When harvesting Jerusalem artichokes, make sure you remove every tuber, even very small ones. Each tuber left will regrow, and artichokes can become a troublesome, invasive weed.

Rhubarb

Force tender stems

Dig up healthy rhubarb crowns and leave them on the soil surface for 7–10 days; exposing them to frost breaks their dormancy. Then put them in pots of compost and leave them in a shed, cellar or garage with a constant temperature of 15–17°C (59–62°F); if it is any warmer, they'll rot. Keep the soil just moist but exclude all light from the rhubarb; ventilate at night to deter rotting.

ROOTS AND STEMS

General

Lift root vegetables

Most roots are best left in the ground and gathered as you need them, but in case a cold spell prevents harvesting or even damages them a proportion can be lifted and stored in a frost-free shed.

Carrots

Sow under protection

Make a sowing of carrots in a cold frame or an unheated or frost-free greenhouse for an early crop.

JERUSALEM ARTICHOKES (above) can be harvested in whole clumps. Each plant will provide about a dozen tubers. Always ensure you have removed every little piece of tuber.

JERUSALEM ARTICHOKE PLANTS (left) mature in autumn, then you can begin to dig out the tubers. They can be left in the ground for digging as and when you need them.

Celeriac

Harvest roots when large enough

Lift celeriac from now through until early spring, when the roots are between the size of an apple and a coconut. On light soil, celeriac can remain in the ground all winter and be harvested when required. On heavier ground, and soil prone to waterlogging, lift it by late autumn and store, because celeriac can be frost-sensitive.

Parsnips

Start lifting roots

Traditionally, parsnips are not harvested until the foliage has died back and the first frosts have arrived, which is a sign that the roots have begun to sweeten. A hard frost will turn the starch content of parsnips into sugars, which is why parsnips make a popular winter vegetable. They are at their sweetest during the coldest weather.

Begin to lift parsnips as required, using a fork to ease them carefully out of the ground. The roots are often extremely long, and may snap off if the fork is not inserted deeply all around each plant in order to get underneath the whole root.

Lift roots for storing

Dig up a few parsnip roots and store them in boxes of sand, soil or compost in a dry shed so that you have some to hand during freezing weather.

TENDER VEGETABLES

General

Clear away crop remains

Plants in the greenhouse and outdoors will have come to the end of their growing season now. Pick off any unripe fruit from peppers, chillies and aubergines and place it indoors to ripen. Clear away all top growth and compost.

Clean greenhouses

Once you have cleared the crops from the greenhouse, clean the staging and the inside of the structure, with a stiff brush; try to get into all the nooks and crannies. Then clean the glass thoroughly. This will help to prevent pests from overwintering in the protected conditions of a greenhouse, ready to attack again next spring.

CELERIAC'S GNARLED APPEARANCE *belies the delicious white flesh with a celery-like flavour beneath. The similarity to celery stops at the taste, because celeriac is a far less time-consuming crop to grow.*

A HARD FROST TURNS THE STARCH OF PARSNIPS INTO SUGARS *so leave them as long as possible in the ground, even after the foliage has died back in autumn. Dig them up only when you want them.*

fruit | WHAT TO DO NOW

TREE FRUIT

Apples and pears

Continue harvesting

Pick apples and pears as they are ready. Harvest time varies greatly depending on variety. To test if an apple or pear is ready to pick, place your hand under the fruit and lift it gently rather than pulling it: if it is ready for picking, the fruit stalk will separate from the tree quite easily.

Order new trees

Order new stock from specialist fruit nurseries for delivery during the dormant season. Take advantage of local apple days to help you choose your varieties; these often include tasting sessions, and there will be experts to advise you and specialist suppliers to consult. Check on pollination groups before completing your order, to make sure you have compatible varieties, and select a rootstock that is appropriate for your circumstances.

Control winter moth

Apply grease bands to apple trees to control winter moth and other insect pests. These bands are strips of greaseproof paper coated with a sticky substance; this traps the wingless female moths as they make their way up the tree trunks from the ground in order to mate and lay their eggs in the branches.

You can buy ready-prepared grease bands, which should be tied round tree trunks about 1m (3ft) above ground level. On older trees with very rough, fissured bark, the moths are often able to find their way behind the sticky paper, and here it is best to apply a fruit tree grease directly to the trunk of the tree.

Inspect stored fruits

Check over fruits in store frequently, removing any rotting fruit straight away so it does not have time to infect adjacent stored fruit.

Keep an eye out for damage by mice, as these often move into sheds at the onset of autumn, and will enjoy

STEP-OVER FRUIT TREES *such as these apples make an unusual, productive yet decorative edging to a garden bed or an allotment plot. It is a particularly useful way of training fruit trees in a small garden or where space is otherwise too limited for larger fruit trees.*

nibbling your stored fruit. Often the first sign of an invasion is small pieces of apple skin on the floor near the storage boxes – mice frequently discard the skin, preferring the juicy flesh underneath.

Prune out dead wood
Cut out dead, dying or diseased shoots as soon as they are seen as well as any crossing or weak growth.

Collect up windfalls
Pick up all fallen fruit, as this often becomes infected with brown rot. Removing the fruit promptly helps prevent the infection being carried over the winter.

Citrus

Change to winter fertilisers
The bulk of flowering and fruit ripening occurs in winter, when citrus plants require a balanced fertiliser. This is the season then to switch from the specialist summer fertiliser to a winter one, swapping back to a summer one in early spring. Citrus plants are unusual in requiring fertiliser all year round. Most large garden centres sell suitable fertilisers, but failing that you can buy them from specialist citrus nurseries or by mail order.

WRAP UP WALL-TRAINED OUTDOOR FIGS *by packing dry bracken, straw or even bubble wrap around each plant and then covering it with horticultural fleece. This will protect the embryo figs from winter frosts.*

Reduce watering
Adjust the amount of water given to citrus trees, allowing the potting compost to almost dry out between waterings until growth starts again in spring.

Figs

Protect outdoor trees
Wall-trained trees can be protected over winter in order to ensure the survival of the embryonic figs. These fruits need to remain on the tree all winter in order to develop fully and ripen next year. In mild areas, a double layer of fleece may be sufficient, but in colder gardens use plastic netting to hold a loose layer of straw, bracken or dry leaves in place around the plant.

Move figs that are growing in pots back into an unheated greenhouse for the winter.

Peaches and nectarines

Control peach leaf curl
Spray trees with mancozeb or copper fungicide at leaf fall to help minimise incidences of peach leaf curl. Remove all fallen leaves and burn them.

Plant new trees
Peaches and nectarines will benefit from warm soil which allows the roots to become established quickly, so they should be planted early in the dormant season.

Plums, damsons and gages

Deal with broken branches
To avoid silver leaf disease, stone fruits should be pruned only in summer, not in the dormant season. However, when trees carry a heavy crop, it is not uncommon for branches to break under the weight of the fruit, and you might find you have a broken branch to deal with now. Cut the branch off cleanly and treat the cut with a proprietary sealing compound to try to prevent disease spores entering the injured stem.

A very heavy crop is often followed by a poor crop the following year (known as biennial bearing): fruit thinning in summer can help to even things out. Otherwise, keep an eye on the developing crop and support heavily laden branches with a firm prop to prevent breakage.

Blackberries and hybrid berries

Prune out old canes

Remove one-year-old canes once they have fruited. Then bundle or train the new canes along the supporting wires.

Black currants

Plant new stock

Plant container-grown black currants from now until late spring. After planting, cut all the stems back to one or two buds above ground level to encourage basal shoots.

Cranberries and lingonberries

Prune plants

Trim plants after harvesting. Every two or three years, thin them to aid air flow and optimise fruit ripening.

Raspberries

Order new stock

Make sure you order certified stock from a reputable supplier so that you start off with disease-free canes.

Strawberries

Care for newly planted beds

If there is a dry spell, newly planted strawberries should be watered carefully to help them get established.

Grapes

Pick remaining fruit

Finish harvesting any remaining grapes now.

Melons

Pick remaining fruits

Take any remaining melons into a warm place to finish ripening (see right). Add the plants to the compost heap.

REMOVE OLD BROWN TUMMELBERRY CANES *by cutting them into shorter sections with secateurs or loppers and then extracting them carefully to prevent their thorns damaging the new green canes.*

PROPAGATING CRANBERRIES

Now the soil is still warm and moist, dig up an established clump of cranberries and gently prise it apart with two garden forks held back to back. Discard the woodier centre and replant the outer, younger divisions. If you don't want to disturb your plant, remove rooted sections carefully from the parent, potting them into a bed or pot of loam-based ericaceous compost topped with grit. Water in well.

| How to store home-grown fruit

Although most fruits freeze well and many can also be dried and made into preserves, this limits their use thereafter because they are no longer in their fresh state. By choosing varieties that have an extended storage life you can continue to eat these fruits raw, and so benefit from their maximum vitamin content.

Apples, pears and quinces are the best crops for fresh storage. Some varieties should be enjoyed immediately, fresh from the tree, while others can only be stored successfully for short periods. But provided you have the right varieties and a suitable area – such as a cool garage or shed – to use as a simple fruit store, you can often enjoy these crops fresh until mid spring.

EARLY APPLES *(above) need to be eaten within one or two days of picking, while some of the later fruit can last for months if stored well.*
CRANBERRIES *(right) can be dried, frozen, eaten fresh, cooked or made into juice. Some of their active chemicals have anti-bacterial properties.*

A SELECTION OF FRUITS WITH LONG STORAGE PERIODS

APPLES	TYPE	SEASON OF USE
'Belle de Boskoop'	Dual-purpose	mid autumn to mid spring
'Bramley's Seedling'	Cooker	Late autumn to early spring
'Court Pendu Plat'	Dessert	Early winter to mid spring
'Edward Vll' (right)	Cooker	Early winter to mid spring
'Idared'	Dual-purpose	Early winter to late spring
'Tydeman's Late Orange'	Dessert	Early winter to mid spring

PEARS	TYPE	SEASON OF USE
'Black Worcester'	Cooker	Mid winter to mid spring
'Catillac' (right)	Cooker	Mid winter to mid spring
'Moonglow'	Dual-purpose	Early autumn to mid winter
'Glou Morceau'	Dessert	Early winter to mid winter
'Santa Claus'	Dessert	Early winter to mid winter
'Vicar of Wakefield'	Dual-purpose	Early winter to late winter

Other storage methods

Freezing

Many fruits such as raspberries and currants freeze very well, and can be defrosted for use in their fresh state. Lay such fruits on a tray so they are not touching, then open freeze them; once frozen, bag them up. Other fruits such as plums and gages can be frozen raw but are best cooked before eating, while yet others such as apples and pears are best frozen in their cooked state.

Preserves

The majority of fruits make excellent jams and jellies. If doing this to use up a glut, don't wait until the fruits are overripe because this can impair their ability to set. This is controlled by the levels of pectin present; fruits with a naturally high pectin content, such as apples, set very readily and can be added to low-pectin fruits, such as strawberries, to improve their setting ability.

Drying

Dried fruits can be used in cakes, breads or similar foodstuffs, or be eaten on their own as a naturally sweet snack. To dry fruits, use a domestic oven on its lowest setting, leaving the door slightly ajar. However, a food dehydrator, with slatted trays that have warm air blown over them for a timed period, is the ideal piece of equipment.

PLUMS AND GREENGAGES *have a moderate level of natural pectin in them so this type of jam is relatively easy to set.*

late autumn

Long, dark evenings reduce the amount of time we can spend in the garden, and dull, cold, wet weather makes working outside a less inviting prospect. But there is still winter digging to be done, and general tidying and clearing of the garden. On a more pleasurable note, this is an ideal time to be planting new fruit trees and bushes, with their exciting promise of new crops to sample next year.

Seed catalogues start dropping through the letter box, and stormy late autumn days can profitably be spent comfortably indoors, planning out what you are going to grow next year. Take into account how this year's crops performed, and try to buy seeds that fit with your crop rotation scheme.

Take advantage of the autumn lull to thoroughly clean your garden tools, replacing any that are worn, and sharpening spades, hoes and secateurs.

vegetables | GENERAL ADVICE

Make your own compost | Use all your garden waste and crop remains to make compost – an invaluable soil conditioner whatever type of soil you have. Buy two compost bins: one to fill while the contents of the other is rotting. Bins should have a capacity of not less than 1cu m (1.3cu yd). Stand them on previously dug-over soil or spread a bucketful of soil under each bin.

Add a mix of organic waste from the garden and kitchen to the bin. About a third of the waste should be soft green nitrogen-rich material such as kitchen waste and lawn mowings; the rest should be straw-like or woody carbon-rich material, such as spent crops. Perennial weeds should not be added to the mix, since they may simply grow there. Keep adding waste until the bin is full, and watering if the contents look dry,

then leave it to rot. Regularly turn the heap with a garden fork. When you have filled one bin, tip its contents into a second, empty bin as a way of turning the heap.

Order seed catalogues | This is the time to start poring over seed catalogues and choosing varieties to grow next year. All the catalogues have their share of novelties; it is always fun to try the latest varieties but be sure to order some well-established varieties too, for their reliability.

Carry on digging | Continue digging areas of the vegetable garden as they become vacant.

GREEN CABBAGES *(right) are best eaten when freshly harvested, but some red and white ones, if large, can be lifted in autumn for storage.*

WORM COMPOST

In small gardens where there is not much room for compost heaps, worm composting in 'wormeries' is another option. Worm bins consist of an upper chamber where the waste is added, and a lower sump where liquid collects. The liquid contains plant nutrients and is watered onto growing crops. Eventually the upper chamber fills with compost, and that's added to the garden. The worms are recovered for the next batch. Even if quite small, bins take useful waste. Both bins and worms can be bought as kits from specialist suppliers.

vegetables | WHAT TO DO NOW

ONION FAMILY

Garlic

Finish planting cloves

In mild areas and in free-draining soils, make a final planting of garlic cloves. Alternatively, plant cloves in modules in a cold frame or unheated greenhouse.

Check new plantings

For the first month or so after planting, regularly check the crop for signs of bird or animal damage; any uprooted bulbs need to be pushed back before they dry out. As garlic is shallow rooting, it dislikes competition so weed the soil regularly – taking care not to damage the bulbs.

Leeks

Lift some plants before bad weather strikes

Dig up a supply of leeks and heel them in to a shallow trench in a patch of light soil near the kitchen. They will keep perfectly well there, and you will always have some plants to hand if the soil freezes solid and prevents you digging the main crop.

HARDY WINTER CABBAGES *can be left where they are growing and harvested only when they are needed for the kitchen. In areas where pigeon attacks occur often, it is best to grow brassicas in a fruit cage.*

THE LEEK IS A VERSATILE AND USEFUL VEGETABLE *that's easy to grow in the right soil conditions. Grown for its stem-like rolled leaves, it can be harvested over an extended period in autumn and winter.*

CABBAGE FAMILY

General

Pigeons are often a problem in cold weather and in rural areas; cover all cabbage family plants with netting where necessary or grow them in a fruit cage.

Brussels sprouts

Remove yellowed leaves

Take off old, yellow leaves from Brussels sprouts plants as you pick the crop. Retain healthy green leaves, as these are required for growth and help to protect the sprouts.

Cabbages

Harvest as required

Hardy winter cabbages can be left where they are growing for harvesting as they are needed, but round-headed, autumn-maturing Dutch white varieties are best cut this

'BLOWN' SPROUTS

Instead of forming tight, firm buttons, Brussels sprouts plants sometimes form loose, leafy, open-centred sprouts that are known as 'blown' sprouts. These are especially common lower down the stems. A major cause is loose soil; all cabbage family plants need to be very thoroughly firmed in, particularly in light soils. On windy sites, the roots can be loosened in the soil by wind rock, and treading round the bases of the plants occasionally will help to refirm them. Poor nutrition is another contributory factor, so grow sprouts in rich, fertile soil and give regular applications of balanced fertiliser. Avoid nitrogen-only fertilisers; although sprouts are greedy plants, an excess of nitrogen can encourage blown sprouts. Modern F_1 varieties are less likely to produce blown sprouts than some of the older types.

month and stored in boxes of straw in a cool, well-ventilated shed or garage. Autumn cabbages for storage include 'Holland Winter White' and 'Hidena'.

Hardy winter cabbages such as 'January King', 'Tundra' and 'Alaska' should stay in good condition in the garden through until early spring, no matter how harsh the weather during winter.

Cauliflower

Protect curds from frost damage

Bend a couple of outer leaves over the top of cauliflower curds, breaking the stems of the leaves but not snapping them through completely. This prevents discoloration.

Kale

Harvest young leaves

Kale is completely frost-hardy, and young leaves can be picked and enjoyed right through autumn and winter until mid spring. Harvest all types while the leaves are still young and tender; older leaves quickly become tough and bitter. Start picking from the crown of the plant and work outwards, removing the tips of the stems with a sharp knife. This will encourage the plant to bush out and produce more sideshoots.

Harvest the crop as required because kale will stay fresh in the refrigerator for only a few days.

REMOVE YELLOWING LEAVES (top) from Brussels sprouts plants and compost them. Tread firmly around any plants with roots that have worked loose in the soil because of wind rock.

YOUNG TENDER KALE LEAVES (above) are delicious in salads or cooked briefly with oil and garlic. Because only a few leaves are cut at a time, kale really earns its keep in the vegetable garden.

BEANS AND PEAS

Broad beans

Sow hardy varieties

In mild areas there is still time to sow hardy broad beans for overwintering in well-drained soil. Protect sowings with cloches. Alternatively, in cold regions or areas with heavy, wet soil, sow beans in pots of seed compost in an unheated greenhouse for planting out in spring.

Peas

Protect overwintering seedlings

If you have sown hardy peas for overwintering, cover the seedlings from cold, wet weather with cloches to help them come through the winter safely.

PERENNIAL VEGETABLES

Jerusalem artichokes

Mulch in cold areas

Cut back the plants to 15cm (6in) above the soil if this has not already been done. The tubers will survive perfectly well in the ground, but to make them easier to dig up in freezing spells it is best to protect them with a mulch of old stems, straw or newspaper.

Harvest tubers

Dig up artichokes as and when they are needed, although they do store fairly well out of the ground with their thick skins. Their flavour is said to improve after a frost. If the soil is likely to be frozen solid, waterlogged or infested by slugs and snails, lift them and store in moist sand in a cool, frost-free place such as a shed. Tubers can also be kept in a perforated plastic bag in the fridge for a couple of weeks. Expect at least a dozen tubers from each plant.

Rhubarb

Plant new stock

Buy dormant crowns for planting now. Provide a sunny position and well-drained, moisture-retentive, fertile soil; avoid heavy soil which can rot the fleshy crown. Add plenty of organic matter, and remove all perennial weeds.

PLANT RHUBARB CROWNS NOW *positioning each one so that the dormant buds are just above soil level. One or two plants should supply sufficient stems for most people's needs during the growing season.*

Rhubarb needs a cold period to break winter dormancy before growth starts, but do not site it in a frost pocket.

Buy crowns from reputable suppliers. 'Timperley Early', 'Victoria' and 'Stockbridge Arrow' are popular varieties. Plant with the dormant buds just above the soil, spacing plants 1m (3ft) apart. Keep well watered for the first growing season.

ROOTS AND STEMS

Carrots

Protect roots

Carrots keep best in the soil. Remove the foliage now and cover rows with 15cm (6in) of straw or a thick layer of cardboard. Keep out rain with some polythene. Where soils become waterlogged in winter, carrots can be lifted and stored in boxes of sand, but their flavour and texture suffer as a result.

Celeriac

Harvest as required

Celeriac is hardy and can be left in the ground over winter, but like carrots the rows are best covered with an insulating layer of straw or similar material to make lifting of the crop easier.

Remove the thick skin from the harvested bulbs and either grate the white flesh for use raw in salads, or dice and cook it. Leave the prepared vegetable under cold water with a dash of lemon juice added to keep the flesh white, otherwise it will turn brown on exposure to air.

Parsnips

Look out for canker

Parsnip canker causes brown or orange, sunken lesions on the roots, particularly at the shoulders. It is a soil-borne fungal disease for which there is no cure, and is worst on heavy, poorly drained soils and in wet weather. Early sown crops and very large roots are particularly prone to the disease.

If parsnips are badly affected by canker, lift the crop and store the roots in just-moist sand, and use them as quickly as possible. Improve soil drainage for next year

A WELL-GROWN, WELL-TENDED CELERIAC *is quite a sight, and can easily rival a coconut in size. When harvesting, ease the roots out of the ground with a fork and trim off the foliage and fine roots.*

and grow parsnips in a different place. Choose resistant varieties such as 'Avonresistor', 'Gladiator' and 'White Gem', and sow them in mid or late spring rather than the more traditional early spring.

Potatoes

Check stored potatoes

Make sure stored potatoes are not exposed to light, which turns them green, and toxic; always fold over the sacks tightly after removing potatoes for use. If you come across any rotten potatoes, or notice an unpleasant smell, tip the tubers out of their sack and go through them carefully, removing any rotting or wet specimens. Allow the rest to dry off, then replace them in thick paper or hessian bags. Never store potatoes in plastic sacks as these hold condensation and encourage rotting.

Swedes

Protect roots from cold

Swedes are hardy and will store well in the soil, but as their shoulders are above ground level they will benefit from insulation in very cold weather. Use a good layer of dry straw, bracken or similar material over the row.

General

Winter salad crops

There is no need for the salad season to have ended by now. Chicory and endive, hardy winter lettuces, corn salad, winter purslane, land cress and winter radish can all keep you supplied with fresh growth through the autumn and winter months.

Chicory

Blanch chicons

Force witloof chicory by covering the roots to exclude light and raise the temperature. Lift the roots now and plant them in deep boxes of moist compost (see page 187). Place in a reasonably warm shed. After several weeks, plump, pointed white chicons will have been produced. Keep them completely dark to reduce their bitter taste.

Blanch endive

Curly-leaved varieties (frisée) are not as hardy as the broad-leaved Batavian types, which can be harvested from now until mid winter. Blanch to reduce bitterness, either by gathering the leaves together and tying them, or by covering the centre of the plant with a large plate. Make sure the leaves are dry before blanching, to reduce the chance of rotting.

WITLOOF, OR BELGIAN, CHICORY *can be forced to develop chicons such as these. Although this can be done outdoors, without having to dig up the roots, better results are often achieved by forcing indoors.*

Lettuces

Harvest autumn varieties

Lettuce in cold frames and unheated greenhouses can be harvested now, as well as hardy varieties outdoors. At this time of year, watch out for botrytis (grey mould) and downy mildew; thin out plants or increase ventilation where these are a problem. Slugs may also be a nuisance.

Radishes

Harvest winter radish

This hardy, usually black-skinned root is much hardier than summer radish. It also forms larger roots, which can be thinly sliced or grated over other food.

Tomatoes

Check fruit ripening indoors

Green tomatoes can be gradually ripened over several weeks indoors, but any tomatoes showing signs of rotting, or that have become wrinkled and withered, should be removed promptly. Large quantities of green fruit at the end of the season are best made into chutney (see left).

SPINACH AND CHARD

General

Continue to harvest spinach and chard before they die down for the winter.

SQUASHES, MARROWS, PUMPKINS AND SWEETCORN

Winter squashes and pumpkins

Check stored fruits

Pumpkins and squashes should be stored in a dry, well-ventilated, cool place; ideally the temperature should be kept at 10°C (50°F). Pumpkins should be used up first, as these do not store as long as most squashes. At the first sign of rotting, remove the fruits, cut away the damaged parts, and use the rest quickly. You may need to protect the fruits from mice.

SOW SPROUTING SEEDS

At this time of year and through the winter and early spring, fresh salad vegetables are scarce, but nothing could be easier than growing sprouting seeds to fill the gap. These are the quickest crops you'll ever grow, and are packed with vitamins as well as flavour.

Special seed sprouters are available, but no special equipment is necessary – just a reasonably large jam jar. Find a (clean) pair of old tights and cut out a circle that will fit over the top of the jam jar and overlap the edge. Rinse the seeds and soak them in clean water in the jam jar for a few hours; fix the circle of tights material over the top of the jar with a rubber band and drain off the water. From then on, rinse and drain the seeds once or twice a day. Keep the jar in a warm place; if you like blanched seed sprouts, keep the jar in the dark, otherwise grow them in the light. Try both ways; the sprouts have a slightly different flavour.

Once the seeds have sprouted sufficiently, they are ready to eat, usually within two to seven days. Alfalfa, mung beans, fenugreek, adzuki beans, broccoli, cress, peas, lentil, mustard, onion, radish and rocket are just a few of the seeds that can be grown in this way

CHARD LOOKS AS GOOD AS IT TASTES, *and is remarkably easy to grow, even tolerating some neglect. It is a useful late autumn vegetable, continuing to crop much later than most other leaf crops, such as spinach.*

| Encouraging natural pest control

Ask any group of gardeners to list the benefits of eating home-grown food and you can bet that somewhere near the top of most people's lists would be the fact that it has been grown naturally, and has not been sprayed with a battery of unknown chemical compounds. While all garden chemicals available today have undergone rigorous testing to ensure they are safe when used as directed, most gardeners would still prefer to eat untreated produce, especially if feeding children.

If you are to win the battle against garden pests without resorting to the sprayer at frequent intervals, you need to enlist all the help you can. Fortunately there are many naturally occurring allies that you can encourage

A POND (above) *provides a habitat in which toads, frogs and newts can breed and is also a water supply for insects, birds and other animals.*
SNAILS AND SLUGS DAMAGE *most plants (right), so at dusk pick them off by hand, with the help of a torch, and destroy them.*

CLOSED BIRDBOXES *(above) with one small entrance hole of no more than 3cm (1¼in) across attract birds such as tits.*

FROGS *(left) reside in warm yet damp, shady places often a considerable distance from ponds, except when breeding in water.*

into the garden. These are unlikely to eliminate your problems entirely, but they will keep pest numbers down.

Natural predators

The majority of garden pests are insects in their various stages. A wide range of natural predators will eat large quantities of both caterpillars and adult insects – common garden birds such as blue-tits, robins and blackbirds; wasps; hoverflies; lacewings; ladybirds; and centipedes and beetles. Hedgehogs are particularly good at disposing of slugs, and frogs and toads also enjoy feasting on slugs and snails as well as a range of insects.

You can attract these useful natural pest controllers into your garden by providing them with a safe environment, an appropriate habitat and breeding area, and a food supply. A garden pond is perhaps the most useful feature you can add, as this provides a home and breeding area for frogs and toads, and a drinking water supply for many other creatures. (Ensure that at least one side of a pond has a shallow 'beach' area or some other way for land animals to escape if they fall in.)

Turn a small corner of the garden into a wild area, with piles of stones, logs and leaves, wild flowers and groundcover plants. Garden centres and specialist mail order suppliers provide wildlife homes such as hedgehog houses and nest boxes for birds, bats and beneficial insects, and many wildlife organisations offer plans for building your own.

Attracting predators

Grow nectar- or pollen-rich flowers that will attract beneficial insects, such as buckwheat (*Fagopyrum esculentum*), poached egg plant (*Limnanthes douglasii*), phacelia (*Phacelia tanacetifolia*) and fennel (*Foeniculum vulgare*).

Putting out food for garden birds all year round will ensure they visit your garden regularly. Peanuts are a useful high energy food, but supply them only in special feeders, as young birds, particularly, can choke on loose nuts, and squirrels are very adept are grabbing large quantities of them. Other suitable foods for birds include mealworms, dried fruit, cheese, stale bread and seeds such as sunflower seeds.

Hedgehogs can also be fed to encourage them into the garden, but never give them milk, which will make them ill. Instead feed them tinned or dry cat or dog food, and always provide a dish of fresh water.

Remember to be extra careful about using garden chemicals – some could be harmful to the creatures you are trying to encourage.

fruit | GENERAL ADVICE

Plant trees | Although container-grown fruit trees can be planted all year round, autumn is the traditional time for planting, and still the best.

If the tree is bare root, measure the spread of the roots so that you know what size hole to dig. Mark out a circle a little wider than the diameter of the roots. Dig the hole out to the correct depth, and fork over the soil thoroughly at the base. If well-rotted organic matter is needed to improve the soil, dig this in prior to planting. To make sure the hole is the correct depth, stand the tree in the hole and lay a planting stick or garden cane across the centre of the hole. The dark soil mark on the tree's stem should be slightly below the level of the stick.

Remove the tree from the hole then hammer in an upright supporting stake. This is done before planting so the roots can be settled in around the stake. If you are planting a container-grown tree, hammer the stake in at a 45-degree angle, since the bulk of the rootball will not enable you to position the trunk close to the stake if it is an upright one. Two or three short stakes about 60cm (2ft) high are sometimes preferred as they give better support.

Then replace the tree in the hole, and return the soil, gently jiggling the tree as you do so to allow the soil to trickle between the roots. Firm the soil into place as you go by gently pressing it. Sprinkle over an application of balanced fertiliser, then return the remaining soil, and when the hole is almost full tread it down more firmly. Attach the tree to the stakes, using tree ties. Water thoroughly.

Guard against rabbits | Rabbits will eat the bark from the base of young trees during the hungry days of autumn and winter, and can easily kill a tree by stripping off a complete circle of bark. Use tree guards to keep rabbits away. There are various proprietary forms available including plastic spiral guards that wrap round the trunk and extend as the tree grows, and wire or plastic mesh guards that encircle the tree.

OVERWINTER CITRUS *under cover in a slightly humid atmosphere, preferably in a conservatory or greenhouse. You should always ensure that you can provide such conditions before purchasing a citrus tree.*

fruit | WHAT TO DO NOW

Apples and pears

Complete picking

Finish picking any remaining apples and pears and store the fruit, or eat it straight away if it is not a long-keeping variety. Pick up and dispose of fallen apples, and pick off and burn any mummified fruit on the trees as this can spread brown rot to the rest of the garden.

Clear up fallen leaves

Leaves infected with scab should be swept up and burned, not left lying under the trees. Good hygiene will help to keep the disease under control in future years.

Get ready for new trees

Prepare sites for planting new trees. Apples and pears are good cool-climate fruit because they tolerate low winter temperatures, and there are varieties that suit most sites and soils. In fact, the choice is so great that it is sensible to consult a local specialist nursery or grower who can recommend varieties that are suitable for your local conditions and that will be able to pollinate each other.

    The ideal position for an apple or pear tree is a sunny, sheltered site, well away from any frost pockets. The perfect soil pH is 6.5. Poorly drained or shallow soils should be improved or avoided.

Plant and prune trees to train as cordons

Cordons are popular tree forms for small gardens, because they fit almost anywhere. Plant a tree to train as a cordon now: a feathered maiden (a branched, one-year-old tree) is the best tree to select, because it will start cropping earlier than a maiden whip (a one-year-old tree without branches).

    If the feathered maiden is wispy with poor branching, lightly prune the leader to encourage more sideshoots and fruiting spurs below; otherwise the leader should be

PLANT AN OBLIQUE CORDON *angled at 30–45 degrees to encourage a system of fruit spurs to develop along its trunk, and tie the leader to a cane, fixed to each support wire by chain-lock ties.*

left untouched. Cut shoots of more than 10cm (4in) in length back to two or three buds.

    If a maiden whip has been bought, shorten the leader by about two thirds to a healthy bud after planting to encourage sideshoots to develop. Thereafter, follow the same procedure as for a feathered maiden.

Prune established cordons

Although the majority of pruning takes place in summer, after a few years it may be necessary to thin out overcrowded spur systems between now and the end of winter. Prune as little as possible in the dormant season, though, as winter pruning stimulates vegetative growth.

    Occasionally wispy growth develops on cordons after summer pruning. This is usually because the pruning has been carried out too early, before the plant has started to slow down for dormancy. If this happens prune back the growth to one bud now.

Plant and prune trees to train as espaliers

Plant against a warm, sunny wall or fence or on open ground. Establish a framework of horizontal wires 45cm (18in) apart, starting from 45cm (18in) above ground level. After planting a maiden whip, cut it back to 45cm (18in) above the ground, to encourage buds to break just beneath the cut. Attach the central trunk to a vertical cane tied to the wires.

Plant trees to train as step-overs

Plant maiden whip apple trees 1.5m (5ft) apart. For each secure a horizontal wire at 45–60cm (18–24in) high, pulled tight between two posts. Gently bend each tree over until it is lying horizontally along the wire. Then attach it securely to the wire using a tree tie. Gently tip-prune the leader to encourage fruiting spurs along the trunk.

Plant trees to train as fans

If buying a feathered maiden, make sure that it has a good pair of sideshoots growing at 35–45cm (14–18in) above the ground. Prepare the soil for trees planted against a wall particularly thoroughly, incorporating plenty of organic matter to hold on to soil moisture.

Plant trees to train as spindles or pyramids

Drive a 2.5m (8ft) long permanent stake 60cm (2ft) into well-prepared ground before planting the tree. After planting a maiden whip, prune it back to 75cm (30in) above ground. Tie the leader to the stake as it begins to grow during summer. After planting a feathered tree, select three or four branches at 60–70cm (24–28in) above the ground to form the first tier of the spindle and remove all others. Leave the retained branches unpruned unless they are spindly, in which case cut each tip at a downward-facing bud. Shorten the leader to 12cm (5in) (about five buds) above the chosen branches.

Apricots

Plant new trees

If you can grow a peach in your garden, then you should definitely be able to succeed with an apricot as they require similar growing conditions – a warm, sheltered site in full sun. Although tolerant of a wide range of soils, apricots prefer well-drained soils but they will struggle in shallow conditions. Dig plenty of well-rotted organic manure into poor soils before planting. Reliable varieties are 'Alfred', 'Flavorcot' and 'Moorpark'.

PLANTING AN ESPALIER

1 CHOOSE A WARM, SUNNY SPOT *on which to transform a young tree into a superb decorative feature, using a method that was a firm favourite in the 19th century.*

2 DIG THE PLANTING HOLE *large enough to accommodate the tree's roots. Sprinkle over controlled-release fertiliser or mix it in with the removed soil. Place the tree in the hole.*

3 TRAIN THE HORIZONTAL BRANCHES *along the supporting wires, tying at regular intervals. Backfill the hole and water thoroughly.*

NATURALLY COMPACT FRUIT TREES *such as this Ballerina apple are excellent choices for gardens with limited space. They are doubly useful as they make good container plants as well.*

Cherries

Plant new trees

Sweet cherries (*Prunus avium*) like a site in full sun, whereas acid cherries (*P. cerasus*) such as 'Morello' are happy to be positioned against a shady wall. Because they flower very early in the year, however, all cherries are best planted in a sheltered position so that pollinating insects (mainly bees) are encouraged to access the flowers. While cherries are tolerant of both acid and alkaline soils they do need good drainage. Cherry tree roots are naturally very shallow, and so any waterlogging will cause them to rot or to succumb to water-borne root diseases.

Figs

Protect trees from cold weather

If you have not already done so, pack fan-trained plants with straw, bracken or even bubble wrap and then cover with horticultural fleece.

Medlars

Plant new trees

Medlar trees crop best if they are positioned in an open, sunny site. Although they will tolerate a position in dappled shade, their flowering, cropping and golden-yellow autumn leaf colours will all be reduced. Avoid frost pockets if at all possible, because medlars flower in late spring. Plant them in moisture-retentive yet free-draining soil. Add bulky organic matter on heavy clay soils prior to planting, to aid drainage. 'Nottingham' produces well-flavoured fruits.

Mulberries

Plant trees

Grow mulberries in well-drained but moist soil with a pH of 6–7. Enrich sandy soils with plenty of bulky organic matter, and avoid chalky soils. In exposed or cool-temperate gardens plant mulberries in a sunny, sheltered spot against a south- or west-facing wall.

Never prune mulberries on planting as they bleed sap badly from both root and shoot pruning cuts.

Peaches and nectarines

Plant new trees

Plant peaches and nectarines. Soils should be well drained but contain plenty of well-rotted humus to help retain moisture. Peach trees will struggle in light, shallow soils, meaning that any underlying compacted soil should be broken up and plenty of organic matter incorporated into the soil before planting.

Peaches and nectarines are best grown as fans on a sunny, south- or south-west-facing wall if the fruits are going to ripen successfully in temperate climates. Peaches can also be grown as free-standing bushes, but nectarines will struggle. A sheltered position will help prevent the leaves and fruit becoming damaged, but exposure to rain will create problems with peach leaf curl. Early spring blossom can easily be damaged by cold, so do not plant these trees in a frost pocket.

Due to their slightly tender nature, both peaches and nectarines can successfully be grown in cool greenhouses, too, but will require particularly diligent watering. Both these fruit trees need a period of dormancy, so do not use a heated greenhouse.

Plums, damsons and gages

Plant new trees

These fruits have quite high moisture demands, so plum, damson and gage trees are best planted on clay or loamy soils. All sites need to be well drained because plums and gages in particular hate waterlogged soils. Add well-rotted, bulky organic matter such as manure to sandy or shallow, chalky soils before planting.

These stone fruits are some of the earliest crops to flower in the fruit garden. While the plants themselves are often extremely hardy, the flowers can easily be killed by frosts. It's therefore essential to position your trees out of frost pockets or windy sites.

A sheltered, sunny spot will encourage insects emerging from hibernation to visit and pollinate the flowers, and also provide some shelter from extremes of cold. Gages in particular are best sited against a south- or west-facing wall to ensure the fruits are exposed to sufficient sunshine and warmth to develop their sweet, rich flavour and to ripen wood.

Grow trees in pots

Plums can also be grown in containers, but make sure the pots are of sufficient size to prevent the potting compost drying out in summer, otherwise flower development and therefore yield will be very much reduced.

Quinces

Plant new trees

Add plenty of organic matter to light or shallow soils before planting quinces. They are happy in most soils, but they are particularly content in those that are relatively moist throughout the summer yet well drained to avoid waterlogging in winter. Mulch the trees thoroughly after planting.

Quinces need a long growing season to ripen well and so are best trained as fans against a south- or west-facing wall in more exposed or northerly gardens. Avoid frost pockets, as quinces flower early and the flowers will be damaged by frost. Gardeners in warmer climates or in sheltered, urban or coastal sites can train their quinces as free-standing trees provided they position them in a sunny location. Free-standing specimens will attain a height and spread of 3.75–5m (12–16ft) at maturity, depending on the rootstock, position and soil type.

TRAIN BLACK- AND HYBRID BERRIES *against a system of horizontal wires to create a framework of annual fruiting branches. These will yield good crops in summer, after which they are cut out.*

SOFT FRUIT

Blackberries and hybrid berries

Plant new canes

Blackberries and their hybrids prefer moisture-retentive but free-draining soil, so dig plenty of bulky organic matter into chalky, sandy or heavy clay soils before planting. While crops can tolerate shade they will be more productive in a sunny, sheltered site. Many varieties, especially the hybrid forms, are extremely vigorous and require at least 3.75m (12ft) between plants when trained against a wall or fence. If blackberries are to be planted near a path, it is a good idea to grow thornless varieties such as 'Black Satin', 'Adrienne' or 'Loch Ness'. This helps prevent the irritation of painful scratches or of clothing being snagged by the thorny stems as people pass by.

Vigorous varieties need a sturdy support system: use a wall or fence with horizontal wires spaced 45cm (18in) apart, with the lowest wire 23cm (9in) from the ground; or run the wires between two strong vertical posts.

After planting, cut all canes down to a healthy bud. This may seem drastic but it will ensure your plant throws up lots of vigorous, healthy suckers in spring.

PLANTING A BARE-ROOT BLACK CURRANT

1 ADD A BALANCED FERTILISER *to the bottom of the planting hole if it wasn't added when the planting area was prepared. Fork it into the soil at the bottom of the hole.*

2 LOOK FOR THE SOIL MARK *on the black currant plant; it should be planted at least 6cm (2¼in) deeper than previously. Place a board across the hole to assess the correct depth.*

3 BACKFILL WITH EXCAVATED SOIL *enriched with well-rotted farmyard manure, then tread the plant in firmly. Water thoroughly so the moisture reaches right down to the roots.*

Black currants

Plant new bushes

Black currants tolerate a wide range of soil conditions but prefer well-drained, moisture-retentive conditions. They like full sun but will tolerate light shade. Avoid frost pockets – frosts can drastically reduce yields, even on some modern varieties that are later flowering.

Plant black currants at any time from now through the dormant season, spacing the bushes 1.8m (6ft) apart. Clear the soil of all perennial weeds and enrich it with a generous amount of well-rotted farmyard manure. Add a compound balanced fertiliser at the rate of 85g per square metre (3oz per square yard). Allow the bed to settle before planting the black currant.

Set each plant at least 6cm (2¼in) deeper than it was previously growing, so that it develops into a multistemmed stool bush. Deep planting encourages young, vigorous shoots to develop from the base. Use a planting stick (or wooden board) to ensure that the plant is at the correct depth. Mix the soil from the hole with well-rotted organic manure and backfill the hole. Firm it in well before watering.

Prune established bushes

Cut back black currants when dormant – from now until late winter. Bushes fruit on the young wood, mainly from one- or two-year-old stems, and it is important to bear this in mind when pruning.

Up to and including the fourth year after planting, remove weak, wispy shoots, retaining a basic structure of 6–10 healthy shoots. After year four, cut out about one third of the older wood at the base, using a pair of loppers or a pruning saw. This will encourage and make room for younger, healthy wood. Also remove weak shoots and low ones leaning towards the ground.

Look out for pest problems

Big bud mite is a serious pest of black currants as it spreads reversion disease, causing a drop in yields and general weakening of the plant. Once the leaves have fallen, check the plant regularly, looking out for affected stems. Buds that contain mites are easily spotted as they are swollen and spherical, instead of slender and pointed. Pick off these buds immediately and burn them. Severely affected plants are best pulled up and replaced.

PLANTING A BLUEBERRY

1 DIG A HOLE *about twice the rootball width and to the depth of the pot, if the blueberry is container grown. Otherwise make the hole wide enough to plant at its original depth.*

2 TEASE OUT THE ROOTS. *Then, using a planting stick or wooden board as a guide, ensure the top of the rootball or the old soil mark is level with the ground.*

3 BACKFILL THE HOLE, *working the soil around the rootball or roots. Firm down the soil with the ball of your foot and water in well so that the soil can settle around the rootball.*

Blueberries

Plant new bushes

Blueberries need moist, well-drained, acidic soil in a sunny, sheltered spot. While they are tolerant of shade, better crops (and autumn colour) are obtained if blueberries are planted in the sun. The pH should be at least as low as 5.5. If your garden soil is very alkaline, grow blueberries in containers of loam-based ericaceous compost (such as John Innes).

When growing blueberries in your garden soil, add plenty of bulky, acidic organic matter such as pine needles or composted conifer clippings. Avoid well-rotted farmyard manure as this is too rich for the plants and will scorch their fine, fibrous roots. Ericaceous compost is useful to help acidify the soil but its structure is very fine and so it will not help create optimum drainage conditions. Space plants at least 1m (3ft) apart to accommodate their spread – further if more vigorous varieties are chosen.

For pot culture use a container 30cm (12in) in diameter for a small plant, and a half-barrel or similarly larger pot for a bigger blueberry plant. Make sure the container is either glazed or lined with polythene sheeting (pierced at the base) to avoid moisture loss.

Blueberries can be grown as single plants, but they will carry a heavier crop if two or more different varieties are planted together for cross-pollination. Make sure you select varieties that flower at the same time.

Cranberries and lingonberries

Plant new bushes

Position cranberries and lingonberries in the same bed as blueberries, because the soil and moisture requirements of all three crops are very similar.

While cranberries and lingonberries tolerate shade, a sunnier position is preferable. Both plants (cranberries in particular) have the ability to layer their stems and form a carpet of growth.

Purchase young, bushy plants. If grown in the open ground, set them 30cm (12in) apart. They will eventually knit together to form a groundcover crop. Minimal initial training is needed: on planting, just clip plants back to ensure they remain compact and bushy.

STAKING A GOOSEBERRY TRAINED AS A STANDARD

1 DRIVE IN TWO STAKES, *one at each edge of the planting hole, using a post-tamper or sledgehammer. Check that the posts will not come above the head of the standard.*

2 PLACE THE GOOSEBERRY PLANT *in the hole, ensuring its rootball is at the same depth as it had been grown in the nursery. Backfill with soil and firm around the stem.*

3 USE TREE TIES *or chain-lock ties to secure the gooseberry plant to the stakes, doing this just below the head of the standard. Then water the new plant very well.*

BEDS FOR ACID-LOVING FRUIT

Blueberries and other acid-loving crops such as cranberries and lingonberries can also be grown in a raised or sunken bed filled with acidic potting compost. Sunken beds are very moisture-retentive so easy to maintain, while raised beds require constant irrigation throughout summer so are more labour intensive.

Make the bed, whether raised or sunk into the soil, at least 60cm (2ft) deep. Line the sides and base with polythene that has been pierced in several places with a garden fork. This piercing is important, as while the aim of lining the bed is partly to conserve moisture in the soil it is also necessary to ensure that there is sufficient drainage to prevent the bed from becoming completely waterlogged. Fill the bed with loam-based ericaceous compost combined with composted bark. If this proves too costly, mix together an equal volume of pH-neutral or acidic soil, composted bark and ericaceous compost. Obtain the soil from a reputable topsoil supplier or, if from the garden, discard the top 7.5cm (3in) as this contains weed seeds.

Gooseberries

Plant new bushes

Gooseberries prefer moisture-retentive yet well-drained soil. Avoid very shallow, dry soils because the roots will dry out quickly, causing problems with American gooseberry mildew. Gooseberries can tolerate some shade and will successfully fruit on a north-facing wall. They can also be grown under fruit trees or in rows under trees in an orchard. Replace a healthy gooseberry bush after 10–15 years, once its regular bumper crops start to fade.

Cordons are the best method of growing these fruits if you want lots of varieties and colours in the garden. Expect a crop of 1–1.5kg (2–3lb) from a cordon. Stretch two wires – one at 50cm (20in) and one at 1.3m (4½ft) – between two posts and tie vertical canes to the wire at the place where each gooseberry is going to be planted.

Before planting, incorporate well-rotted manure into the soil, and add a balanced granular fertiliser to poor, nutrient-deficient soils at a rate of 100g per square metre (3oz per square yard). Plant single, vertical cordons 30cm (12in) apart and bushes 1.5m (5ft) apart. Set the related jostaberries and worcesterberries 2.1m (7ft) apart.

Raspberries

Plant new canes

When ordering new raspberry canes, always buy from a supplier offering certified stock. This ensures that your canes will be free from virus infections, to which raspberries are particularly prone and which can severely deplete yields.

Raspberries prefer slightly acid soil that retains moisture well, particularly in the summer when the fruits are swelling. Add plenty of bulky organic matter to the planting site, particularly to chalky or sandy soils, which should have a good depth of fertile topsoil. The plants will tolerate some shade, but will crop better in an open, sunny position in the garden or allotment.

Summer raspberries require a sturdy support system: run two horizontal wires – one 60cm (2ft) high and the other 1.5m (5ft) high – along the length of the row. Autumn raspberries don't need support.

Clear the site of perennial weeds before planting as these are difficult to control once raspberries are established. Plant bundles of bare-root canes now, spacing the new raspberry plants at least 30cm (12in) apart. Then add a mulch, 7.5cm (3in) thick, of well-rotted, bulky organic matter such as garden compost. Avoid mushroom compost (which is too alkaline) or overly rich farmyard manure (which tends to burn off the new shoots as they push through the mulch layer).

Plant in containers

In small gardens, raspberries will grow surprisingly well in containers. Use a 30cm (12in) pot filled with a half-and-half mix of good-quality soilless potting compost and John Innes No. 3. Plant three canes to each pot now. Keep the plants moist during the growing season and feed them with a high-potash fertiliser.

Red and white currants

Plant new bushes

Red and white currant bushes are hardy plants that thrive in open, sunny positions. They are tolerant of moderate shade and so make attractive features when fruiting on a north-facing wall. Avoid frost pockets and exposed windy sites. Incorporate well-rotted organic matter into the soil before planting, and set the bushes 1.5m (5ft) apart.

Red and white currants, and the less commonly grown pink currants, are all grown in the same way. However, while they are closely related to black currants, it is important to remember that black currants are pruned completely differently, so do not get the two groups of currants confused.

Strawberries

Protect potted plants

Strawberries that have been potted up for forcing in late winter should be protected from excess rain, which can cause them to rot, but do not put them in a greenhouse because they require a cold period outside to fruit well.

PLANT BARE-ROOT RED CURRANTS NOW. *Having dug the planting hole, check its depth against the plant's old soil mark. To do this, hold the plant against a planting stick placed across the hole.*

VINE FRUIT

Grapes

Clean up greenhouse vines

Carefully remove the old, loose bark of indoor vines in order to deter overwintering pests.

Plant new vines

Choose a warm, sheltered, sunny location, such as a south- or southwest-facing wall or fence. Dig over the planting site and break up any compacted soil. Add a bucketful of grit to the planting hole on heavy, clay soils. The vine roots should be encouraged to seek out their own nutrients from deep down in the soil, so do not incorporate manure or compost. Nor should fertiliser be added to outdoor grapevines.

NUTS

Almonds

Plant new bare-root trees

Although a container-grown tree can be planted at any time of year, this job is still best done now or in spring with a bare-root specimen. Grow in well-drained, humus-rich soil against a south- or west-facing wall. Failing this a sheltered, sunny spot would be sufficient. Avoid exposed, windy sites or frost pockets.

THE INDIVIDUAL FLAVOUR OF WINE is based very much on the unique soil characteristics of the place in which the grapevine is planted, and they are derived from they natural nutrients in the soil.

PLANTING A CONTAINER-GROWN GRAPEVINE

1 DIG A HOLE into prepared soil at least 30cm (12in) in front of a single vertical cane attached to the horizontal wire support on the wall. Add grit if the soil is heavy.

2 PLACE THE ROOTBALL of the grapevine into the hole, angling the main stem towards the vertical cane. Backfill the hole once the plant is at the same depth as previously growing.

3 TIE THE MAIN STEM to the vertical cane and lowest wire using string or garden twine in a figure-of-eight loop. Then apply copious amounts of water around the vine.

| Grow your own pear varieties

Despite their delicate aromas and their buttery-rich flavours, pears are less popular than apples. Therefore, there are less likely to be other pear trees growing nearby and this is important when selecting a tree as it will need pollinating (see page 78). Fortunately, a wide range of pear varieties is available. Bear in mind that pears often give lower yields than apples, and that the blossom is more sensitive to frost because it opens earlier in the season.

With the exception of a few cooking varieties such as 'Catillac', pears do not store nearly so well as apples. They remain in peak condition for eating for a very short time, so must be looked over regularly if they are not to become overripe and 'sleepy' in texture.

HARVEST PEARS (above) *just before they are fully ripened. They should be firm and swollen, with a subtle colour change to their skin.*

A GLUT OF PEARS (right) *will need to be stored carefully. Spread them out evenly and ensure they do not touch each other.*

Dessert varieties

'Beth'

(pollination group late, pick late summer, store until early autumn) Pale yellow skin and delicious, white flesh. The fruits are small, but the crops are heavy and regular. Has an upright growth habit.

'Beurré Hardy'

(pollination group mid, pick early autumn, store until mid autumn) Excellent flavour, a vigorous pear with no graininess in the flesh. The large, yellowish green fruit has reddish russeting on the skin.

'Concorde'

(pollination group mid, pick early autumn, store until late autumn) A fine, compact hybrid (of 'Conference' and 'Doyenné du Comice') bearing heavy yields of medium to large fruits that are sweet and juicy.

'Conference'

(pollination group mid, pick early autumn, store until late autumn) It is a popular commercial variety due to its reliable, heavy crops. The greenish fruit is distinctive due to its elongated shape. It is self-fertile, and will also bear 'parthenocarpic' fruits without being pollinated at all.

'Doyenné du Comice'

(pollination group late, pick mid autumn, store until early winter) Pick 'Doyenné du Comice' for its outstanding flavour and perfumed aroma. Needs a warm, sheltered site, so train against a south-facing wall as a fan or an espalier.

'Louise Bonne of Jersey'

(pollination group early, pick early autumn, store until mid autumn) It has good flavour and produces heavy yields. Although partially self-fertile, it is better grown with another variety in the same pollination group.

'Onward'

(pollination group late, pick early to mid autumn, store until mid autumn) A delicious, juicy pear with reliable crops. The fruit does not store well at all so needs to be eaten almost straight away.

Cooking varieties

'Black Worcester'

(pollination group mid, pick mid autumn, store until early spring) A very old variety and one of the best, most flavourful culinary pears.

'Catillac'

(pollination group late – triploid, pick mid autumn, store until mid spring) Reduces down to an attractive, pink colour after a couple of hours' cooking. 'Catillac' is heavy cropping and has a vigorous habit.

'Gorham'

(pollination group late, pick early autumn, store until mid autumn) Dual-purpose pear that ripens early. Moderate crops of sweet fruits.

'Hessle'

(pollination group late, pick mid autumn, store until mid winter) Dual-purpose variety suitable for dessert and cooking. Juicy and aromatic. Grows well in cooler areas.

early winter

Make out your seed and plant order as soon as you can. The earlier you can order, the better – you will be more sure of getting the varieties you want, as popular or new varieties often sell out quickly. This is the time to get ready for the busy sowing season ahead, cleaning greenhouses and cold frames, making sure heated propagators are in good working order and buying in stocks of seed trays, pots and sowing compost.

There is still digging to be done when the weather allows. There is no point in trying to work frozen soil, and treading over heavy, very wet soil will ruin its structure. There are usually some bright, dry days in early winter when working outside is a tonic, with the air just crisp enough for you to enjoy the warm glow that hard exercise brings.

vegetables | GENERAL ADVICE

Get ready for spring | Dig over vacant ground, spread organic manures, incorporate green manures, check the pH and add lime if required, and make sure the soil is in the best condition for an early start next spring. Keep weeding the vegetable patch.

Use winter crops | Gather winter vegetables and eat those in store, discarding anything rotten.

Turn compost | Empty compost bins, mix the contents and refill them. This will help to speed up decomposition and give a better end product.

Order seeds | Draw up plans for next year's vegetable garden, and order seeds. Check you'll have sufficient canes, stakes, netting, fertiliser and pesticides. Bear in mind that mail-order suppliers and gardening clubs and societies can often offer significant savings over retail outlets. When seed arrives, store it in cool, dark, dry conditions until you are ready to use it.

SEED PACKETS FEATURE AN EXPIRY DATE, *but the actual viability of the seed after this date will depend on how it is stored and the type of seed it is. Large seeds usually last longer than small ones.*

vegetables | WHAT TO DO NOW

Garlic

Plant garlic indoors
In mild areas plant garlic cloves in modules under cover.

Leeks

Prepare the planting site
Leeks do best in a sunny site on any reasonable soil that doesn't become waterlogged in winter, although the ideal soil is heavy and moisture-retentive. Dig the planting site now and leave it rough in clods so that winter frosts can help to break the soil down to fine crumbs. On free-draining ground it's important to add plenty of well-rotted organic matter to produce a good crop.

Onions and shallots

Check overwintering onions
Keep overwintering onions free of weeds and check for signs of disease.

ONIONS ARE SHALLOW ROOTING *and should be weeded regularly to avoid competition for water and food. To avoid damaging overwintering onions, do this by hand, assisted by a fork.*

Plant shallots
In mild areas with free-draining soil, shallots can be planted now. Space rows 30cm (12in) apart with sets 15–20cm (6–8in) within the row.

General

Protect crops from pigeons
As the weather gets colder, pigeons cause more and more damage to all cabbage family crops. If it is not possible to grow crops in a fruit cage or under netting, various other methods can be tried to scare pigeons away, though results are often variable. Most deterrents rely on movement, sound and flashing lights to scare the birds off, but pigeons do eventually tend to get used to them all.

One deterrent you could introduce is a humming line, where a plastic tape like cassette tape is stretched taut between posts, where it vibrates and hums in the breeze. Another is a series of brightly coloured spiral rods or old CDs hung around the plants; these will twist and flash in the sun. Also, the movement and buzz of children's windmills may have some effect. Other products rely on scaring birds by imitating predators such as hawks and cats. Using a range of different deterrents and changing them over frequently will have the optimum effect.

Broccoli and calabrese

Plant calabrese for a spring crop
Transplant calabrese that was sown in modules during mid autumn, setting plants out in a cold frame or an unheated greenhouse. They will be ready for harvesting in spring, when other fresh green vegetables are scarce.

As with all brassicas, be sure to firm the plants into the soil thoroughly. Keep the soil moist, but not wet, throughout the winter.

| Grow your own root crops

Root crops provide some of our most useful staple vegetables. They are invaluable in winter, when they provide the basis of many hearty, warming soups and casseroles. Packed with comforting carbohydrates, root crops are ideal vegetables to enjoy on cold, winter days. Many varieties are completely hardy and can be pulled straight from the ground all winter, or a supply can be lifted in autumn and kept in store in a shed or under a pile of soil near the kitchen door so they are always near at hand. However, roots are not just winter fare; they are also delicious when pulled young and tender. With a little careful planning and staggered sowings it is easy to have fresh roots available for harvest all year round.

BEETROOT AND CARROTS (above) *intended for storage are best lifted by gently easing them up with a fork to avoid damaging the roots.*

CARROTS ARE READY FOR HARVESTING (right) *about 12–16 weeks after sowing. Young carrots can be pulled up carefully by hand.*

Beetroot

The roots may be round or long, and are usually deep red though a bright yellow-orange variety is also available. Harvest them from the mini 'baby beet' stage until they are the size of a tennis ball for the most succulent, tender roots. Mature roots can be stored through the winter.

'Pablo'

A very early variety with smooth skin (below), fine colour and no internal rings. Good resistance to bolting.

'Boltardy'

Recommended for early sowing, this is a smooth-skinned, bolt-resistant variety with a fine colour (below).

Carrots

Choose the right varieties and you can harvest carrots from late spring right round to early spring. They store well over winter and come in a range of shapes and colours, from red to yellow to purple.

'Adelaide'

Excellent crop, suitable for sowing in cold frames (below). This variety forms stump-ended roots, is almost coreless and has fine tops. One of the earliest maturing varieties available.

'Flyaway'

Midlength maincrop variety with stump-ended roots and sweet flesh. Good resistance to carrot fly attack.

'Maestro'

Blunt, smooth-skinned carrot that is uniform in shape and size.

'Parmex'

Round-rooted carrot ideal for shallow soils and containers (below). It has good uniformity and core colour.

Parsnips

Parsnips are extremely hardy and can be left in the ground over winter for harvesting as needed. They like well-drained soils, ideally ones that are light and sandy. The seeds are very slow to germinate.

'Javelin'

Wedge-shaped, canker-resistant variety with long, tasty roots.

'Countess'

Reliable, smooth-skinned, canker-resistant parsnip with a lovely sweet, pale cream flesh. The yields from 'Countess' are very good.

'Gladiator'

Good for light soils, this variety is early to mature, resistant to canker and has large, smooth, white roots with a sweet flavour.

'Excalibur'

Long, cream-coloured parsnip (below) suitable for harvest from early autumn onwards. Canker-resistant roots of sweet flavour.

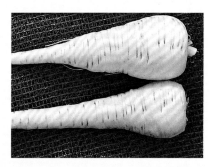

Swedes and turnips

Good swedes to try include 'Magres' (below) and 'Ruby'; both have foliage that is resistant to powdery mildew. 'Primera' and 'Oasis' are useful turnip varieties, with good yields.

Brussels sprouts

Continue to pick sprouts
Harvest sprouts as required when they are large enough, starting from the lowest sprouts and working upwards.

Remove yellowed leaves
Pick off yellowing leaves to prevent the spread of fungal diseases in the sprout patch.

Refirm and stake plants
In exposed areas, tread round the base of sprout stalks to refirm them and prevent root rock. Stake plants if this has not already been done.

Cabbages

Cut leafy greens
Spring cabbages that had been planted out in autumn can be used as winter greens as soon as they are large enough. Leave alternate plants to heart up in spring.

Cauliflower

Protect curds
Continue to protect the curds of winter-hearting cauliflowers from discoloration by breaking a leaf over the top of the plant.

CHOOSE BRUSSELS SPROUT VARIETIES *to extend the season from autumn right through to early spring. Try 'Nelson' or 'Franklin', then 'Trafalgar' and Hastings', followed by 'Agincourt'.*

Kale

Continue harvesting
Remove leaves from the plants as required, taking a few from each plant.

KALE IS ONE OF THE HARDIEST VEGETABLES *and can always be relied on to provide a constant supply of fresh produce whatever the weather – during even the harshest of winters.*

BEANS AND PEAS

Broad beans

Protect overwintering crops
If this has not already been done, place cloches or polythene tunnels over autumn-sown hardy varieties.

Peas

Sow under cover
Sow peas in a greenhouse for planting out after germination. An easy method is to fill a length of plastic guttering with moist potting compost, taping the ends to keep the soil in place. Sow two staggered rows of peas in the gutter, spacing the seeds 5cm (2in) apart. Place the gutter in a bright spot at a temperature of 10°C (50°F) or slightly higher. Also protect the growing site outdoors with cloches now to keep the rain off.

Jerusalem artichokes

Continue to harvest tubers
Dig up Jerusalem artichokes as they are required. Be careful to remove all the tubers to prevent unwanted regrowth from missed tubers next year.

Look out for slugs
In wet soils, slugs can inflict a lot of damage on Jerusalem artichokes. If the problem is severe, dig up all the tubers and keep those of good quality in store.

Rhubarb

Plant new crowns
Rhubarb can be planted at any time during the winter. Space the crowns 75–90cm (30–36in) apart in well-prepared, free-draining soil.

Expose the crowns
Rhubarb can be forced outdoors, where it is growing, as well as being moved inside. Before rhubarb can be forced, it needs to experience a certain amount of cold weather; how much depends on the variety. Remove all dead foliage and debris from the top of the crowns to expose them to as much frost as possible and prepare them for forcing *in situ* from mid winter.

JERUSALEM ARTICHOKES *are extraordinarily productive even in poor soil, and they require just the minimum amount of work. They store well, providing invaluable tubers right through the winter months.*

General

In mild spells, lift a supply of roots and either heel them in to a shallow trench in an area of light soil near the kitchen, or store them in boxes of damp sand, soil or coir compost in a shed.

Celeriac

Protect plants
If this has not already been done, protect the plants with a layer of straw in really cold spells.

General

Harvest leafy crops
Leafy salad crops such as corn salad (also called lamb's lettuce) and land cress will be available for harvest through the winter.

Continue sowing
Most sprouting seeds take less than a week to produce a crop. Keep sowing a range of different seeds (see page 225) so that you always have a ready supply for salads.

Chicory

Continue forcing
Keep forcing witloof chicory to produce chicons for winter salads (see page 187).

Perpetual spinach and Swiss chard

Protect crops
Although spinach will produce leaves all winter without any special treatment, the leaves are more tender if they have some protection. Either use a polytunnel or cover your row with a cloche or tunnel of fleece.

| Grow your own potatoes

Potatoes are one of our staple foods. Whether eaten with butter and mint in spring, with salads in summer, or roasted or baked in the cold, dark days of autumn and winter, few days go by without potatoes appearing on our plates in one form or another.

While they are the most readily available of all vegetables, and usually cheap to buy, it is still worthwhile growing your own. The flavour of the bland supermarket potato bears no resemblance to the wonderfully rich taste of potatoes freshly dug from the soil. Growing your own allows you to choose exactly the variety you want, and to try out unusual shapes and colours to liven up the dinner table. And there is always something truly exciting about harvesting the potato crop, uncovering the cache of hidden treasures nestled beneath the soil.

WHEN HARVESTING POTATOES (above) dig very carefully into the surrounding soil, to avoid spearing the tubers with your garden fork.

Different varieties of potato are often suitable for different uses. Catalogues from companies selling seed potatoes will tell you whether each variety is good when mashed or roasted or made into chips or potato salad; some varieties are good all-rounders. If you are interested in something a little out of the ordinary, some specialist producers also sell long-established heritage varieties, or novelty varieties with deep blue or red flesh and skins.

Varieties are divided into groups of first early, second early and maincrops, according to the length of growing season required. Quick-growing first earlies are dug as new potatoes; as potatoes are not hardy, they need protection from spring frosts. Second earlies extend the new potato season and can also be left in the ground to bulk up and use as maincrops. Maincrop potatoes are lifted in late summer or early autumn before the first frosts and are stored for use over winter.

Recommended varieties

'Kestrel'
A second early variety. This is a smooth-skinned potato with good slug resistance. Its versatility in the kitchen makes it a popular choice.

'Picasso'
An early maincrop variety. This is one of the heaviest-cropping potatoes, with creamy skin and bright red eyes. Resistant to eelworm and common scab, it is good for dry soils.

'Charlotte'
A long, oval variety, producing yellow-skinned, waxy potatoes with creamy yellow flesh. 'Charlotte' is excellent when eaten hot as well as when used cold in salads.

'Accent'
First early variety, with creamy, waxy flesh and good scab and eelworm resistance. A very tasty new potato.

'Anya' AGM
An excellent salad potato, with a lovely nutty flavour, pink/beige skin and waxy, cream flesh.

'Dark Red Norland'
Heavy-cropping variety with a dark red skin, pure white flesh and good flavour; use for boiling and roasting.

'Lady Christl'
A second early potato, long and oval in shape, with pale yellow skin, firm flesh and shallow eyes. It has good scab and eelworm resistance. An excellent variety for growing in containers where space is limited.

'Cherie'
This potato gives a heavy crop of medium-sized, red-skinned, oval tubers. The creamy coloured flesh has a waxy texture, making it an excellent salad potato, and it has a good flavour. Prefers a moist soil.

'Cherie'
A first early salad potato with medium-sized, oval tubers. The skin is a glowing rose-pink and the flesh creamy coloured, with a firm texture and a delicious flavour. Plants provide a good yield.

fruit | GENERAL ADVICE

Buy new plants | Take delivery of and plant nut and fruit trees and bushes. If the soil is too wet for planting or is frozen, heel the new plants in until conditions improve. Keep the new plants in a frost-free place and ensure the roots don't dry out if the plants are bare root.

Winter wash trees | Use a winter wash on dormant trees to control pests that overwinter in nooks and crannies on the trunk and branches. A winter wash based on plant oils has replaced the traditional tar oil winter wash, which is no longer available.

THE PRINCIPALS OF PRUNING

Because pruning stimulates growth, give vigorous trees only a light trim to avoid an excessive reaction. Alternatively instead of pruning, festoon the branches, that is, train them downwards towards a horizontal position to encourage fruiting instead of vigorous growth (see page 97). Trees lacking in vigour should be pruned back hard to stimulate more growth.

Research shows that trees recover better when wounds are left unpainted. The paint can sometimes seal in infections and can also inhibit the tree's natural ability to callus over the pruning cuts. Therefore only use a wound paint when it is essential to prune stone fruits during the dormant season.

When to prune: Apple and pear trees were traditionally pruned during winter, when it was easy to see the shape of the tree as it was leafless. Free-standing trees are still pruned in winter for this reason. However, restricted forms of apples and pears are pruned in late summer. Not only is the weather more pleasant but vigorous trees also put on less growth when pruned at this time of year. Summer pruning can help to prevent biennial fruiting (fruiting every two years), too.

Stone fruits such as cherries, peaches, plums and apricots should always be pruned when the plant is in growth. This is to avoid disease problems that enter pruning cuts made in the dormant season.

Tools

Secateurs: These should be used for thinning out fruiting spurs and cutting branches no thicker than 2cm (¾in) in diameter. A good-quality pair with sharp blades is essential for making clean cuts. Bypass secateurs are the best type as

they make a clean cut. Avoid anvil secateurs as these tend to crush the branch.

Pruning saws: On branches that are too thick for secateurs, use a pruning saw. This is long and narrow so its blade will fit between the narrow angles made by branches. Bow and panel saws should be used only to cut up large pieces of wood once they have been removed from the tree.

Extended saw: Sometimes called a pole saw or long-armed saw, the extended saw is useful for cutting branches above head height. It is far safer to prune from the ground and therefore an extended saw is a better option than climbing a ladder and using a shorter saw. Always wear head and eye protection when using this tool.

Loppers: These are useful for chopping up prunings once they have been removed from the tree and can occasionally be helpful when actually pruning. However, they don't make as clean a cut as a pruning saw. Never use loppers from a ladder as they require two hands to operate them, meaning that it is not possible to hold onto something else while pruning.

Ladders: Sometimes ladders are needed to reach high branches. Three-legged stepladders (tripods) are best because they are easiest to get in close to the tree and among the branches. Only use ladders on level ground and make sure that the legs are fully extended. Never overstretch or lean out too far over the sides. Very large fruit trees will need to be pruned by a professional tree surgeon. Don't risk it yourself.

Basic safety

Protection using a pair of thick gloves is particularly important when pruning thorny plants such as gooseberries and blackberries. Gloves will also reduce the risk of cutting your hand with secateurs or a pruning saw. Wear eye protection to prevent sawdust blowing into your eyes or a sharp branch scratching them.

General guidelines

Although each tree should be treated individually when it comes to pruning, there are some general guidelines that should be followed.

Remove long, heavy branches in stages to avoid tearing the bark with their weight. If pruning a branch back to the trunk, leave a small collar because this will help the tree to callus over the wound.

When cutting back, always check that a replacement branch is growing in the required direction and that it is at least one third the width of the branch that has been removed.

Make pruning cuts with secateurs at an angle just above a bud – never through a bud. Slant the cut downwards from 5mm (⅕in) above the bud, sloping away from the bud.

Where there are opposite buds, make a flat cut at a similar distance above the buds, that is 5mm (⅕in). A long stub left between the cut and the bud may cause the branch to die back, increasing the risk of disease.

Maximise crops

Once you understand how your tree produces its fruit, you can then prune it to maximise potential yields (see page 280). Peaches and acid cherries, for example, bear fruit mainly on wood from the preceding year, so on such tip bearers you must ensure that plenty of new shoots are retained for next year's crop. Sweet cherries, however, develop their fruit on a series of spurs built up over the last two or three years, so a system of spur pruning is necessary.

Summer-fruiting raspberries bear fruit on canes produced the previous year whereas autumn-fruiting ones form fruit on the current season's growth.

Grapevines bear fruit on shoots produced in the current year. Prune them annually in winter to encourage new, healthy canes, and avoid using water shoots (canes coming directly off the central trunk) because they will contain far fewer clusters of grapes. Instead, try to select canes coming off the spurs of the trunk.

fruit | WHAT TO DO NOW

Apples and pears

Deal with canker

Canker is a very common and damaging fungal disease. Malformed, swollen areas appear on the trunk and branches; they are cracked and fissured and sometimes white or red pustules are visible.

Prune out cankers seen on branches and twigs, cutting back into healthy wood. On trunks and larger branches, cut out the cankered areas with a sharp knife, paring back to healthy tissue. Apply a canker paint to the cut surfaces, and collect up and dispose of all the affected tissue that has been removed.

Check stored apples

Make regular inspections of your apples, checking them carefully for any sign of disease or discoloration, such as bitter pit, which may show up as small, sunken, dark brown spots on stored fruit. Use up affected fruit quickly, cutting out the pitted areas. Make a note to apply a controlled-release fertiliser in spring to the trees that have produced affected fruit, and to ensure they do not run short of water next season. Mulching is beneficial, too, as it helps to conserve soil moisture.

Clear up fallen leaves

If you have not already done so, pick up fallen leaves from below fruit trees. If the trees were affected with diseases such as scab, burn the collected leaves rather than putting them on the compost heap. This will help to prevent the disease from being carried over to the following season.

Prune cordon-trained trees where necessary

Thin out congested spurs to stimulate growth (see box, right) and help to rejuvenate the apple or pear tree. Don't carry out major pruning of restricted forms in winter as

APPLES AND PEARS *are often affected by fungal canker, which can eventually kill the tree. It causes depression and cracks within the branches, often near pruning cuts. Treat canker promptly.*

SPUR THINNING

Mature cordons and espaliers benefit from their spurs being thinned every two or three years in winter, when their shape can be seen better because the leaves have fallen. Where the swollen, short sideshoots are crowded, remove the older spurs in favour of the younger wood, to encourage new growth to replace the old spurs.

this will stimulate excess growth; the main pruning is carried out in late summer.

Carry out formative pruning of espaliers

Cut back the central stem to a healthy bud 45cm (18in) above the highest established tier (at the height of the next tier wire). This will encourage buds to break below the cut; these will form the next tier. Repeat this process each year until the desired number of tiers have been created on your apple or pear espalier.

Carry out formative pruning of fans

Tip-prune the branches that have developed by removing about one third of the new growth, ideally to an upward-facing bud.

Prune established fans

When they are the desired length, prune the main branches on apple and pear trees and thin the spur system (see box, left). If the fan is predominantly a tip bearer (see page 280), use a form of replacement pruning whereby some of the older fruiting branches are removed to create space for younger shoots.

Prune established spindles

Once established, prune a spindle-trained tree to keep the upper branches shorter, in order to maintain the cone shape and allow sunlight to reach the lower tiers.

    On the top tiers cut back the older branches every two or three years to ensure shorter branches and a regular supply of cropping wood each year. Cut out any vigorous leader that exceeds the height of the stake and replace it with a more spindly, weaker leader.

    On the lower tiers, remove some of the older branches to make space for new ones and tie them down if there is space. Remove completely or cut back other branches to three or four buds to encourage fruiting spurs to form.

Train trees as bush forms

An apple or pear tree trained as a bush with a short stem and open centre is the traditional method of growing apples and pears. Not only do they look attractive but their open structure also allows for good air circulation. To do this, you need to create a basic structure of about four strong branches that will form the open shape and regularly bear fruiting sideshoots and spurs.

WHEN FORMING A SPINDLE *(top) cut overly long branches back to a downward-facing bud in winter; otherwise leave them unpruned. Tie down the branches as they grow.*

TO MAINTAIN THE VIGOUR OF A MATURE SPINDLE *(above), renew the cropping wood from time to time by removing older branches and training new growth in their place.*

If a maiden whip was planted in autumn, prune back an apple tree on 'M26' or 'MM106' rootstock and all pear trees to 76cm (30in); shorten trees on 'M27' and 'M9' rootstock to 65cm (26in). Thereafter, follow the same procedure as for a two-year-old feathered maiden.

If a feathered maiden was planted in autumn, remove the leader, cutting back to three or four good strong branches above ground level. These branches should ideally form a wide angle with the trunk. They will become the primary branches of the tree and will form part of its permanent structure. Remove any other branches from the trunk. Cut back any vigorous branches by one half to an outward-facing bud and shorten less vigorous ones by two thirds.

By the following winter, the three or four branches chosen the previous winter should have developed a few sideshoots of their own. Select two or three equally spaced sideshoots from each of these branches; you should avoid those growing into the centre of the bush. Cut back the selected sideshoots by one third and shorten any other shoots to three or four buds, to encourage them to develop as fruiting spurs. Prune back the main branches by one third, and remove any new shoots that have formed lower down the trunk.

By the third winter after planting, the tree should have a well-established framework of branches. Continue to extend the network of branches by tip-pruning new, well-spaced sideshoots by one third. Reduce other sideshoots to short spurs of three or four buds or remove them completely. Also cut out branches that are crossing or growing into the centre.

Prune established bush forms

Continue to keep the centre of an apple or pear bush open by removing branches growing into the centre, with a pruning saw. Lightly prune vigorous trees; those that are making poor growth can be pruned harder. Cut out all diseased or dead wood.

If the tree is predominantly a spur bearer, such as 'Cox's Orange Pippin', 'James Grieve' and 'Sturmer Pippin', tip back one third of the new sideshoots to three or four buds to encourage fruit buds, and eventually spurs, to develop along their length; leave shorter sideshoots alone.

On predominantly tip-bearing apple or pear trees, remove any dense or crossing branches; leave unpruned any remaining sideshoots or new growth to avoid removing potential fruits that form in the tips. Tip-bearing apple varieties include 'Cornish Gilliflower', 'Fuji', 'George Cave', 'Gladstone', 'Irish Peach', 'Lady Sudeley', 'Tydeman's Early Worcester' and 'Worcester Pearmain'. Only a few pear varieties are tip bearers – 'Jargonelle' and 'Josephine de Malines' being the best known.

Remove some of the older branch framework on an apple or pear bush to make way for new, younger shoots. Also cut away all water shoots growing directly from the trunk flush with the trunk. Do this before they spoil the look of the tree.

Training and pruning a standard

Standard and half-standard trees are essentially bush trees but on taller stems so that the branches start at a different height. The training and pruning methods are the same (see page 253).

REMOVE CROWDED AND CROSSING BRANCHES on established bushes and standard trees, in winter. Aim to keep the centre of the tree open to allow for good air circulation and therefore healthy growth.

FRUIT BUDS ARE FAT as they contain not only next year's leaves but also the flower buds. When pruning an apple or pear tree, it is important to distinguish these from growth buds, which are smaller and thinner.

WHEN PRUNING BACK LARGE BRANCHES *leave an angular cut and try not to damage surrounding bark. Clean cuts using sharp tools should heal quickly.*

Rejuvenate neglected trees

Restore an old or neglected tree to its former glory gradually and in stages over a few years (see page 256). Making lots of large cuts and removing all the large limbs will stress the tree, causing it to overcompensate the following year by sending out an excess of branches.

That said, apple and pear trees are resilient and can deal with far more pruning than other trees. Dispense with secateurs and use only a pruning saw. Tree restoration requires big decisions and usually big cuts. Snipping away with secateurs will just encourage more vigorous growth to develop.

Once the leaves have fallen off the tree and you can see its framework, assess the tree from the ground, looking at the overall shape. Identify the original shape of the tree – was it supposed to be open centred or have a central leader? Which branches are making the tree look unbalanced or lose its shape? If the tree is too high for picking the fruit or for spraying, decide how to cut branches back to lower limbs. Are any of the large branches dead or diseased?

BEFORE STARTING TO RENOVATE A TREE *(top) study it carefully when it is dormant and you can see its branch structure. Usually, this is a tangle of twiggy branches. Then thin out the crown (above) and remove dead, diseased and crossing branches. Never cut out more than a quarter of the branches in one growing season.*

DEALING WITH OLD TREES

There are a number of reasons why apple and pear trees benefit from rejuvenation. Congested canopies cause poor air circulation, which can potentially encourage a build-up of pests and diseases: they also create shade, which reduces the light levels necessary for fruit-bud initiation and ripening and therefore causes low yields. Furthermore, whatever fruit there is is usually undersized, has poor colour and rarely tastes good because the tree hasn't been able to produce adequate sugars.

Oversized, congested apple trees often dominate older gardens, and the question of whether they are worth restoring is often an issue confronting the owner. An oversized tree in a small garden can certainly be a problem, with it casting too much shade or its roots absorbing too much moisture and nutrients at the expense of the rest of the garden. Mature trees will never be as fruitful as young trees – most apple and pear trees are most productive for their first 8–20 years. However, they can still continue to give large, healthy crops for considerably longer if looked after properly. Old trees can also create an invaluable habitat for wildlife, and they can make attractive features with their old, gnarled trunks. Climbing plants such as roses and clematis can be trained up into them to compensate for any lack of blossom.

If the decision is made to remove an apple tree completely it is worth consulting a fruit expert to discover whether the variety is rare – many old varieties have been lost and it would be tragic to lose yet another one. One method of preserving the variety would be to save a few branches and send them off to a fruit nursery to be propagated (either by grafting or budding) onto dwarf rootstocks, which can then be replanted in the garden at a more manageable size.

REMOVE DYING BRANCHES *close to their base, where they join the main framework of the tree. Use a sharp and clean pruning saw for this pruning task and protect your hands with gloves.*

THIN OVERCROWDED STEMS *growing into the centre of the tree and those that are rubbing against other stems. Such crossing stems are vulnerable to damage, and this provides a potential entry point for disease.*

REMOVE WATER SHOOTS *growing from the main trunk, below the main network of branches, as early as possible. At the same time prune out suckers and clear competing weeds around the base of the tree.*

Once the main limbs have been identified, use a tripod stepladder to get in close to the tree and begin to saw out selected branches. Always cut back to another branch. Don't leave large stubs because these will die back and can cause problems with diseases. When in the canopy of the tree it will also be easier to identify crossing branches that have been rubbing against each other and therefore causing damage to the bark. Remove these initially, as well as dead and diseased branches such as those riddled with canker. Cut out large branches in many sections, making undercuts to prevent the bark from tearing.

Over a period of several years, prune most branches lower down close to the crown of the tree. A useful rule of thumb is to remove no more than a quarter of the branches in one pruning season. Don't make the mistake of cutting back all the tips on the growth – a bit like hedge trimming – because the tree will regenerate from the cuts, making it top-heavy, which will cause shading and poor fruiting.

Keep getting down from the ladder to reassess the tree, which will look very different from the ground than from up close when you are on a ladder.

HANDMIST CITRUS PLANTS *regularly with tepid water in order to provide the humid atmosphere that they need, especially when in flower, because this aids pollination and fruit set.*

Citrus

Bring trees under cover

While some species are comparatively cold-tolerant, none is fully hardy and so all citrus benefit from being brought into a frost-free environment for winter. Despite often being marketed as such, citrus generally don't make good house plants where there is a dry atmosphere caused by central heating. The plants do not like hot conditions; they need to be kept frost-free, but cool.

To ensure adequate pollination keep the atmosphere humid in winter, when plants flower. Regular handmisting with water, standing plants on trays of moist gravel and grouping plants together will all help raise humidity levels and ensure good fruit set.

Most citrus plants are self-pollinating, and as long as the atmosphere is sufficiently moist they do not need any special pollination techniques in order to set fruit.

Peaches and nectarines

Move containers under cover

If this has not already been done, move container-grown trees back under cover without delay.

BULLFINCHES AND FRUIT

Bullfinches are beautiful birds with brilliant pink breasts and a striking, black cap. Occasionally in winter, when their normal food supplies are low, they attack fruit trees and bushes, nipping out the buds all along the stems so that they can eat the developing centres. This can have a devastating effect on the fruit crop, particularly as the birds often work in groups.

However, bullfinch numbers have fallen dramatically in recent years, and if you see a bullfinch in your garden you are very lucky; they can no longer be considered as pests. Help them to survive – and incidentally prevent them from attacking fruit buds – by supplying alternative food sources such as bird seed and sunflower seeds.

Quinces

Carry out formative pruning

Quinces bear their flowers singly at the tips of one-year-old stems and to a lesser extent on short fruiting spurs. Carry out formative pruning now. Aim to create a system of well-spaced branches on a clear stem, as for apples and pears (see page 253). The erratic growth of quinces means that you'll occasionally have to remove wayward stems as they're produced, but it is better to sacrifice an inappropriate shoot in the initial stages of training rather than trying to remedy the situation once the tree's framework is otherwise well established.

Prune established quinces

Established pruning simply consists of removing dead, diseased and damaged growth, along with thinning out congested or unproductive stems. Pull off any suckers as soon as they develop at the bottom of the trunk.

General

Take hardwood cuttings

Gooseberries, red and white currants and black currants can all be propagated by hardwood cuttings now. Push the cuttings, each 20cm (8in) long, either into a trench lined with sharp sand in the open garden or in deep pots of sandy compost that are then placed in a cold frame. Insert the cuttings with two thirds of their length below the soil and firm them in well.

Gooseberries

Prune established bushes

Shorten last summer's new shoots back to one or two buds and prune back the branch leaders by one quarter.

Raspberries

Prune autumn-fruiting varieties

Cut all the canes, which will have fruited, back to ground level between now and late winter.

Red and white currants

Prune established bushes

Red and white currants should be pruned in exactly the same way as gooseberries (see above).

Grapes

Prune cordon vines

On vines that were planted last autumn, prune back the leader by about one third. Shorten any lower growth back to one or two buds. On established cordons, cut the leader back to one bud above the top wire and shorten the other shoots to two buds. Thin congested spurs.

Prune guyot vines

Continue to replace and tie in the fruiting arms, selecting new ones that are strong and vigorous.

PRUNE GOOSEBERRIES (top) by cutting new sideshoots back to one or two buds to concentrate growth from the spurs and keep plants compact. Wear gloves to protect your hands.

AUTUMN-FRUITING RASPBERRIES (centre) fruit on the current season's canes, so all this year's canes can be cut to ground level between now and late winter. New canes will grow in spring.

PRUNE RED AND WHITE CURRANT SIDESHOOTS (bottom) back to two buds in winter to keep the plant compact and ensure that growth is concentrated from the spurs.

PRUNING A KIWIFRUIT

1 SHORTEN WELL-PLACED NEW SHOOTS to 12–15cm (5–6in) to encourage new spurs and fruit production.

2 THIN OUT SOME OF THE OLDER SPURS. This will encourage air flow around the kiwifruits and remove congested and unproductive growth.

GUYOT-TRAINED VINES

AFTER PLANTING A VINE TO BE TRAINED USING THE GUYOT SYSTEM, tie the leader to the first fixed wire. Then prune it back to the first healthy bud above the lowest wire. Remove any other shoots.

ON ESTABLISHED GUYOT-TRAINED VINES, remove all other stems except for one or two in the centre, which should be cut back to two or three buds. The fruiting arms should each form an arc. Tie these in.

Kiwifruit

Prune plants

Pruning can be quite drastic each year once a framework of branches has been established.

NUTS

Cobnuts and filberts

Plant new trees

After planting, cut the stems back by half their length to encourage sideshoots to form.

Prune back brutted stems

On established plants, shorten stems to 10–12cm (4–5in) that were brutted in late summer (see page 181).

EXTENDING THE RASPBERRY SEASON

Autumn raspberries bear most of their fruit on the current year's canes, but they can be forced to crop like summer varieties by careful pruning. This allows a single autumn variety to yield both summer and autumn crops, thereby extending the season in minimum space, and so is a particularly useful technique for small gardens. Good autumn-fruiting varieties include 'Autumn Bliss', 'Fallgold', 'Heritage', 'September', 'Himbo Top', 'Polka' and 'Joan Squire'.

Instead of cutting all the canes down to the ground by late winter, remove the fruited, upper section on a few of them. Because the lower section of these canes did not bear the fruit in the previous autumn, they will produce fruiting shoots in spring – much as summer varieties do. Once harvested, cut these canes back to soil level.

mid winter

The weather is usually at its coldest now, and it is a good idea to make regular checks on tender fruit such as figs to ensure that the protection is still doing its job. There are several crops that can be sown now in a warm greenhouse, or even on a brightly lit windowsill. Store the rest of the seeds in a dry, cool place until they are needed. If you're impatient for spring to arrive, cover an area of soil on the vegetable plot with plastic sheeting, to dry and warm the soil for early sowings. Seed potatoes may arrive soon, too; set these up in a bright place to sprout.

Hardy winter root crops are still available for harvest, but it's always a good idea to bring a few days' supply under cover, just in case the soil freezes solid, locking them in. Protect early sowings of peas and beans with cloches or horticultural fleece during cold spells.

In the fruit garden, take full advantage of dry, reasonably mild days to get underway with the pruning of soft and tree fruit.

vegetables | GENERAL ADVICE

Sow early crops under glass | Broad beans, Brussels sprouts, early summer cabbage, calabrese, cauliflowers, leeks, onions, peas, radishes, shallots, spinach and turnips can be raised under cover. Windowsills are rather dark and seedlings suffer if grown on them for prolonged periods. Greenhouses offer better conditions, but some heating is needed to produce healthy, well-grown plants.

Continue clearing the vegetable plot | Clear away crop debris and weeds and carry on digging over the soil, harvesting winter root vegetables for use in the kitchen or for storage, incorporating manure where appropriate. Work out your rotation plan (see box, right) so that you know where manure and lime should and should not be incorporated.

Prepare for early sowings | After digging, cover areas of the soil with clear polythene where you want to make early sowings. This will keep the soil dry and help it to warm up and so assist plant growth.

Keep off wet soil | No matter how keen you are to prepare the soil for spring, do not work on very wet, heavy, clay soil. Trampling over it when it is sodden will destroy the soil structure. Walk or wheel a barrow on a wooden plank over it to help to distribute your weight and prevent compaction.

If your soil is badly drained, work in as much organic matter as possible to improve it. Consider whether installing a drainage system might be worthwhile.

KEEP CROPS ON THE MOVE

Moving crops to different areas of the vegetable garden is important in order to avoid the build-up of soil-borne diseases. It also helps to ensure that greedy crops such as brassicas do not deplete the soil of nutrients. You need to have decided where each crop is planned to go as you dig, so you know whether to add manure to the soil or not.

There are several different schemes for crop rotation, but a simple one is a three-year rotation, dividing the vegetable plot into three equal-sized beds, and grouping crops into roots, brassicas (cabbage family) and everything else. In year one, grow roots in bed one; do not add lime or manure to the soil but add a balanced fertiliser in spring. Grow brassicas in bed two, digging in manure or compost in autumn and adding lime (depending on soil pH) in spring. In bed three, add balanced fertiliser in spring and grow all the other crops such as beans, peas, onions and salads. The following year, move the roots to bed two, the brassicas to bed three and everything else to bed one; the year after that, move roots to bed three, brassicas to bed one and everything else to bed two. Your crops have now been fully rotated round the vegetable plot. Then repeat this cycle.

PARSNIPS can be harvested and stored for use throughout the winter. If there is a hard frost, the ground will freeze and they will be difficult to harvest, so make sure you have enough in storage during cold spells.

vegetables | WHAT TO DO NOW

ONION FAMILY

Leeks

Sow for an early crop

To get an early crop to mature from late summer to autumn, sow leeks in a seed tray from now until late winter in a heated greenhouse or on a bright windowsill. Prick out the seedlings into modular trays or space them 5cm (2in) apart, and continue growing them under cover before hardening them off in a cold frame for planting out in mid spring.

Onions and shallots

Sow onions under cover

For large onions, sow seed now in a heated greenhouse or propagator. If you want to try your hand at growing extra large bulbs for the show bench, choose varieties such as 'Ailsa Craig' and 'The Kelsae'.

CABBAGE FAMILY

General

Continue harvesting crops

Keep cutting cabbages, cauliflower, sprouting broccoli and kale, and picking Brussels sprouts.

Cauliflower

Sow seed under glass

Summer cauliflower varieties can be sown in pots in the greenhouse at 10–16°C (50–60°F). When sufficiently large, harden off the young plants ready for planting out from early spring for harvesting in early summer.

If club root is a problem, you could try the late summer variety 'Clapton', which is resistant to the disease.

CUT OFF EACH CABBAGE *(top) close to the ground with a sharp knife. If it is not to be used immediately, remove some of the outer leaves, then store it in a straw-lined box in a cool, dry place.*

SOWING IN SEED MODULES *(above) means that seedlings do not need transplanting until they have outgrown their individual cell, but you must thin them regularly to leave only one plant per cell.*

BEANS AND PEAS

Broad beans

Sow under cover

Sow broad beans in individual pots in a cold frame or unheated greenhouse, ready for planting out in spring.

PERENNIAL VEGETABLES

Rhubarb

Force plants outdoors

Forcing rhubarb encourages earlier, more tender stems; early-cropping varieties are most suitable. To do this, cover healthy crowns with a rhubarb forcer or large, tall pot now. Forcing can be further hastened by mounding farmyard manure or garden compost around the forcer to heat it. Shoots will begin to appear from late winter. Do not force the same crowns year after year or they will become exhausted.

ROOTS AND STEMS

General

Continue harvesting roots or using from store

In many areas root vegetables can stay in the ground all winter, but in colder regions it is advisable to lift the majority of the crop and keep it in store. Insulating crop rows with straw or similar material will also help.

IT IS TIME TO START EATING UP TURNIPS *and any other stored root vegetables before they begin to deteriorate in the warmer spring weather, which is now only a month or so away.*

DIVIDE RHUBARB CROWNS

If you want to increase your stock of rhubarb plants, lift healthy crowns now, trying to avoid damaging the roots as much as possible. Use a sharp spade to split the crown into sections, each section having some strong roots and a healthy growth bud. Replant the sections straight away.

RHUBARB PLANTS *should be divided every three or four years otherwise they can become congested and weak. If dividing large clumps, discard the older, less productive centre portion.*

Choose potato varieties

Decide which potato varieties you are going to plant in the new growing season, so that you can purchase the tubers from a reliable source.

Different varieties are suitable for different cooking methods: for example, 'Charlotte' and 'Pink Fir Apple' are good for salads; 'Kestrel' for roasting and for chips; 'King Edward' for baking; and 'Rooster' for mashing. Specialist suppliers will be able to recommend the best types.

SALADS

Chicory

Continue to force plants

Keep forcing witloof chicory in boxes of compost in a warm place, for winter salads (see page 187) or braising. Ensure all light is excluded to keep the chicons white and to reduce their bitter flavour.

fruit | GENERAL ADVICE

Use winter washes | Apply winter washes to fruit trees and bushes to kill overwintering pests. Always do this job only when plants are fully dormant, as winter washes will scorch young growth.

Feed with potash | Apply a topdressing of sulphate of potash to all fruits and nuts. Potash is the main nutrient that promotes good flowering and fruiting, as well as the ripening of wood.

Plant new stock | Plant nut trees as well as fruit trees and bushes in suitable weather – do not plant when the soil is frozen or waterlogged.

Check stored fruit | Continue to make regular visits to any places where fruit has been stored. Check each type is still in an appropriate temperature and that the environment is dry. Keep an eye out for mice or other rodents. Remove rotten or diseased pieces of fruit; feed them to garden birds.

SURROUND BLACK CURRANT PLANTS *with well-rotted bulky organic matter such as garden compost or manure. Keep the mulch away from the actual plant stems to prevent them rotting.*

fruit | WHAT TO DO NOW

TREE FRUIT

General

Check tree stakes
Ensure tree stakes and ties are firm and sound. Loosen ties where they are constricting the tree trunk.

Mulch fruit trees, bushes and canes
Use a generous amount of well-rotted garden compost or manure to mulch around fruit plants.

Protect tender fruit
Erect a lean-to cover of clear plastic over peaches, almonds, apricots and nectarines, or place pot-grown fruits in an unheated greenhouse.

Apples and pears

Collect shoots for grafting in spring
If you have a fruit tree that you want to propagate, whip-and-tongue grafting is a good way to do it. On a dry day, cut some shoots 23cm (9in) long from the tree you want

COLLECT GRAFTING SHOOTS *from young and healthy hardwood stems that you wish to propagate by whip-and-tongue grafting (see page 73). Bundle them together and then store until spring.*

REMOVE AFFECTED BRANCHES *as soon as symptoms of fungal canker occur. These show as depresssions and cracks within the branches on apple and pear trees, often near pruning wounds.*

to increase. Store them in a plastic bag in the bottom of a refrigerator to ensure they remain dormant.

Buy a suitable rootstock from a specialist fruit nursery and plant this out now, ready to be grafted in spring.

Prune out canker
Continue to prune out fungal cankers from apple and pear trees. Destroy all affected wood. Disinfect tools before using them on healthy trees.

Check grease bands
Grease bands may become covered in dead insects, leaves and general debris, forming a bridge for pest species to get safely across. Renew the bands where necessary.

Citrus

Harvest fruits
Pick citrus fruits once mature, using secateurs to cut them with a short stem rather than pulling them from the plant. Leave them on the plant as long as possible, as they do not continue to ripen once picked.

Peaches and nectarines

Control peach leaf curl
Erecting a plastic cover over wall-trained trees (see page 282) is one of the best ways of reducing peach leaf curl. However, if this is not possible, spray the plants with mancozeb or copper fungicides now.

SOFT FRUIT

GENERAL

Continue pruning
If you have not done so in early winter, it is now time to prune currants and gooseberries unless there are freezing conditions; if there is a severely cold spell, wait until the weather is warmer.

Take hardwood cuttings
Use some of the prunings from currants and gooseberries to increase your stock by hardwood cuttings. Make each cutting 25cm (10in) long, cutting just below a bud at the base of the stem and just above a bud at the top. Insert the cuttings in a trench or large pot of sandy soil and leave until next autumn, when they should have rooted.

Raspberries

Prune canes
If this has not already been done, cut out all canes that have fruited. Remove all canes from autumn-fruiting varieties down to ground level, while on summer-fruiting varieties prune out only those canes that bore fruit last summer; these can be identified because they are a darker brown than the new canes.

SOME SPECIES OF CITRUS *are comparatively more cold-tolerant, but none is fully hardy and so they benefit from a frost-free environment in winter if you are to enjoy fruit such as these oranges.*

late winter

No matter how bad the weather, there is still a real note of optimism this month. You know that the worst of the winter is behind you, yet sometimes the hardest thing to do at this time of year is to control your impatience. After a long winter it seems as though spring may never arrive, but it really isn't far away. The shortest day is long past, and the lighter evenings are now really noticeable.

It is a mistake to do too much too early, however, because winter can still have a few unpleasant tricks in store. Cold spells this month are common, sometimes with the temperature not rising above freezing for days at a time. But there are still plenty of crops to harvest from the garden, with winter brassicas and roots shrugging off the harshest weather. You should still be enjoying your stored harvests, too, though it pays to use these up quickly before they deteriorate too much.

vegetables | GENERAL ADVICE

Order seeds | Check the catalogues and websites of suppliers of vegetable seeds. Since seed can be stored in cool, dark, dry conditions, it is worth buying in as wide a selection as you have room for, saving surplus seed for future years. Seed packets usually have some kind of expiry date and, though it is true that old seeds are less likely to germinate than new ones, they are likely to be viable for several years. To help you choose vegetables, the RHS regularly tests different kinds and publishes lists of recommended varieties on its website (www.rhs.org.uk/plants), giving its Award of Garden Merit (AGM) to the very best. AGM plants do not require highly specialist growing conditions or care.

ORDER PLUG PLANTS

It is sometimes more convenient to buy plants in spring than to raise your own from seed for which you may not have appropriate growing conditions. Many of the major seed catalogues also feature plug plants – young plants grown in individual cells that are sent out ready for potting on or planting out. Order these at the same time as your seeds to make sure you get the varieties you want.

Wait for spring | By now there is an almost irresistible temptation to start sowing and planting. While you can begin sowing early crops under glass, either on a windowsill or in a greenhouse, you should wait for the warm weather of spring before planting anything unless your garden is unusually well-drained and in a sheltered, mild district.

ALL TYPES OF BROCCOLI *should be harvested when the flower shoots are well developed but before the flowers actually open.*

vegetables | WHAT TO DO NOW

ONION FAMILY

Leeks

Continue harvesting
Keep on pulling leeks, making sure you use them up before the plants begin to grow again in spring. Once they start into growth they produce a flower stem which forms a firm, dense core in the centre of the leek; these are still edible, but they are not of such good quality.

Onions and shallots

Plant shallots
Plant in well-drained soil, setting the bulbs 23cm (9in) apart in rows 30cm (12in) apart.

Thin overwintered onions
Onions such as 'Senshyu Yellow Globe' that were sown in late summer can be thinned to their final spacing, 8–10cm (3–4in) apart, or slightly wider if you want to encourage larger bulbs.

CABBAGE FAMILY

Broccoli and calabrese

Keep picking
Harvest the flower shoots of purple-sprouting broccoli regularly to keep it going into spring. The less common white-sprouting broccoli should be ready for picking by now. Regular picking can extend the cropping time for up to an invaluable eight weeks, at a season when other fresh vegetables are becoming very scarce.

An occasional application of a balanced general fertiliser, plus watering if the weather should be particularly dry, will help to encourage the formation of new shoots to keep the season going even longer.

LEEKS SHOULD BE HARVESTED *(top) before they start to bolt in the warmer spring weather, when they will have developed a solid flowering stem in the centre of the plant.*

PURPLE-SPROUTING BROCCOLI *(above) produces smaller flowerheads than calabrese. It is an invaluable crop in late winter and spring, when it can be boiled, or eaten with butter like asparagus.*

Brussels sprouts

Continue harvesting
Keep picking Brussels sprouts, working your way up the stems from the bottom. Refirm the plants in the soil if they have been loosened by wind. Once all the sprouts on a stem are picked, don't forget to cut and eat the tops of the plants; they make a good leafy green vegetable. Some varieties produce an almost cabbage-like head.

Cabbages

Sow summer varieties

Sow cabbages either into a prepared seedbed outdoors, into seed trays or modules for later planting, or directly where they are to grow. Summer cabbages can be sown from now until late spring.

Cut spring greens

Cut overwintered cabbages for use as spring greens as soon as they are ready for harvesting.

BEANS AND PEAS

General

Continue sowing peas and broad beans

If you have not already done so, sow peas and beans in pots in the greenhouse for planting out in spring.

PERENNIAL VEGETABLES

Asparagus

Sow seed indoors

Soak the seed overnight, and then sow 1cm (½in) deep into 7.5cm (3in) pots of seed compost. Water well and keep at 14°C (57°F). 'Martha Washington' and 'Connover's Colossal' are long-established asparagus varieties that can be grown from seed; 'Marte' and 'Jersey Knight' are newer, all-male hybrids (see box, above right).

MALE AND FEMALE ASPARAGUS

Asparagus produces male and female flowers on different plants. Male plants are more desirable: they have thicker spears, which tend to emerge earlier in the spring, and the plants are often longer lived. Another advantage of male asparagus plants is that they do not produce berries (as female plants do); these are a nuisance when they self-seed. Always look for all-male plants when buying asparagus crowns or seed varieties.

DESIGNING RAISED BEDS

If you are making more than one raised bed, sketch out plans on graph paper to scale to ensure that they fit the site. This will also help when ordering the materials as it will give you a clear idea of the quantities and sizes of the materials you need. Before purchasing these, however, mark out the area for the raised beds in the garden itself with canes and string to check that your calculations are correct and that you are happy with the plan.

Prepare new beds

Dig over the soil, adding well-rotted organic matter. If your soil is heavy, consider making a raised bed (see box, above).

Globe artichokes

Sow seed indoors

Sow globe artichoke seeds between now and early spring, placing one seed in each 9cm (3½in) pot filled with seed compost. Leave in a place at 15°C (59°F) to germinate.

ALTHOUGH CALLED SPRING GREENS, *this type of small, pointed cabbage should be ready for harvesting in late winter. When you pick them, remove alternate plants, leaving the others to heart up.*

HARDY PEA VARIETIES *will rot if sown in cold, wet soil so they are best started off in a greenhouse. In the seed compost, make a drill 5cm (2in) deep and set the peas 5cm (2in) apart.*

Jerusalem artichokes

Plant tubers

Plant Jerusalem artichoke tubers in a sheltered spot. The top growth is very tall, so bear in mind that the plants may cast shade on other crops growing nearby. However, the stems can make a useful windbreak.

You can plant tubers obtained from the greengrocer, but a better crop will be obtained by choosing a named variety from a specialist supplier. 'Fuseau' is the most popular; this has long, smooth-skinned tubers that are easier to clean and peel than the very knobbly tubers of the common variety of Jerusalem artichoke.

Rhubarb

Continue forcing

Keep on forcing rhubarb for tender, early stems. Make regular inspections of plants that are being forced to ensure they are not rotting. Start picking rhubarb stems as soon as they are large enough.

BEETROOT SEED

For many beetroot varieties, each corky 'seed' is in fact a cluster of seeds, which produces several seedlings. These seedlings will need thinning shortly after germination if the remainder are to have room to develop into healthy plants. However, modern varieties such as 'Solo' and 'Moneta' are 'monogerm', which means that only one seedling is produced, saving the trouble of thinning them out so early in the growing process.

Beetroot

Sow for an early crop

The first sowing of beetroot can be made under cloches, horticultural fleece or cold frames. If you live in a very mild area it may soon be possible to sow outside, but beetroot doesn't germinate well below 7°C (45°F).

Sow beetroot seed 2.5cm (1in) deep in rows 30cm (12in) apart, spacing seeds about a thumb's width apart. The large, corky-textured seed is easy to handle but can be slow to germinate (see box, below).

Carrots

Sow in a cold frame

Sow carrots in a cold frame or unheated greenhouse to harvest during late spring.

Parsnips

Continue harvesting

Keep lifting parsnips that have been left in the ground. Once they start into growth again in early spring, their roots become flabby and unappetising, so make sure you have used the crop before this happens.

TAKE CARE WHEN DIGGING UP PARSNIPS *as canker can develop in any roots damaged when adjacent ones are dug up. Some varieties such as 'Countess', 'Javelin' and 'Gladiator' have good resistance to canker.*

| How to store vegetables

Most vegetable growers would love to be able to provide their family with fresh produce straight from the vegetable garden every week of the year, but even the best organised and largest of gardens would be hard pushed to achieve this. The majority of crops are produced in summer and early autumn. A few can be harvested through the winter, and even less during early spring, a time traditionally referred too as the 'hungry gap'.

Fortunately many crops can successfully be stored for use through the leaner winter and spring months. There are several methods of storage, some very simple, others requiring more preparation. Whichever method you use, select only sound, undamaged produce for storage.

LEEKS (above) *have a big advantage: they can be harvested over a long period, from autumn to winter, remaining 'stored' in the ground.*

ALLOW POTATOES TO DRY (right) *after harvesting before bagging them up in a paper or hessian sack or wooden boxes.*

Storage methods

In the ground

This is often the best, and certainly the easiest, method of storing many vegetables – just leave them where they are growing. Root crops such as parsnips, carrots, swedes and turnips, brassicas such as winter cabbages and Brussels sprouts, and hardy crops such as leeks can all be left where they are and harvested as required. However, when so left they are more prone to weather and pest damage, and in some areas may be inaccessible because they are frozen into the ground during cold weather.

In clamps

This is a traditional method that is useful if you don't have much space for storing roots under cover. In a sheltered spot outdoors, make a conical stack of roots and cover it with a layer of straw and then with a thick layer of sand or light soil, patted firmly into place. For ventilation, pull a tuft of straw through the soil at the top of the stack.

In boxes or sacks

Use sturdy wooden boxes for preference. In a cool but frost-free shed or garage, put a layer of slightly moist sand, light sandy soil or peat substitute in the base of the box, lay the vegetables on top so they are not touching and cover them with more sand, soil or peat substitute. Potatoes store well in hessian or strong paper sacks (not plastic, which will encourage rotting).

On the shelf

In a cool, frost-free shed, garage or cellar, set up a system of slatted wooden shelves, which will allow a

STORED VEGETABLES AND FRUIT *will start to deteriorate once the weather starts to warm up, so finish them off quickly before they start to shrivel or sprout.*

good flow of air round produce and encourage it to last throughout the winter months. Produce such as mature marrows, pumpkins and squashes, winter cabbages, onions, garlic and shallots will all keep well in such a store.

When produce is stored for a long time on shelves, it can start to rot underneath, where the wooden slats press against it. Hanging the produce in nets or stringing up onion family members in ropes or plaits gets round this problem.

In the kitchen

Many fresh vegetables in optimum condition after harvesting are best frozen as they deteriorate quickly (for example, peas, beans, asparagus and sweetcorn). Otherwise dry them (for example, herbs, tomatoes, chillies) or turn them into pickles and chutneys.

MAKE PICCALILLI *and other pickles, chutneys and relishes with vegetables that deteriorate quickly once harvested.*

Potatoes

Start to sprout seed potatoes

Buy certified seed potatoes that are free from viruses. Start them into growth by sprouting, or 'chitting', them four to six weeks before planting. Set the tubers on end, in egg boxes or seed trays, and place in good light in a cool room. Usually most of the eyes are at one end of the tuber (known as the rose end), and this end should be set uppermost.

The advantage of chitting potato tubers is that it gets them into early growth, ready for the season ahead; each tuber will develop sturdy, green shoots to give them a head start when planted out.

Turnips

Start sowing now

As with most root crops, turnips do not transplant well and must be sown outdoors directly where they are to grow. It is best to sow the crop in gradual succession over a number of months, so that gluts are avoided and you can continually harvest the emerging young plants while the roots are at their most tender.

Make the first sowing now, in suitable weather. Sowing can continue right through to the end of summer, with at least two weeks between each sowing. Sow thinly in drills 1cm (½in) deep, spacing rows 23–30cm (9–12in) apart. Thin

THE SEED LEAVES OF CUCUMBER *look very different to the true leaves of this plant once it is mature. Pot on seedlings into 13cm (5in) pots only once the true leaves have started to develop.*

the emerging seedlings in stages until the plants are about 10–20cm (4–8in) apart. Use horticultural fleece to protect the rows from frost.

SALADS

Cucumbers

Sow seeds under cover

Sow cucumber seeds in pots in a frost-free greenhouse or heated propagator; an early sowing will give you the longest harvest season. Alternatively, you could buy ready-grown plants in spring and early summer from a garden centre or mail-order supplier.

Lettuces

Sow seed under cover

Sow lettuces for an early summer crop in trays of seed compost in a frost-free greenhouse. Prick the seedlings off to wider spacings as soon as they are large enough. These will be ready for transplanting outside in mid to late spring, once there is little risk of frost.

THIN TURNIP SEEDLINGS *as they develop to prevent overcrowding. Do this by protecting the adjacent seedlings so they are not disturbed when the surplus seedlings are removed.*

Radishes

Sow seed under cover

Sow early varieties in modules in a frost-free greenhouse for planting out in mid spring. They can also be sown in the greenhouse border for an early crop.

Tomatoes

Sow seed in warmth

If you have suitable facilities, you can sow greenhouse tomatoes now. Sow in trays or pots of seed compost at 15–30°C (59–86°F) in a heated propagator, and grow the seedlings on at 21°C (70°F) in good light.

If you cannot provide these warm conditions, delay sowing for a few weeks.

SPINACH AND CHARD

Spinach

Sow seed outdoors

In mild areas with light soil, spinach can be sown thinly in 1cm (½in) drills in rows 30cm (12in) apart where it is to crop. It will germinate best in soil that has been covered with cloches or clear polythene.

TENDER VEGETABLES

Peppers and chillies

Sow under cover

Sow seed at 20°C (68°F) in pots or modules of seed compost. Sow the very hot chilli varieties early, because they can take 30 days to germinate. During this time the seed can rot, which means you will have to try sowing them yet again.

Sow milder chillies and sweet peppers from now until early spring. Transfer into individual 9cm (3½in) pots when large enough, and grow on at 18°C (64°F).

Growing peppers and chillies from seed offers by far the widest choice of varieties, although you can buy ready-grown plants if just a few are needed or you can't provide the high temperatures needed for germination at this time of year.

ONCE TOMATO SEEDLINGS EMERGE (top) *move the container to a warm, well-lit spot and let the seedlings grow. Pot them up individually into 8cm (3in) pots as soon as they are large enough to handle.*

SWEET PEPPERS CAN BE SOWN (above) *from late winter to early spring. Once seeds have germinated, leave them on a sunny windowsill until the weather is warm enough for them to grow in a greenhouse.*

| Grow your own brassicas

The brassica family includes many crops that form the mainstay of the vegetable garden. Although it is often referred to as the cabbage family, it includes broccoli, Brussels sprouts, cauliflower and kale as well as cabbage. In addition to these leafy and flowering crops, the root crops swede and turnip are brassicas, too. This makes the brassica family a very large and diverse group of plants.

However, all brassicas do share a number of cultivation requirements. They like similar soil conditions and are prone to the same pests and diseases, so it is convenient to group brassicas together in the crop rotation scheme. Whatever brassicas you are growing, the following tips will help to ensure you get good results from this sometimes rather difficult-to-manage family.

BRASSICAS (above) are among the most useful of all vegetable crops, providing a fresh, nutritious harvest all year round.

CABBAGES (right) are particularly welcome from winter to early spring when there is little else available in the vegetable garden.

Success with brassicas

Nutrients

Brassicas are hungry crops, and require large amounts of nitrogen. They thrive on soils that have been improved with generous quantities of organic matter such as well-rotted garden compost or manure. They also like an open, sunny position.

Avoiding club root

One of the most important factors in growing good brassicas is avoiding the disease club root. This is a soil-living fungus that only affects plants of the cabbage family, and it can do serious damage. It thrives in acid soil, which is why brassicas should be grown in neutral or alkaline soils. In many gardens this means applying garden lime to the area in which brassicas are to be grown, in order to bring the soil pH up to the correct level of 6.5–7.5. Also, to deter club root, follow a crop rotation plan (see page 262) to ensure that brassicas are not grown on the same piece of ground in successive years.

Club root is often brought in on the roots of plants that have been raised elsewhere, on infected ground. For this reason, you should either raise your own plants from seed, or buy them from a reputable source, making sure they have been raised in sterile potting compost. Accepting kindly meant gifts of plants from friends or neighbours is one of the most common ways for club root disease to be introduced.

KEEP CABBAGE SEEDLINGS *(top right) free of competing weeds by regular handweeding or hoeing. Take care not to damage the stems.*

WHEN HARVESTING CAULIFLOWERS *(right) retain some of the leaves intact around the head to protect it during handling.*

Plant firmly

When planting any brassica, do make sure that the ground is firm. Although walking on the soil destroys its structure, brassicas need firm planting, so don't be afraid to use your feet when planting to firm them in around the base of the stems. If brassicas such as cauliflowers, calabrese and broccoli work themselves loose, they will develop poor root systems and leaf structure so that they flower prematurely and produce small, poor-quality heads. After planting, tug gently at a leaf – the leaf should tear rather than the plant move in the soil.

Brassicas need good amounts of space between plants to allow air to circulate around them and to help prevent diseases from taking hold. For the same reason, it is also important to remove weeds and any old, withered leaves as they appear.

Protect against pests

The best defence against the three main brassica pests – caterpillars, cabbage root fly and pigeons – is enclosing the plants in a cage covered by insect-proof netting.

To prevent cabbage root fly, place a 7.5cm (3in) disc or collar of roofing felt or carpet underlay around the base of the stem when planting out to prevent the fly laying its eggs. Proprietary collars are also available.

fruit | GENERAL ADVICE

Last chance to prune | Finish pruning apples, pears, medlars and quinces before the trees start into growth in the spring.

Untie festooned trees | Untie festooned fruit tree branches that have set into position (see page 97).

Plant bare-root trees | Get all bare-root fruit trees planted as soon as possible now.

Use high potash fertiliser | Apply a topdressing of sulphate of potash to all fruits and nuts if this has not been done in the last month.

Check newly planted fruit | Fruit trees and bushes that have been recently planted may have been lifted by frosts, which cause the soil to expand. Tread round the root area to firm them into place again. Also check that all ties are secure and not rubbing.

FRUITING SPURS OR FRUITING TIPS?

Successful fruit pruning depends on having a basic understanding of a plant's physiology. Fruit trees – particularly apples – fall into two categories as to how they produce their flowers and therefore, after pollination, their fruit: these are spur bearers and tip bearers. Most fruit trees form both types of growth but are usually prone to producing more of one type than the other. Spur bearers, which are the most common, bear their fruit on short, stumpy shoots (the spurs), which are usually more than two years old. The fruit of the tip bearers develops on shoots that were formed during the previous season. Trees that are mainly tip bearing in habit, such as a 'Bramley's Seedling', are unsuitable for growing as restricted forms (see page 58).

VISUAL IDENTIFICATION

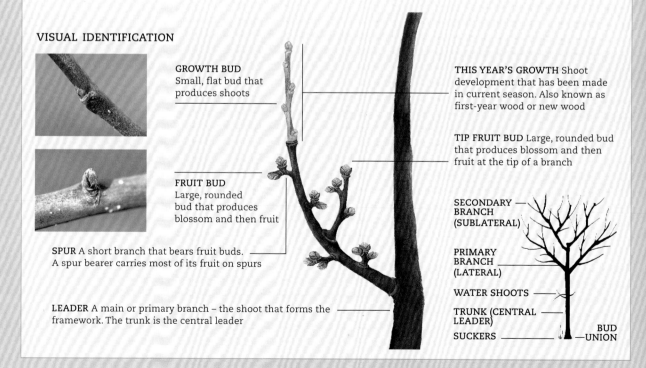

GROWTH BUD Small, flat bud that produces shoots

FRUIT BUD Large, rounded bud that produces blossom and then fruit

SPUR A short branch that bears fruit buds. A spur bearer carries most of its fruit on spurs

LEADER A main or primary branch – the shoot that forms the framework. The trunk is the central leader

THIS YEAR'S GROWTH Shoot development that has been made in current season. Also known as first-year wood or new wood

TIP FRUIT BUD Large, rounded bud that produces blossom and then fruit at the tip of a branch

SECONDARY BRANCH (SUBLATERAL)

PRIMARY BRANCH (LATERAL)

WATER SHOOTS

TRUNK (CENTRAL LEADER)

SUCKERS

BUD UNION

fruit | WHAT TO DO NOW

TREE FRUIT

Apricots

Feed trees

Apricots benefit from a granular feed using a general compound fertiliser now, followed by mulching around the rooting area with well-rotted farmyard manure.

Protect blossoms from frost

Apricots flower very early, and their flowers must be protected against frost if their blossoms are to survive and set a good crop. Erect a double layer of horticultural fleece over the trees, supporting it so that it does not touch the flowers. Remove this during the day in mild weather so that insects can access the flowers to pollinate them. If insects are scarce, hand pollinate the flowers using a soft paintbrush (see page 282).

Citrus

Prune trees where necessary

Because most citrus are bought as established plants, often no formative pruning is required. However, regular pruning is required to maintain the shape of the many citrus trees that are trained as standards. When pruning, take care to avoid the vicious thorns that many citrus bear; wear a pair of stout, thornproof gloves.

This is the main pruning period – just before the plants come into growth. Thin out congested shoots and prune back leaders to maintain a balanced head, using a pair of sharp secateurs.

Mist flowering plants

Spray plants with tepid water when they are flowering, to help ensure good fruit set.

Continue harvesting

Continue to pick citrus fruits as they ripen.

CITRUS FLOWERS APPEAR IN CLUSTERS *in late winter and need misting. As well as developing into fruits, they also emit a deliciously sweet perfume, which hangs in the surrounding air.*

Figs

Repot container-grown plants

Container-grown figs usually need repotting every other year. Turn the tree carefully out of its pot and crumble away loose compost from around its rootball. Trim back very thick roots with secateurs.

Repot with fresh loam-based compost such as John Innes No. 3, either into a pot one size larger than previously, or in the same size pot. This job must be done while the tree is dormant.

Mulberries

Finish pruning

Mulberries do not normally need regular pruning, but any pruning necessary – removing dead, diseased, overcrowded or crossing branches – must be finished now. If this is done when the tree is not fully dormant it will bleed sap from the pruning cuts.

Peaches and nectarines

Protect trees from disease

Erect a polythene structure over the top and the front of wall-trained trees to keep rain off them until spring. This helps to prevent peach leaf curl.

Protect blossoms from frost

Cover the blossom of peaches and nectarines so it is protected against frost, removing it during the daytime in mild weather. Hand pollinate the flowers if necessary.

Spray against peach leaf curl

If appropriate, make a second spraying against peach leaf curl, following the manufacturer's directions (see page 267).

Quinces

Feed trees on light soils

An application of sulphate of ammonia or other high-nitrogen fertiliser every three or four years will be beneficial, especially on light, sandy soils. Quinces also appreciate sulphate of potash to help boost yields.

PROTECT PEACH TREES (top) *from peach leaf curl and peach blossom from early spring frosts by covering them with polythene secured to a frame. Remove this during the daytime so insects can access the flowers.*

PEACHES FLOWER EARLY IN THE YEAR (above), *when there may be a lack of pollinating insects. To aid pollination, transfer pollen from one flower to another using a soft brush.*

SOFT FRUIT

General

Finish pruning

Complete the pruning of black currants, gooseberries, red and white currants and raspberries.

Hand weed and mulch bushes

Hand weed around black currants, gooseberries and red and white currants. Feed with a balanced compound fertiliser at a rate of 100g per square metre (3oz per square yard). Mulch with well-rotted manure or compost.

Black currants

Weed bushes carefully

Hand weed round the base of black currant bushes. Avoid hoeing as the blade might cut through new shoots developing at the base of the plants.

Blueberries

Prune plants

Keep plants productive by taking out a proportion of the older wood; cut out two or three of the oldest stems to their base. At the same time tip back vigorous, new shoots to a plump, healthy bud to encourage side branching.

Take hardwood cuttings

Use prunings of one-year-old wood as hardwood cuttings. Cut them into 20cm (8in) lengths and insert into a trench of moisture-retentive but well-drained acidic soil so that only the top 7.5cm (3in) is above ground.

Gooseberries

Give balanced fertiliser

Apply a balanced fertiliser around the base of gooseberry bushes. Avoid feeding gooseberries with too much nitrogen as this can encourage wispy, sappy growth, which is prone to gooseberry mildew.

Raspberries

Prune back canes

Tip back summer-fruiting raspberry canes to 15cm (6in) above their top support wire.

Strawberries

Plan for early crops

Move pot-grown strawberries into a heated greenhouse for an early forced crop, keeping them at a temperature of 10–16°C (50–61°F). You will probably need to hand pollinate the flowers when they open.

Order cold-stored runners for planting out during spring. They will fruit 60 days after planting.

VINE FRUIT

Grapes

Mulch greenhouse vines

Apply a generous thickness of mulch such as well-rotted manure or garden compost round the base of the vine. Do not let it touch the stem.

Prune guyot-trained vines outdoors

On established grapevines, untie the lower, fruiting arms and prune off, replacing them with two reserved shoots (see page 258). It is better to do this before late winter but it can still be done now if the job has been left. Do not leave any later or the sap will bleed, wasting the plant's energy.

HARVESTING STRAWBERRIES IS USUALLY MUCH EASIER *when they are grown in special strawberry planters, but at this time of year they will need cold-weather protection if you are to force an early crop.*

Kiwifruit

Feed plants

Apply a topdressing of high-potash fertiliser such as sulphate of potash now and follow it up with a more balanced feed in early spring.

NUTS

Cobnuts and filberts

Prune out older stems

Nuts will develop on established plants along the length of one-year-old wood and on fruiting spurs. To encourage the production of new, more floriferous growth on established trees, remove older, thicker stems; these can be used for hurdles or plant supports. Do this now, while the trees are flowering, because in the process their pollen is likely to be dislodged from the male flowers and transferred to the females on the remaining stems.

The male flowers of these nuts are the familiar catkins, but the female flowers are much less conspicuous, being very small red tufts on the branches. Because they flower so early, cobnuts and filberts are pollinated by wind rather than by insects.

| Vegetable sowing and harvesting chart

Plan your vegetable production with the help of this chart, which shows the main periods when crops should be sown or planted and when they can be harvested. The actual times will vary according to the climate in the area where you garden, and also the weather conditions in any particular year. The crops have been listed in alphabetical order so you can easily find the vegetable you are after and never miss a sowing or harvesting date again.

		EarlySpr	MidSpr	LateSpr	EarlySu	MidSu	LateSu	EarlyA	MidA	LateA	EarlyW	MidW	LateW
Asparagus	Plant:	•	•										•
	Harvest:		•	•									
Aubergines	Sow:	•	•										
	Plant:			•	•								
	Harvest:					•	•	•	•				
Autumn cabbage	Sow:	•	•	•									
	Plant:			•	•								
	Harvest:							•	•	•			
Beetroot	Sow:	•	•	•	•	•	•						•
	Harvest:				•	•	•	•	•				
Broad beans	Sow:	•	•						•	•	•	•	•
	Plant:	•	•	•									
	Harvest:			•	•	•	•						
Broccoli	Sow:		•	•	•	•							
	Plant:			•	•	•							
	Harvest:	•	•			•		•	•	•	•	•	•
Brussels sprouts	Sow:	•	•	•									
	Plant:				•	•							
	Harvest:	•							•	•	•	•	•
Carrots	Sow:	•	•	•	•	•						•	•
	Harvest:	•		•	•	•	•	•	•	•	•	•	•
Cauliflower	Sow:		•	•					•	•	•	•	
	Plant:	•	•	•	•	•	•						
	Harvest:	•	•	•	•	•	•	•	•	•	•	•	•
Celeriac	Sow:	•	•										
	Plant:		•	•	•								
	Harvest:	•	•						•	•	•	•	•
Chicory	Sow:		•	•	•	•	•						
	Plant:		•		•								
	Harvest:				•	•	•	•	•				
Courgettes, marrows, summer squashes	Sow:		•	•	•								
	Plant:			•	•								
	Harvest:					•	•	•	•				
Cucumber	Sow:	•	•	•									
	Plant:			•	•	•							
	Harvest:					•	•	•	•				
Florence fennel	Sow:		•	•	•	•							
	Plant:			•	•	•							
	Harvest:				•	•	•	•	•				
French beans	Sow:		•	•	•								
	Plant:				•	•							
	Harvest:				•	•	•	•	•				
Garlic	Plant								•	•	•	•	•
	Harvest:				•	•	•						
Globe artichokes	Plant:	•	•										•
	Harvest:			•	•								
Jerusalem artichokes	Plant:	•	•	•									•
	Harvest:								•	•	•	•	•
Kale	Sow:		•	•	•								
	Plant:				•	•	•						
	Harvest:	•	•	•					•	•	•	•	•
Leeks	Sow:	•	•									•	•
	Plant:			•	•	•							
	Harvest:	•	•	•					•	•	•	•	•

		EarlySpr	MidSpr	LateSpr	EarlySu	MidSu	LateSu	EarlyA	MidA	LateA	EarlyW	MidW	LateW
Lettuce	Sow:	•	•	•	•	•	•	•					
	Harvest:			•	•	•	•	•	•	•			
Okra	Sow:	•	•										
	Plant:			•	•								
	Harvest:					•	•	•					
Onions	Plant sets:	•						•	•	•			
	Sow:	•					•	•					•
	Harvest:			•	•	•	•	•					
Parsnips	Sow:	•	•	•									•
	Harvest:	•						•	•	•	•	•	•
Peas	Sow:	•	•	•	•	•							
	Harvest:				•	•	•	•	•				
Peppers and chillies	Sow:	•	•										•
	Plant:			•	•								
	Harvest:					•	•	•	•				
Perpetual spinach	Sow:		•	•	•								
	Plant:			•	•								
	Harvest:			•	•	•	•	•	•	•			
Potatoes	Chit:	•										•	•
	Plant:	•	•	•									
	Harvest:				•	•	•	•	•	•			
Radishes	Sow:	•	•	•	•	•	•	•					
	Harvest:			•	•	•	•	•	•	•	•	•	
Rhubarb	Plant:	•		•					•	•	•	•	•
	Harvest:			•	•	•							
Runner beans	Sow:		•	•	•								
	Plant:				•	•							
	Harvest:				•	•	•	•	•				
Spinach	Sow:	•	•	•	•	•	•	•					
	Harvest:		•	•	•	•	•	•	•				
Spring cabbage	Sow:					•	•						
	Plant:								•	•			
	Harvest:		•	•									
Summer cabbage	Sow:	•	•	•									•
	Plant:			•	•								
	Harvest:				•	•	•	•	•				
Swedes	Sow:			•	•								
	Harvest:							•	•	•	•		
Sweetcorn	Sow:		•	•	•								
	Plant:			•	•								
	Harvest:					•	•	•	•				
Swiss chard	Sow:		•	•	•	•	•						
	Plant:			•	•								
	Harvest:	•	•	•	•	•	•	•	•	•	•	•	•
Tomatoes	Sow:	•	•										•
	Plant:			•	•								
	Harvest:					•	•	•	•				
Turnips	Sow:	•	•	•	•	•	•						•
	Harvest:			•	•	•	•	•	•	•	•		
Winter cabbage	Sow:			•	•								
	Plant:				•	•							
	Harvest:	•								•	•	•	•
Winter squashes and pumpkins	Sow:		•	•	•								
	Plant:			•	•								
	Harvest:					•	•	•	•				

| Fruit production chart

Knowing when each crop is likely to be available, either fresh from the tree or from store, will help you plan for the inevitable gluts and shortages. Most fruit is ready to harvest in late summer and early autumn, but freezing and jam-making means you can enjoy it for much longer.

* from store • fresh

	EarlySp	MidSp	LateSp	EarlySu	MidSu	LateSu	EarlyA	MidA	LateA	EarlyW	MidW	LateW
Almonds								••	*	*	*	
Apples (see right)	*	*				•	•	••	*	*	*	*
Apricots					•	•	•					
Blackberries					•	•	•					
Black currants					•	•						
Blueberries					•	•	•					
Cherries				•	•	•						
Citrus	*										•	••
Cobnuts							•	••	*	*		
Cranberries							•	•				
Damsons						•	•					
Figs						•	•					
Filberts							•	••	*	*		
Gages						•	•					
Gooseberries					•	•	•					
Grapes							•	•	•			
Hybrid berries					•	•						
Kiwifruit							•	••	*			
Lingonberries							•	•				
Medlars								*	*	*		
Melons					•	•	•	•				
Mulberries					•	•						
Nectarines					•	•	•					
Peaches					•	•	•					
Pears	*	*				•	•	••	*	*	*	*
Plums						•	•					
Quinces							••	*	*		*	*
Raspberries				•	•	•	•	•	•			
Red currants					•	•						
Strawberries			•	•	•	•	•	•				
White currants					•	•						

| Pests and diseases

Both fruit and vegetable plants may be attacked by a wide range of pest and disease organisms. Sometimes these are of little consequence, but there are other times when their effects can be devastating.

A pest or disease may have its effect simply by weakening the plant, slowing or halting its growth and development. Diseases such as mildew, which reduce a plant's ability to photosynthesise, and sap-sucking pests such as aphids, can be included in this category. This will obviously lead to lower yields than would be obtained from healthy plants. Other pests and diseases may have a direct effect on the crop itself; botrytis makes fruits inedible, and cabbage caterpillars munch their way

through brassica leaves and spoil what remains of the yield with their excrement. Even if the crop is not completely destroyed, its eating or keeping qualities may be badly affected.

It is almost inevitable that at least a proportion of your fruit and vegetable plants will become a victim of some form of pest or disease during their lives, but there are preventive measures you can take to avoid attack and ways to reduce the damage caused to plants once they have been affected.

This chapter will help you to understand the various pests and diseases that pose a risk to your crops and the most effective methods of dealing with them.

CATERPILLARS ON CABBAGE (top) are voracious feeders, and can very quickly reduce a brassica crop to a lacework of tattered leaves if they are not controlled at an early stage.

WOOD PIGEONS (above) are particularly damaging to cabbage crops during cold spells in the winter. Growing winter brassicas in a fruit cage may be the only answer in some areas.

NEWLY EMERGING LEAVES (top) on fruit trees are vulnerable to attack by winter moth caterpillar. These are up to 2.5cm (1in) long and pale green, and walk with a looping action.

MICE (above) can be a nuisance when they dig up and eat newly sown pea and bean seeds. They also frequently attack fruit and vegetables in store in sheds and outhouses over the winter.

Avoiding problems

Encourage healthy growth Provide the best possible conditions for plants and you will give them a head start in being able to fight off pest and disease attacks. Grow them in well-prepared, fertile soil at the correct spacings and keep them weed free. Apply fertilisers where necessary and provide protection from adverse weather conditions.

Suit plants to their environment Don't try to grow plants where you know the conditions are not to their liking. Tender plants will suffer in cold areas; plants such as blueberries, which require acid soil, will never thrive in chalky soil, and so on. Plants that are already weakened by struggling to grow in unsuitable conditions are much more likely to be seriously affected by a pest or disease.

Practise good hygiene Creating wild areas will help to attract beneficial wildlife, but limit them to a specific corner of the garden and keep the rest of the growing area clean and tidy. Slugs, snails and various other pests enjoy the protection of dense weed cover and piles of debris where they can hide.

Remove and destroy any diseased plant tissue and disinfect pruning tools between trees when a disease such as canker present. Avoid importing problems such as club root by raising your own plants from seed, or ensuring that bought-in plants are free of symptoms.

Grow resistant varieties If specific pests or diseases have struck in previous years, look for varieties that are resistant to the particular problem concerned. For example, the carrots 'Flyaway' and 'Resistafly' are less likely to be affected by carrot fly: maincrop potato 'Sarpo Mira' has good resistance to both blight and slug attack; parsnip 'Lancer' is resistant to parsnip canker; and tomato 'Ferline' is resistant to blight.

Choose sowing and planting dates carefully. Sometimes the peak season for a particular pest or disease can be avoided by adjusting the date of sowing or planting – for example peas should be sown early or late in the season to avoid them flowering in mid summer, at the peak time for pea moth to be on the wing.

VELVET MITE *(magnified, top) is not to be mistaken for red spider mite, which is brown. Its presence is signalled if the leaves take on a silvery sheen and fine silky white webs appear around the shoot tips.*

BOTRYTIS *or grey mould (above) causes fruit such as strawberries to rot in damp conditions. Remove the affected fruits promptly to stop the fungus spreading.*

| Dealing with pests and diseases

When a pest or disease does strike, early detection and prompt action can make all the difference. It is important to inspect plants regularly, particularly at the times you know pests and diseases are likely to occur – for example, aphids are very likely to be found on the fresh young growing tips of broad bean plants in late spring, and potato blight can be expected in warm, wet weather in summer. Walk among your plants and look them over frequently. Do not forget to check the undersides of the leaves because this is often where a pest or disease symptom can first be spotted.

When you do identify a problem, decisions need to be made. Is the effect likely to be serious enough to warrant taking action? Sometimes a small amount of damage can be tolerated if you think it is unlikely to get any worse. At other times, however, it is vital to act swiftly – give a cluster of cabbage white butterfly eggs or tiny, newly hatched caterpillars on the underside of a cabbage leaf a week or two and they will reduce the plant to a tattered skeleton.

The next decision to be made is what type of control method you are going to use. Simple, non-chemical controls can be tried first; if these fail to overcome the problem you might then want to consider using proprietary products. Organic gardeners need not feel that all pest and disease control products are unsuitable for their use; increasing numbers of products are made from naturally occurring substances that break down

BLACK CHERRY APHIDS *(top) attacks the growing points of cherry trees in large numbers in spring. The aphids distort the foliage and can weaken the growth of the tree.*

CHOCOLATE SPOT *(above) tends to occur on broad beans in damp, humid weather early in the season and is visible as brown spots. Usually this isn't severe and is therefore not worth treating.*

IRON DEFICIENCY *(top) can occur when acid-loving plants, such as this citrus, are grown in the wrong pH. Ensuring plants have the right conditions will increase their immunity to pests and diseases.*

AMERICAN GOOSEBERRY MILDEW *(above) is less of a problem on varieties with resistance, such as 'Invicta'. Plants suffering from drought stress are more vulnerable so keep well mulched and watered.*

A **BEER TRAP** *can be used to attract and kill slugs. This and other traditional remedies such as half-grapefruit skins are worth a try if you are averse to all other methods, but expect to lose some of your crops.*

YOUNG FRUIT TREES *are particularly prone to damage by rabbits: they eat the bark, which can kill the tree. Trees are easily protected by a simple plastic tree guard.*

quickly and are perfectly suitable for use in an organically cultivated garden.

Non-chemical control methods

Provided you spot problems early enough, these methods can be very effective. Pinching out and destroying a shoot tip clustered with aphids; hand-picking cabbage caterpillars or slugs; washing aphids off runner beans with a strong jet of plain water; and using sticky yellow traps to keep down whitefly in the greenhouse are all useful ways of dealing with problems.

It is also a good idea to put up physical barriers to protect plants from attack in the first place – low fences of fleece or fine netting around carrots help to keep carrot fly at bay, while felt discs around the stems of newly planted brassicas will stop cabbage root flies laying their eggs.

Chemical controls

Where other methods fail, chemical pesticides can be used to clear pests and diseases from crops. All pesticides available today have passed stringent tests to ensure they are safe, but they must be used as directed – and that means always reading the instructions and following them. Choose non-persistent pesticides that break down rapidly after use and time your treatments so that you put beneficial creatures at minimum risk (by not spraying insecticide while plants are flowering, for instance).

Prevention and cure

Insecticides should be used only where a problem has been clearly identified; fungicides, on the other hand, can sometimes be used as a preventive before symptoms appear. Biological controls can also be used in certain situations; they tend to be particularly successful in greenhouses, where the introduced predator or parasite can be contained more easily than in the open air. Biological controls for red spider mite and whitefly were among the first to become available to gardeners but now there are also controls for a much wider range of garden pests such as aphids, caterpillars, slugs and even vine weevil.

| Vegetable pests and diseases chart

Some vegetable crops are far more prone to pest and disease problems than others, but with all crops, growing them in the best possible conditions will help to limit the amount of damage that occurs. When using chemical controls, always take particular care to observe the minimum time between spraying and harvesting.

Pests	Symptoms	Control
Aphids	Soft-bodied insects, usually green or black, cluster on new growth of many crops in spring and summer. Growth is weakened and aphids often spread virus diseases.	Spray with pyrethrins, fatty acids or plant oils. Bifenthrin and thiacloprid can be used on some crops (check the label).
Asparagus beetle	Small black, yellow-spotted beetles and dark-grey larvae eat asparagus foliage and stems.	Hand pick both from late spring or spray with pyrethrins. Cut off and burn stems in autumn.
Cabbage white caterpillars	White butterflies lay eggs on all cabbage plant crops. Black and yellow caterpillars feed voraciously and severely damage the plants.	Hand pick caterpillars and crush eggs. Spray with pyrethrins or bifenthrin. *Bacillus thuringiensis* is no longer available for garden use, but there is a biological control that uses nematodes.
Cabbage whitefly	Small white moth-like flying insects affect all cabbage-family members, weakening plants by sucking sap.	Spray heavy infestations with bifenthrin or pyrethrins.
Carrot fly	As well as carrots, celery, parsnip and parsley may be affected. Larvae mine the roots; signs include red-tinged leaves and poor growth.	No chemical control. Fleece or fine-mesh netting helps keep flies away. Avoid handling foliage as the scent attracts flies. Grow resistant varieties.
Celery leaf miner	Affecting celery, parsnips and parsley. Larvae eat the leaf from within, causing dead patches and weakened growth.	There is no chemical control. Pick off and destroy affected leaves.
Cutworm	Caterpillars live below soil, severing young plants from the roots and eating holes in root crops. Affects many, particularly cabbages and lettuce.	Search the soil near damaged plants and destroy the caterpillars. There is a biological control containing nematodes.
Flea beetle	Tiny black beetles eat characteristic small round holes in the foliage of cabbage-family crops; rocket is often particularly badly affected. The beetles jump like fleas when disturbed.	Provide good growing conditions to get plants through the young seedling stage as quickly as possible. Spray heavy attacks with pyrethrins. Clear crop debris at the end of the season.
Mice and voles	Large seeds such as beans, peas and sweetcorn are dug up and eaten after sowing. Mice also damage stored vegetables in winter.	Only set traps indoors. Outside, cover seedbeds with small mesh wire netting or lay prickly prunings such as holly along newly sown drills.
Millipede	Feed mainly on decaying plant tissue but occasionally damage seeds and young seedlings.	Remove weeds and refuse to keep the growing area tidy and millipede numbers down.
Onion fly	White larvae eat through the roots and bulbs of onions and related crops.	Cover with fleece to stop adults laying eggs. Grow onions from sets for higher resistance.
Pea moth	Whitish caterpillars feeding on developing peas within the pod remain hidden until harvesting.	Avoid peak egg-laying season with early or late sowings. Pea moth traps help control the adults.
Pigeon	Winter brassicas are eaten, especially in spells of cold weather, when damage can be very severe.	Use bird scarers. Protect crops with netting or grow in a fruit cage.
Rabbit	Rabbits will eat a wide range of crops, especially young plants, biting them down to ground level.	Fencing is the best method but extend it underground to prevent rabbits burrowing beneath it.
Red spider mite	Serious greenhouse pest. Leaves appear dry and speckled; shoot tips are spun with webbing; tiny green or red-brown mites can be seen.	Keep humidity high to discourage pests. Spray with plant oils or fatty acids, or use the biological control *Phytoseiulus persimilis*.
Slugs and snails	Damage a large number of crops, especially young seedlings, eating them off at ground level. Soil-living slugs also damage potato tubers.	Remove weeds and debris. Metaldehyde pellets can be used but may harm pets; aluminium sulphate and ferric phosphate are alternatives. Beer traps and hand picking are possibilities, and there is a biological control that uses nematodes.
Wireworm	The larvae of click beetles; wireworms damage root crops, especially carrots and potatoes, and eat seedlings off at ground level.	Dig the soil to expose the larvae to birds. Harvest potatoes and carrots as soon as they are ready as they are more susceptible left in the ground.

Disease	Symptoms	Control
Anthracnose	Fungus disease particularly affecting dwarf beans and cucumber. Discoloured, sunken patches appear on leaves, stems, pods and fruit. Leaves may die and plants are weakened.	Remove affected parts of plants and get rid of badly affected plants altogether. In the greenhouse, increase ventilation.
Blight	Affects potatoes and outdoor tomatoes (greenhouses can be affected in some years). Leaves rapidly yellow and wilt. Top growth of potatoes soon collapses completely. Potato tubers and tomatoes develop sunken brown patches of rot.	Occurs in warm, humid weather. Regular sprays of copper fungicide or mancozeb protects crops but won't control it once present. When found on potatoes, remove and burn all top growth to prevent the spores washing down to the tubers.
Blossom end rot	Disorder affecting tomatoes, peppers and aubergines. Brown shrunken patches develop on the blossom end of the fruits. Caused by lack of water at a critical time of fruit development.	Ensure plants are kept moist at all times when flowering and fruiting. Plants in growing bags are particularly susceptible; it helps to mix water-retaining granules with the compost.
Botrytis (grey mould)	Fluffy grey fungus on dead and damaged plant tissues quickly spreads in cool, damp conditions. Affects many crops, especially courgettes outdoors and cucumbers and tomatoes under glass.	Remove all plant debris and affected parts promptly. Increase the air flow around plants and raise temperatures in the greenhouse in autumn, when botrytis is most prevalent.
Chocolate spot	Chocolate-brown spots appear on the leaves of broad beans; stems, flowers and bean pods are also affected. Plants are weakened and may die.	The fungus is worst in humid conditions, so grow plants at the correct spacing and remove weeds. Destroy affected plants and remove and burn debris as the spores can overwinter on it.
Club root	A serious disease of all cabbage-family plants. First signs are usually plants failing to thrive and wilting in hot weather, with swollen, distorted roots. Likes acid soil, long lived and easily spread.	Improve drainage on heavy soils and add lime to reduce acidity. Once present, raise plants in pots so they have a good rootball when planted out and earth up stems to encourage new roots to form. There are no chemical controls.
Damping off	Young seedlings collapse at soil level where stems have rotted. Common in seed trays and encouraged by overcrowded conditions.	Sow thinly using sterile compost and clean trays; give plenty of light and good ventilation. Spray with copper fungicide after sowing.
Downy mildew	Causes discoloured patches on leaves with fungal growth on the underside. Common on spinach and lettuce, but affects many crops.	Remove affected foliage. Increase air circulation and reduce humidity by no overhead watering. Mancozeb can be used.
Leaf spot	Affects various crops including beetroot and celery. Brown spots can spread to the whole leaf and weaken plants, but the effect is often slight.	Remove affected foliage as soon as it is seen.
Leek rust	Leek leaves develop orange pustules containing numerous spores, turn yellow and die. Usually the inner leaves are unaffected, but the whole plant may rot from secondary infections.	Worst in crowded, damp conditions, so space plants correctly and control weeds. Remove and destroy affected leaves at harvest. Rotate leeks to a new area each year. Grow resistant varieties.
Onion white rot	White fungal growth at the bulb's base; yellow wilting leaves. Spores persist in the soil for years.	Destroy affected plants (do not compost) and grow onions in another area in future.
Parsnip canker	Brown, sunken areas appear on the roots, especially the shoulders. The disease often begins at a site of damage.	Avoid damaging the tops of roots by cultivation or hoeing. Improve drainage in heavy soils. Avoid very early sowings. Grow resistant varieties.
Potato common scab	Tubers develop scabby patches and need thicker peeling, and may not store well. Swedes and turnips can be affected. Thrives in alkaline soil	Do not lime the soil for potatoes and improve light soils with organic matter. Keep plants moist during dry spells. Look for resistant varieties.
Powdery mildew	White, powdery growth on foliage of a range of plants; marrows and courgettes are often badly affected. Severe infections weaken growth.	Remove affected growth and plant debris. Keep the soil moist, but do not splash water on the foliage. Can be treated with sulphur fungicide.
Sweetcorn smut	Most common in hot summers. Some kernels become hugely swollen and deformed and turn grey then burst to release black powdery spores.	Pick off affected cobs before the spores are released. Burn infected plant debris and grow sweetcorn in a different area next year.
Violet root rot	Affects many crops, especially asparagus. Plants fail to thrive; foliage yellows; roots are covered in violet-coloured strands of fungal growth.	Burn affected plants and crop debris. Improve drainage and add rotted organic matter to the soil. Grow the crop in a different area next year.
Virus	Many crops affected, particularly potatoes and marrow family. Distorts, marks and curls foliage. Plants are often severely weakened or killed.	Control sap-sucking pests such as aphids, which spread viruses. Remove and destroy (do not compost) affected plants as soon as they're seen.

| Fruit pests and diseases chart

Listed below are some of the common problems that can affect fruit trees and bushes. Some pests and diseases are specific to particular crops while others are more general.

Early diagnosis gives the best chance of successful treatment, so inspect crops regularly. Prompt action can avoid the need to use chemical controls altogether.

Pests	Symptoms	Control
Aphids	Small, soft-bodied insects on shoot tips and leaves. Weaken growth and can transmit viruses.	Squash colonies between finger and thumb or spray with pyrethrins, bifenthrin or thiacloprid.
Big bud mite	Swollen buds develop on black currants, filled with tiny mites that spread reversion virus, which can severely reduce cropping and is incurable.	Pick off affected buds in winter, before bud burst. Destroy heavily infested plants.
Birds	Birds eat many fruits, particularly cherries, blueberries, raspberries and strawberries. They also peck fruit buds in winter.	Erect taut netting over vulnerable crops in late winter (buds), or as soon as the fruits begin to show colour. A fruit cage gives best results.
Brown scale	Small, convex brown insects attached to the bark of fruit trees and bushes. The foliage is covered with honeydew that attracts sooty moulds.	In mid summer, spray affected plants with fatty acids or plant oils.
Codling moth	Larvae tunnel into the centre of apples and pears to feed on the core. The tunnel also encourages secondary rotting so damaged fruits won't store.	Erect codling moth traps in late spring to catch male moths and spray in early and mid summer with bifenthrin, before larvae tunnel into fruits.
Fruit tree red spider mite	Mainly affects apples and plums, especially in hot dry summers. Leaves are flecked and mottled with dozens of tiny mites on the undersides.	Spray affected plants with bifenthrin or plant oils.
Glasshouse red spider mite	Greenhouse and outdoor crops in a sheltered spot are at risk. Foliage is flecked and mottled, fine webs appear and tiny mites can be seen.	The biological control *Phytoseiulus persimilis* is effective if introduced early on; alternatively spray with bifenthrin, fatty acids or plant oils.
Gooseberry sawfly	In early summer, shoots of gooseberries and red and white currants suddenly appear defoliated. Green caterpillar-like larvae, up to 2cm (¾in) long, can be found on the leaves.	Pick off light infestations by hand and spray plants with pyrethrins when damage is seen.
Mealybug	Citrus, figs and grapes are most at risk. White fluffy insects can be seen in and around leaf axils and midribs. Leaves are covered in a clear, sticky residue, which attracts black sooty moulds.	Treat greenhouse infestations with the biological control *Cryptolaemus montrouzieri*. Alternatively, spray plants with fatty acids or plant oils.
Rabbit	Especially damaging to newly planted trees. The outer layer of bark is eaten away, weakening growth. Trees can die if stripping is severe.	Erect rabbit-proof fencing around multiple fruit trees or use spiral guards on individual trees.
Shothole borers	Tree-fruit branches become peppered with tiny holes where larvae have tunnelled into and fed on the wood. They emerge as adult beetles.	More likely to affect trees that are already weak, so address problems such as lack of pruning or inadequate nutrition. Prune out affected growth.
Tortrix moth	Green caterpillars spin webs on apple leaves to feed on them and graze developing fruits.	Pick off and destroy affected leaves.
Wasps	The high sugar content and odour of ripening fruit attracts wasps, which damage the fruit.	Hang traps in trees and harvest crops as soon as they ripen; don't leave windfalls on the ground.
Winter moth	Pale green caterpillars damage the newly emerging leaves on many types of fruit tree.	Place grease band around trunks in mid autumn to stop the flightless females laying eggs. Spray newly hatched caterpillars with bifenthrin.
Woolly vine scale	Flat, brown insects are seen on the bark of bush and vine fruit. In spring, females lay masses of white, woolly eggs bound in cotton-like threads.	Spray affected plants with plant oils or fatty acids in early and mid summer.

Disease	Symptoms	Control
Bacterial canker	Affects stone fruit. Areas of bark are flattened and gum oozes from the main limbs or trunk.	Prune out affected areas, limiting pruning times to the summer months to deter re-infection.
Blossom wilt	Blossom withers and rots soon after emerging, then remains hanging on the tree. The fungus travels to the foliage, causing it to brown.	Prune out affected stems. Just before flowering, spray Bordeaux mixture for apples, sweet cherries and plums, or copper oxychloride for peaches.
Botrytis (grey mould)	Fungus most prevalent on soft fruit, encouraged by high humidity. Fruit and other soft tissues develop a fuzzy grey covering and decay.	Ventilate covered crops well to decrease humidity and water from below rather than overhead. Remove affected plant parts promptly.
Bracket fungi	Flattened, single or overlapping, horizontal fungus appear on a fruit tree's trunk or main limbs. Some cause wood decay, weakness of limbs and eventual death, but this takes years.	There is no cure for bracket fungi. The main concern is that the tree can become unstable and so pose a safety risk. Therefore, check it regularly and fell the tree if necessary.
Brown rot	Fruit turn brown near harvest time and become covered in grey, raised, circular spots.	Avoid damage to fruit which allows the fungus in. Remove affected fruit as it can overwinter.
Coral spot	Orange-pink raised dots appear on dead stems of woody plants. Left unchecked, dieback can continue down the stem and become extensive. It enters through untidy pruning wounds.	Using sharp secateurs, cut out all affected growth well into healthy tissue, then burn it.
Crown gall	Large woody swellings near the base of fruit plants or on roots, especially in wet soils. Galls rarely affect the vigour of the host but can lead to secondary infection when they disintegrate.	Remove affected plants promptly to prevent the spread of the disease.
Downy mildew	Common on grapes and melons. Irregular, yellow patches on upper leaf surfaces have downy grey growth on the undersides.	Remove affected leaves and ventilate covered plants to reduce excess humidity. Water from below, not overhead.
Fireblight	Apple, pear and quince are susceptible. Flowers wilt and subsequent dieback then progresses down the stems. Bacterial ooze can sometimes be seen, along with discolouration under bark.	Prune out growth well back into healthy tissue, burning prunings and sterilising tools after use. A notifiable disease in some areas.
Fungal leaf spot	Irregular, brown/purple spots in yellow rings can appear on fruit including black- and hybrid berries, currants, cherries, figs and strawberries. Spreads rapidly during warm, humid weather.	Remove infected plants promptly and avoid replanting in that site.
Honey fungus	Causes weakness and eventual death. Clumps of toadstools appear around the base of plants in autumn. A white fungal layer smelling of mushrooms is found under the bark of larger roots.	Remove infected roots and replace with resistant plants.
Phytophthora	All woody fruits are at risk, especially on waterlogged soils. Plants weaken and die. Root cores are often stained orange and emit a sour smell.	There is no control for this fungus, so affected plants must be disposed of. Improve drainage and avoid replanting on affected soils.
Powdery mildew	Leaves develop a milky white covering, which eventually yellows and dries out the foliage. The skin of affected fruit often cracks.	Plants suffering from drought stress are more susceptible, so keep well mulched and watered. Spray with sulphur or grow resistant varieties.
Replant disease	Most tree fruit are vulnerable when planted on a site that has previously supported the same crop. Trees are weak and fail to put on new growth.	Various soil factors are to blame, including fungi and nematodes. Avoid planting on old sites or change the soil to a depth of 45cm (18in).
Rust	Attacks most cane fruit, plums and pears. Orange pustules on the leaf in early summer turn brown. Leaves fall early, reducing vigour.	Remove and burn affected leaves promptly and protect with copper-based fungicide on soft fruit (black currant, gooseberry and raspberry).
Silver leaf	All stone fruit, almonds and apples are vulnerable. A silver sheen appears on the foliage or all branches and the tree is weakened.	Prune stone fruit immediately after harvest in summer. Mild cases can be suppressed with feeding, otherwise remove the tree.
Virus	Stunting, distortion, blistering, or yellowing of foliage are common and yield is often reduced.	Dispose of affected plants. Control virus-spreading pests and purchase certified virus-free stock.

| Glossary

AGM The Award of Garden Merit is awarded by the Royal Horticultural Society (RHS) to plants that are judged to be of outstanding all-round excellence.

Bare-root A tree or shrub lifted from the open ground for sale during the dormant season, rather than being grown in a pot.

Basal cluster The lower cluster of leaves on a branch or stem of a plant.

Biennial bearing Where fruit is borne every two years instead of each year.

Biological control A method of controlling pests using predators and parasites instead of chemicals.

Bleeding The loss of sap from plant tissues after damage or pruning.

Bolting The premature production of flowers and seed which, in the case of lettuces, for example, makes the leaves taste bitter.

Botrytis Fungal disease most commonly seen as grey mould, usually attacking decaying or damaged parts of a plant.

Brutting The fracturing of young shoots (usually on hazelnuts) to restrict growth.

Bud A protrusion on a stem containing embryonic leaves and/or flowers. Fruit buds contain flowers and they often differ in shape to leaf buds.

Cane Straight stem of cane fruit such as raspberries and blackberries.

Catch crop A quick maturing crop for growing between the harvesting of one crop and the growing of the next.

Cloche A low glass or plastic covering used to protect young plants from adverse weather conditions early or late in the season.

Cold frame An unheated outdoor frame in which young (often tender) plants are placed to acclimatise them to outdoor conditions.

Collar A point on the main plant stem where the roots and stem meet.

Cordon A tree or bush trained against a support to form a single rod or stem. U-shaped cordons have two stems. The stems of oblique cordons are set at an angle.

Crop rotation Growing annual vegetables in a different site each season, primarily to prevent the build-up of pests and diseases and maintain the nutrients in the soil.

Cross-pollination The transfer of pollen between two separate plants of the same species.

Cultivar A word derived from the contraction of 'cultivated variety' to specify that a variety arose in cultivation rather than in the wild. In this book, 'variety' and 'cultivar' are used interchangeably.

Damping off When a fungal disease destroys emerging seedlings by rotting the stems at soil level.

Downy mildew Fungus disease causing discolouring and blotches on the upper leaf surface, most commonly on young plants and those grown with poor ventilation.

Drill Groove or furrow for planting seed.

Earthing up Drawing up soil around a plant, for example potatoes, to stop the tubers turning green, but also to help anchor some in the ground and prevent rocking in the wind.

Ericaceous compost Lime-free potting compost with a pH below 7, suitable for plants such as blueberries that need acid soil.

Espalier A fruit tree or bush trained against a support with an upright trunk, from which horizontal lateral branches arise to create a tiered effect.

F1 hybrid Plants or seeds that have been bred under strict conditions to create a crop that is uniform, vigorous and high yielding. Seeds gathered from F1 hybrids will not come true, so you will need to buy fresh stock for the next year.

Family tree A fruit tree in which several different varieties have been grafted on to the same rootstock. It is useful in small gardens where two or more varieties are required for pollination, but there is space for only one tree.

Fan A fruit tree or bush trained against a support, with branches splayed out to form a fan shape.

Feathered maiden A young fruit tree, usually in its first year after grafting, with branches along its length. Each branch is sometimes referred to as a feather. See also Maiden whip.

Festooning The practice of training fruit tree branches horizontally in order to increase the yields of fruit.

Forcing The practice of accelerating plant growth and fruit production by manipulating the growing environment.

Freestanding A fruit bush or tree grown without any support such as a stake or fence.

Hardening off The process of acclimatising tender or half-hardy plants raised under glass to outdoor conditions by gradual exposure to lower temperatures.

Hardwood cutting A method of plant propagation using woody stems.

Heeling in Planting in a temporary location, for example when soil conditions aren't suitable for the permanent planting of a fruit tree, or when crops such as leeks are lifted before freezing weather and brought to a position nearer the house.

Intercropping Growing a quick-maturing crop between slower-growing ones.

John Innes composts A suite of potting compost recipes invented by the John Innes Horticultural Institute, each one designed to suit particular needs.

Lateral A stem or branch arising from a main stem or leader. See also Sublateral.

Leader A primary branch from which lateral branches are produced. Central leaders form the main stem or trunk at the centre of the plant.

Maiden whip A young fruit tree, usually in its first year after grafting, without branches. See also Feathered maiden.

Mulch A thick covering over the soil, usually of well-rotted compost. Its many advantages include locking moisture in the ground in spring, ideally after a period of heavy rain, by reducing evaporation; insulating plants' roots in cold winters; blocking out weeds; and improving soil structure. Black polythene can also be used but won't improve the soil.

Offset Young plant attached to the parent, which can be separated and grown on.

pH A scale that is used to measure acidity and alkalinity of a soil. It ranges from 1 (acid) to 14 (alkaline) with 7 being neutral.

Perennial A plant that lives for several years.

Pinch out Remove the growing tip by nipping it off with finger and thumb, encouraging the growth of sideshoots.

Pollination The transfer of pollen from the anther to the stigma, which, if successful, leads to flower fertilisation and fruit set.

Powdery mildew Fungus disease creating a powder-like white to greyish-white cover on the leaf surface.

Puddling in The practice of applying a heavy soaking of water at the time of transplanting seedlings. Traditionally done with plants in the cabbage family.

Red spider mite Tiny, sap-sucking, spider-like mites often found in hot, dry conditions in greenhouses.

Rootstock The lower part of a grafted fruit tree or bush onto which the scion or top part is joined. The type of rootstock chosen controls the vigour of the tree or bush.

Runners Surface-running stems that grow from a parent plant (such as a strawberry). Runners bear young plants at the end, which root into the soil.

Scion The above-ground part of a grafted fruit tree or bush, which joins the rootstock.

Seed, running to See Bolting.

Seep hose A hose with pinprick holes that allow moisture to seep out of the full length of the hose for irrigation.

Self-fertile A plant that is able to pollinate its own flowers.

Self-infertile (or self-sterile) A plant that is unable to pollinate its own flowers and depends on the presence of another tree of the same or closely related species nearby.

Sideshoot see Sublateral.

Softwood cuttings A method of plant propagation using young and soft, unripened growth.

Spindle A compact fruit tree form that retains its central leader. The tree is trained in a cone shape so sunlight can reach fruit both at the top and the bottom of the tree.

Spur A short branch or network of branches of a fruit tree, bush or vine. Spurs bear an abundance of fruit buds and therefore carry the flowers and fruit.

Spur thinning Pruning to thin out a congested system of fruit spurs. This encourages good air flow around the fruit, deterring pest and disease attack and encouraging even ripening and fruit size.

Standard A fruit tree or bush grown on an upright, leafless trunk.

Step-over A compact form of apple or pear tree with a single clear stem to a height of 40–60cm (16–24in). This terminates in a horizontal stem, which bears fruit.

Stigma The female part of a flower, which receives the pollen. See also Pollination.

Stone fruit Trees or shrubs belonging to the cherry family, including peaches, nectarines, plums, damsons and almonds.

Strig A cluster or string of currants.

Sublateral A sideshoot arising from a lateral stem. See also Lateral.

Successional sowing Making sowings at regular intervals to ensure a continuous supply of the crop and avoid one big glut.

Sucker Any shoot that arises directly from the root or rootstock of a woody plant.

Thinning Removing some seedlings or plants to ensure that those left are evenly spaced with enough room to grow and access adequate light and food supplies. Also refers to removing some flower or fruit buds to improve the size and quality of the fruit that is left.

Tip-layering A method of plant propagation where tips of stems are made to root while attached to the main plant.

Topdressing Fertiliser applied to the soil after planting.

Transplanting Moving a seedling or plant from one place to another, for example, from a small to a larger pot or out into the garden.

True leaves The first set of leaves on a seedling, after the appearance of the seed leaves.

Variety See Cultivar.

Water shoot Young branches that arise directly from a bare stem or trunk of a fruit tree.

Index

Page numbers in *italics* refer to captions.

Acknowledgements

Vegetable text written and compiled by: Guy Barter, Alison Mundie, Amy Lax, Andrea Loom, Lia Leendertz, Sue Fisher, Lucy Halsall and Simon Maughan.

Fruit text written and compiled by: Simon Akeroyd, Lucy Halsall and Simon Maughan.

Photographic acknowledgements

Key: a above, b below, c centre, l left, r right

Fotolia AlcelVision 223br, Alla Salamaha 78a, Anna Khomulo 156a, b.neeser 164a, Becky Swora 276bl, Birgit Kutzera 193bc, Canoneer 227al, cherie 265bl, Christopher Howey 9a, Dan Marsh 288bl, Daniel Schmid 192br, Dolnikov 156 br, eAlisa 170br, Edsweb 44bl, Egidijus Mika 71cr, Elena Elisseeva 226a, Elena Moiseeva 227ar, Elena Ray 133bl, 201bl, Eric Pothier 184br, Florin Capilnean 148b, Fotolia XIII 133cl, Hamiza Bakirci 193bl, Hazel Proudlove 43bcl, 163ar, 192a, 271cr, Karin Lau 193ac, Kerioak 274a, Kirsten Alexander 288al , klikk 132a, Konstantin Sutyagin 228, Larry Ye 150ar, Lezh 248a, Marc Roche 243bl, Margit Fürnhammer 75b, Maria Brzostowska 220 ar, Mario 193cr, Martina Berg 209bl, Michel Bazin 277ar, Microgen 214br, Monkey Business 275br, Pavel Bernshtam 98ar, PJGCC 221ar, Profotokris 133ac, ril 66bl, Rudolf Ullrich 278a, Scott Prokop 201br, Sergey Shaklein 133al, Stef Run 200a, Stefano Tiraboschi 237ar, Stephen Vickers 264cr, Stocksnapper 193c, superfood 193br, 279br, tadamee 193cl, Thomas Oswald 238br, Ukr_photographer 226 br, Veronica 193ar, Vladimir Korostyshevskiy 288br, Vyacheslav Osokin 173ac, weim 51b, Zigurds Folkmanis 200br

Gap Photos Elke Borkowski 36, Graham Strong 92a, 93al, John Glover 198bl, Rice/Buckland 274br

Garden World Images Nicholas Appleby 147tr

Jim Arbury 157br

Marianne Majerus Garden Images Andrew Lawson 158–9, Marianne Majerus 182–3, Marianne Majerus/Helen Pitel 134–5, Marianne Majerus/Joanna Crane 104–5

Marshall's Nursery (www.marshalls-seeds.co.uk) 79bl

Octopus Publishing Group Jane Sebire 8, 18, 27, 28, 29a, 31l, 39, 40, 42, 43, 45, 47, 48b, 49, 65l, 67, 68l, 69b, 84, 85, 107, 108b, 109, 111, 112, 113al & b, 116l, 117a, 118, 119, 131bl, 137, 138, 139l, 141, 142al & r, 143, 144a & c, 162bl & r, 169ar, 166–8, 169 ar, 170a, 171a, 172br, 177, 178a, 180b, 185, 189, 205a, 206r, 208, 218, 223a, 263, 277b, Stephen Robson 2, 11, 12, 15, 16, 23, 32, 35, 58a, 60–61, 65r, 69a, 80–1, 92b, 94, 102, 103b, 110, 115l, 121, 136, 140, 146, 161, 169 br, 172a, 173al, bl & br, 178b, 188, 194, 204, 207a, 221b, 225, 240–1, 250, 260–1, 299, Torie Chugg 17, 20, 21a & c, 22, 24, 25, 26r, 29b, 30l, 31r, 33b, 52–55, 57, 58b, 73, 74, 76, 79l & ar, 95, 96a, 97, 98b, 99, 100al & b, 103a, 123–30, 131a, bc & br, 133ar & bl, 142b, 144b, 149, 150b, 151r, 152–154, 175, 176, 179, 180a,

181b, 195b, 196b, 197l, 198, 199, 201ar, 201cl, 207b, 210–213, 229–236, 237b, 251–6, 257l, 258–9, 266–7, 281–3, 288ar, 289b, 290al, ar & br, 291

Paul Jasper (www.jaspertrees.co.uk) 239al

Photolibrary Garden Picture Library/Christopher Gallagher 19, Garden Picture Library/David C Phillips 96bl, Garden Picture Library/Francesca Yorke 242r, Garden Picture Library/Gary K Smith 48a, Garden Picture Library/Howard Rice 115ar, Garden Picture Library/James Guilliam 273bl, Garden Picture Library/Juliette Wade 165br, Garden Picture Library/Linda Burgess 275ar, Garden Picture Library/Maxine Adcock 249br, Garden Picture Library/Michael Howes 66br, Garden Picture Library/Stephen Hamilton 222bl, 265ar, Garden Picture Library/Lynn Keddie 289ar, Garden Picture Library/Maxine Adcock 290 bl, Garden Picture Library/Mayer/Le Scanff 157ar

Shutterstock 7716430100 145ar, 8781118005 171b, Alex Kuzovlev 13ar, Andrew Chambers 21b, Anna Chelnokova 63, Anne Kitzman 270r, Ariy 278br, ason 91br, Bochkarev Photography 120a, Borislav Borisov 257r, Charlotte Erpenbeck 77br, chudoba 10, clearviewstock 71br, David Kay 187bl, Denis and Yulia Pogostins 71bl, 87ar, Dewitt 46bl, Dianne Maire 238a, Dusan Zidir 86bl, eleana 133br, Elena Moiseeva 197ar, Elena Ray 56, fotoar 44 br, Fotocrisis 201al, Fotosav 106r, Gavrila Bogdan 201cr, George Green 174r, George Vollmy 205bl, Gleb Semenjuk 276ar, Hamiza Bakirci 146a, Heather Barr 216–7, Inc 244br, Ivaschenko Roman 173cr, 201ar, James Doss 122r, Jasna 162a, 193al, Jim Mills 117br, Jirsak 72, Joe Gough 272bl, Johanna Goodyear 70ar, John Kershner 77br, khwi 93br, Krzysztof Slusarczyk 264ar, KSLight 246bl, Lezh 187bcl, LianeM 26bl, Lindsay Noechel 195ar, Liz Van Steenburgh 191, Marek Pawluczuk 83, 271ar, Marilyn Barbone 30br, Mauro Rodrigues 181ar, Microgen 201ac, Monkey Business Images 247bl, Nic Neish 116br, Nicholas Rjabow 64ar, Nicola Keegan 88bl, Petar Tasevski 196ar, Peter Baxter 169al, Peter Polak 209br, Pontus Edenberg 215br, Rachell Coe 101, Rafa Fabrykiewicz 45 bl, Rimantas Abromas 214a, 287, Robert Taylor 206al, Robyn Mackenzie 201cc, Ruta Saulyte-Laurinaviciene 68br, S Fierros 113ar, 244a, 272 br, Sally Wallis 273br, sevenke 155bl, Sharon Kingston 100ar, Simon@naffarts.co.uk 186br, slowfish 108ar, 219, Stale Edstrom 201bc, stocksnapp 114bl, Sviecia 139br, TW 140br, Teodor Ostojic 279cr, Tereza Dvorak 33ar, Todd S Holder 145br, Tomas Smolek 151al, Vakhrushev Pavel 224, Vera Bogaerts 6b, vesilvio 6a, Vitelle 246ar, Vladimir Sazonov 181al, zimmytws 202–3

RHS Collection 41l & r, 165ar & cr, 245ar, 249ar & cr, Tim Sandall 190, 220b, Harry Smith Collection 147cc, 165cl & cc

RHS Herbarium 157ar, 215c, 239bc & ar, Graham Titchmarsh 79ac & bc, 157al, ac, bl & bc, 215a, 239ac & bl

Suttons Seeds (www.suttons.co.uk) 41a & c, 86a, 147ar, ac, cl, cr, bl, & bc, 165ac, bl & br, 245al & ac, 249al, cc, bl & bc

Thompson & Morgan (www.thompson-morgan.com) 165al, 245ac & br, 249al & ac